INSTRUMENTS OF THE ORCHESTRA

# THE OBOE

*Also in this Series*

THE CLARINET
*by F. Geoffrey Rendall*

# THE OBOE

*An Outline of its History, Development
and Construction*

PHILIP BATE

LONDON
ERNEST BENN LIMITED

*First published by Ernest Benn Limited 1956*
*Bouverie House · Fleet Street · London · EC4*
*Printed in Great Britain*

To
M. B. and S. G. B.

# Contents

# Illustrations

[*These plates are inserted immediately preceding Chapter One*]

# Introduction

'ONE would wonder the French Hautboy should obtain so great an esteem in all the Courts of Christendom as to have Preference to any other single Instrument. Indeed, it looks strange at first Sight; But on the other hand, if a Man considers the Excellency and Use of it, this wonder will soon vanish. . . .' Thus wrote 'J.B.' at the beginning of his preface to *The Sprightly Companion,* which contains the earliest known instructions for the instrument. The initials J.B. most probably represent John Banister the younger, violinist and wind-player, and *The Sprightly Companion* was published by Henry Playford of London in 1695. Now, we have good reason to believe that in 1695 the French *Hautboy* was still a comparatively new instrument—less than forty years old— yet evidently in that short time it had achieved some prominence. Of course Banister wrote in an age of hyperbole, when literary dedications and commercial puffs alike were set out in the most flowery of language, but his preface nevertheless indicates the position that the new instrument had attained. It is clear that it had already proved itself superior to the older reed instruments and that men were beginning to find in it an adaptability, fluency, and expressiveness which are just those qualities we esteem in the oboe today.

To give some account of the three hundred years that have transformed the French Hautboy into the modern oboe, and to explain its behaviour in terms of modern knowledge, is the purpose of the following chapters. The story is far from being simple and direct, nor does it fall easily into chronological sections. Useful artificial divisions can, however, be made at the end of the 18th century and again near the beginning of the 20th, and for convenience these have been adopted.

The writing of this book has been a task undertaken with some misgiving—misgiving which I think the reader will understand if he cares for a moment to examine the kind of material which must form the basis of the historical part. The principal sources of information about the development of any musical instrument are of three sorts: first, actual examples from public or private collections together with descriptive matter and photographs; second, descriptions, instruction books, fingering charts, makers' lists, etc., and illustrations from contemporary sources; and third, music composed at different times expressly for the particular instrument. Of these three sources the first is naturally the most satisfactory. Here we have actual concrete objects which we can compare, measure, and test in various ways. We may even find specimens preserved in playable condition. The difficulty is that in the course of time some physical characteristics may have changed due to such causes as decay, the natural shrinkage of wood, etc., or to the actual loss of detached sections.

Let us, for example, consider the case of a reed instrument. The reed has always been an expendable commodity, physically delicate and liable to damage, and not worth keeping when past its best; yet without its appropriate reed we cannot submit an old instrument to any really convincing test. Here, then, our most obvious source of evidence may fail us and we must search elsewhere. Perhaps our second source may help us to decide what the appropriate reed looked like so that we may reconstruct it. Suppose we find a picture in a catalogue or instruction book. In the first case we do not know what degree of accuracy in illustration was originally required; in the second we may assume that little more than a diagram served. We decide, however, to make up a reed according to our chosen picture. We fit it to our old instrument and on test find that we can sound only certain notes. Was this, then, the whole compass of our instrument? or is there something wrong? We must turn for answer to the third source of evidence and enquire what range of notes was demanded of our instrument by typical contemporary music. Thus by degrees we arrive somewhere near the truth.

The above is a hypothetical case and over-generalised, but it does show clearly that the task of the instrumental historian extends far beyond the mere setting down of accepted facts. His work is really that of a musical and scientific detective. The clues may or may not exist. They may be buried in the most unlikely places, as, for example, Ambrosio's account of the Phagotum, which is incorporated in a 16th-century treatise on the language of the Chaldees. Even when unearthed they may prove inadequate. There are still some problems regarding the oboe which cannot be answered except by deduction guided by experience. In the following pages I have offered a number of conjectures, and I hope I have made it clear where I have done so. I have also felt obliged in one or two matters to challenge the accepted interpretation of evidence. I do so well aware that my own conclusions may in turn be challenged.

During the last hundred years the interest of musical scholars has been increasingly directed towards wind instruments and much has been written on various aspects of the subject. The bulk of this material is, however, distributed through encyclopædias, periodicals, pamphlets, and catalogues, and is not very easy to find. Too much of it also consists of mere repetitive assertions passed on from book to book, dictionary to dictionary, by writers who were out of touch with original sources; many of these authors, who should have known better, have been content to quote earlier writers without either acknowledgment or attempt at verification. As a result, many statements which began only as suggestion or surmise (whether well or ill founded) have gained currency and are now accorded the respect due to proven fact. Much of our information about musical instruments is traditional, and tradition is respectable. We should be wrong, however, always to accept tradition without reasonable and, if possible, unprejudiced enquiry.

Finally I must say that this volume makes no pretence to being a treatise. Today such a work would require a writer who is both a scholar and a performing musician of high ability and experience. The example has been set, possibly for all time, by Rockstro in his monumental book on the flute. All I can claim is to have set down duly considered information and conclusions that have come to me during a good many years as a student of woodwind instruments. In doing so I have tried to fill in some measure a gap in the literature of musicology, for I believe that no comprehensive study of the oboe has been published since that of Bechler and Rahm in 1914. Since then our knowledge, especially in the field of acoustics, has widened a great deal. If I have given any pleasure, or have stimulated others to further research, I shall be amply rewarded.

## Acknowledgements

In preparing this book I have enjoyed the encouragement of many good friends who have most generously made me free of their libraries, their collections, and their own researches. I thank them all, in particular Messrs. A. C. Baines, Edgar Brackenbury, Adam Carse, R. B. Chatwin, W. A. Cocks, J. Gosden, Lyndesay G. Langwill, J. McGillivray, B. Manton-Myatt, Josef Marx, R. Morley-Pegge, E. O. Pogson, the late F. G. Rendall, Anthony

Winter, Prof. Bernard Hague, the late Herr Wilhelm Heckel, Herr Franz Groffy, Sir Edward Salisbury, Director of the Royal Botanic Gardens, Kew, and M. Maurice Selmer. The quotation from H. S. Williamson's *The Orchestra* is made by permission of the Sylvan Press. I am specially indebted to Mr. Eric Blom, the Editor, and Messrs. Macmillan and Company Limited, the publishers of *Grove's Dictionary of Music and Musicians* for permission to quote verbatim certain paragraphs from my contribution to the fifth edition of that work. These include in particular the technical descriptions of the different French oboes of the 19th century. My thanks are also due to the Curators of the Rijks Museum, Amsterdam, the Gemeente Museum, The Hague, and the Brussels Conservatoire Museum for allowing me to illustrate instruments in their care and to Mr. Paul Wilson of London for photographing specimens from my own collection.

PHILIP BATE

## *NOTE*

CERTAIN important references are given in italic at their first appearance, and in roman thereafter ; this has been followed also in the corresponding indices.

THE tonality or pitch of an oboe is indicated by a Capital, e.g. oboe in C or C oboe. To save innumerable musical examples, the following method of staff notation has been adopted

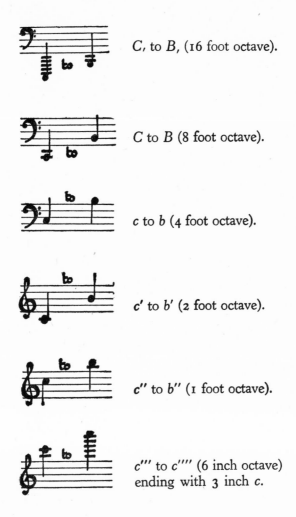

C, to B, (16 foot octave).

C to B (8 foot octave).

c to b (4 foot octave).

c' to b' (2 foot octave).

c'' to b'' (1 foot octave).

c''' to c'''' (6 inch octave) ending with 3 inch c.

PLATE I

# THE OBOES OF THE MODERN ORCHESTRA

1. Bass (Baritone) in C.  *Cabart, Paris*
2. Cor Anglais in F.  *Lorée, Paris*
3. Oboe d'amore in A.  *Louis, London*
4. Soprano in C.  *Lorée, Paris*
5. Heckelphone in C.  *Heckel, Biebrich a/Rh*

The four oboes are all of the 'Brussels Conservatoire model. No. 1 has only the essential keywork of the type, the others are fitted with additional trill-keys.

For convenience Nos. 1 and 5 are reproduced to ⅘th the scale of the others. *Photograph by courtesy of E. O. Pogson, Esq.*

PLATE I

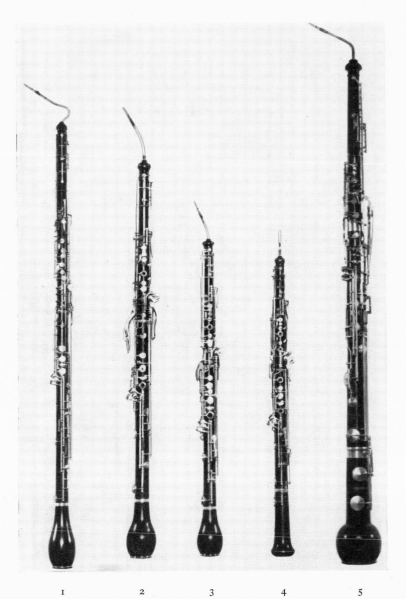

1          2          3          4          5

PLATE II

16TH- AND 17TH-CENTURY DOUBLE-REED
INSTRUMENTS

1. Tenor Pommer. *Anon.* ⎱16th century. *Brussels*
2. Discant Schalmey. *Anon.* ⎰ *Conservatoire Collection*
3. Deutsche Schalmey. *R. Haka,* ⎫ *Gemeente*
   *Amsterdam.* Later 17th century ⎬ *Museum,*
4. Oboe. *C. Rijkel, Amsterdam. c.* 1695 ⎭ *The Hague*
5. Oboe. *I. C. Denner, Nürnberg.* pre-1700
6. Oboe. *T. Stanesby senior, London.* pre-1700. *F. G.
   Rendall Collection*

Nos. 1 and 2 reproduced to ½ scale of the other instruments.

In this and subsequent plates instruments not otherwise
attributed are from the author's own collection

PLATE II

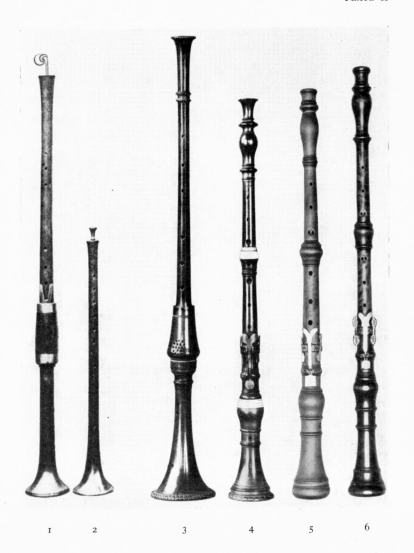

PLATE III

# 18TH-CENTURY OBOES

1. Dark wood (ebony?) inlaid with ivory. Silver keys. *French?* Early 18th century. *Edgar Brackenbury Collection*

2. Ivory, silver keys. (Several later additions.) *Debey, Paris? c.* 1730

3. Stained pear? wood, silver keys. *T. Stanesby junior, London.* pre-1754

4. Boxwood, ivory mounts, silver keys. *T. Lot, Paris. c.* 1775

5. Stained boxwood, brass keys. *W. Milhouse, Newark.* pre-1789

6. Boxwood, silver keys. *T. Collier, London. c.* 1780

PLATE III

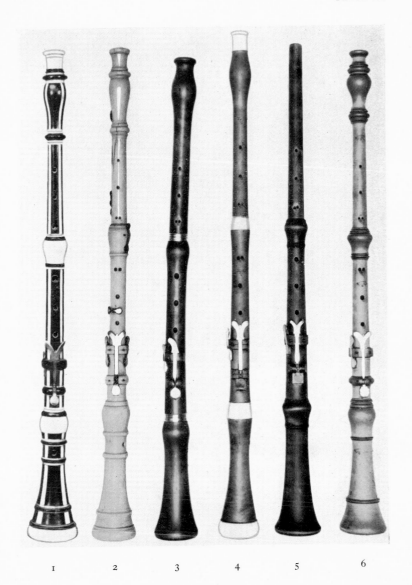

1        2        3        4        5        6

PLATE IV

## 19TH-CENTURY OBOES. A

1. Boxwood, silver keys. *Milhouse, London.* *c.* 1820
2. Rosewood, silver mounts and keys. *Wylde, London.* *c.* 1830
3. Ebony, German silver mounts and keys. *S. Koch, Vienna.* *c.* 1825. ('Sellner's 13-keyed oboe' shown with the tuning slide extended.)
4. Boxwood, ivory mounts, silver keys. *Bormann, Dresden.* *c.* 1840. (Shown with supplementary tuning joint)
5. Rosewood, ivory mounts, German silver keys. *A. Morton, London.* *c.* 1860. *E. Brackenbury Collection*
6. Blackwood, German silver mounts and keys. *Zuleger, Vienna.* Late 19th century

Nos. 2–6 show the development of German characteristics during the century.

PLATE IV

PLATE V

## 19TH-CENTURY OBOES. B

1. Violet wood ?, ivory and silver mounts, silver keys. *H. Brod, Paris.* pre-1839

2. Boxwood, brass keys. *Triébert, Paris. c. 1855.* (Presumed experimental model)

3. Blackwood, German silver keys. *A. Morton and Sons, London. c. 1872.* (Military thumb-plate model)

4. Rosewood, silver mounts and keys. *Triébert, Paris.* Barret's model of 1860

5. Stained Maple wood, German silver keys. *L. A. Buffet jeune, Paris.* (Boehm system as patented by Buffet in 1844)

6 and 7. Cocus wood, German silver keys. *Anon.* Two Boehm system instruments to low A♮ associated with A. J. Lavigne's later experiments. Late 19th century

PLATE V

PLATE VI

# TENOR OBOES

1. *R. Wyne, Nijmegen.* Early 18th century? *Gemeente Museum, The Hague*
2. *J. H. Rottenburgh, Brussels. c. 1750*
3. 'Vox Humana.' *Longman and Broderip, London. c. 1785. Boosey and Hawkes Collection*
4. 'Cor Anglais Modèrne.' *H. Brod, Paris.* pre-1839
5. Cor Anglais. *Triébert, Paris. c. 1875*

PLATE VI

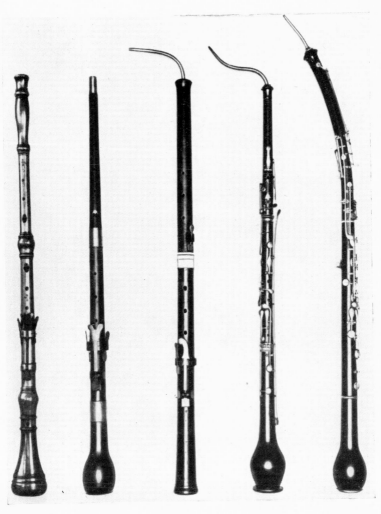

PLATE VII

# CORS ANGLAIS, CURVED AND ANGULAR TYPES

1. Hardwood, leather covered. Ivory mounts and keys. *Italian.* Early 18th century. The instrument is thought to have been repaired and later marked by *Fornari of Venice*

2. Stained wood, brass keys, some late additions. *P. di Azzi, Venetian Republic.* Late 18th century

3. Maple wood ?, leather covered, ivory mounts, brass keys. *Anon. Austrian ? c.* 1830

4. Stained Maple wood, ivory mounts, brass keys. *J. Uhlmann, Vienna. c.* 1850.

5. Maple wood, leather covered. German silver mounts and keys. *Triébert, Paris. c.* 1850

PLATE VII

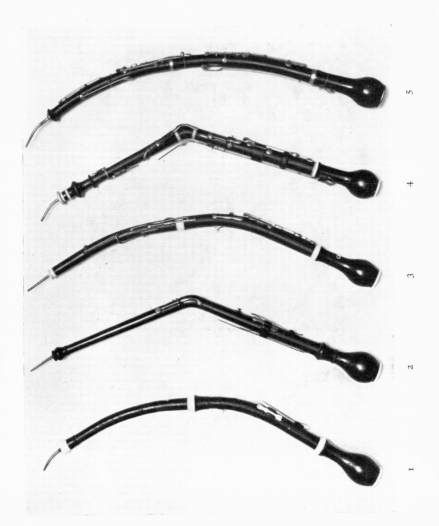

PLATE VIII

## OBOI D'AMORE AND BASS OBOES

1. Stained wood, brass keys. *P. Wolravpier, Brussels?* Early 18th century? *Brussels Conservatoire Collection*

2. Cocus wood, German silver mounts and keys. *V. Mahillon, Brussels. c. 1890. Bernard Hague Collection*

3. 'Hautbois Baryton,' brass keys. *C. Bizey, Paris. c.* 1740

4. 'Hautbois Baryton,' brass keys. *G. Triébert, Paris. c.* 1823

*Paris Conservatoire Collection*

5. 'Hautbois Baryton,' German silver mounts and keys. *F. Triébert, Paris.* Mid 19th century

Nos. 3–5 approx. $\frac{5}{8}$ scale of 1 and 2

PLATE VIII

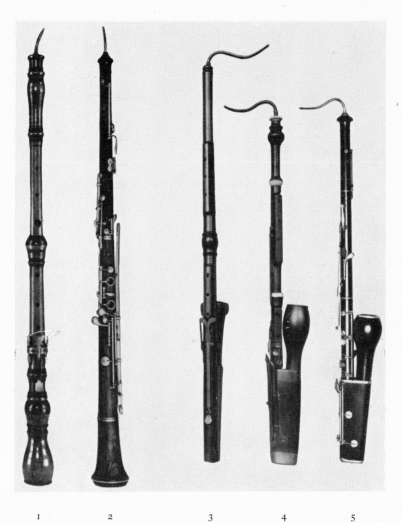

1       2       3       4       5

# Definitions and Descriptions

To claim pre-eminence for any particular musical instrument would seem to be both ungracious and unwise: ungracious since all instruments of cultivated music are equally the products of man's artistry; unwise because tastes and fashions change with successive generations. The flute fever which affected Europe, and particularly England, in the first half of the 19th century has gone, leaving, it is true, the flute as the most highly organised of the woodwinds,[1] but without lasting influence on music in the widest sense.[2] The craze of the restless nineteen-twenties for the saxophone has passed, leaving even less trace on musical literature, but the instrument itself is now valued more nearly at its true worth and as its inventor would have wished. So it has been also with the oboe, and the modern musician would probably hesitate to endorse John Banister's eulogy. In spite, however, of latter-day re-assessments, the oboe remains one of the most valued of all wind instruments, whether as a solo voice or for ensemble use in the full orchestra and the chamber group. In the words of H. S. Williamson, 'The bitter-sweet oboe which is first heard marshalling the orchestra to tune, continues, as the music proceeds, to assert its small but inexpressibly poignant voice whether it is heard singing plaintively to a hushed accompaniment or whether under the passionate surge of the strings it is heard calling, as it seems, from the innermost secret places.' The writer of that passage has sensed unerringly the quality and place of the oboe in our music, and, though different schools of playing tend to cultivate different ideals of tone with subtleties that are more easy to recognise on hearing than to define in words, his description still holds good.

The oboe is the type instrument of what is commonly called the 'double-reed' family. As constructed nowadays it consists of a slender tube of dense hard-wood (occasionally of metal or ebonite) some 59 cms. long, made in three sections united by tenon-and-socket joints. The bore, which is narrow and conoidal, expands fairly regularly for about five-sixths of its length, and then opens out more rapidly to form a moderate bell. In playing, this part of

the instrument behaves as a resonator and its dimensions govern
the note sounded. The effective length of the tube is variable by
means of sixteen to twenty-two side-holes, six of which are controlled directly by the player's fingers and the rest indirectly with
the help of key mechanism which is sometimes most ingenious and
complicated. There are at the present day at least four recognised
systems of keywork applied to the oboe, and these are described in
some detail in subsequent chapters. The instrument is sounded by
means of a reed formed of two thin blades of 'cane' bound with
thread to a narrow tapered metal tube which forms an extension of
the bore. This tube is called a staple. When placed between the
player's lips and gently blown, the blades of the reed vibrate together and in turn energise the air in the tube. The proper
management of this very delicate apparatus is probably the most
difficult part of oboe technique for the beginner to acquire or for
the teacher to impart.

The compass of the modern oboe extends from *b♭* below the
stave to *a* in the fifth space above it—in all thirty-six notes, of
which the first sixteen are fundamental tones, each sounded by its
own appropriate length of tube. The remainder are harmonics of
the notes actually fingered and are produced by changes of 'lip' on
the reed, helped by the opening of certain special keys. (See
'Octave or Speaker Key' in Chapter 'Acoustics'.) Certain of the
highest notes may be sounded in several different ways.

( —————————— Fundamental tones ———————————— )

Fig. 1. Compass of the oboe

*Construction of the scale*

In addition to the treble or soprano pitched in C, we have at the
present day several deeper-toned oboes. Those recognised for

orchestral use are: (1) the Oboe d'amore in A, usually regarded as an alto but sometimes as a mezzo-soprano; (2) the cor anglais, or English Horn, in F, the tenor of the group, also at times called an alto; (3) the Bass (Baritone), also in C. The larger oboes are almost always built today with a pear-shaped bell having a constricted opening, and on this characteristic some scholars have felt it necessary to base a sub-group within the main family. In terms of the most strict classification this is probably justified, but for the purposes of this book I have found it unnecessary, and I have preferred to group the instruments only according to their pitches. The bulb-bell is discussed under several headings in subsequent chapters.

All modern oboes are in direct descent from a much simpler instrument which first appeared in France in the latter half of the 17th century. The first, and indeed the only nearly contemporary description we have of it is in English, and appears in the Harleian Manuscript 2034, f. 207b, preserved in the British Museum. This is the *Academy of Armory*, written by the third Randle Holme some time prior to 1668 and, in addition to a brief text, it contains an excellent sketch of the instrument. Our next detailed information is also in English and is found in the James Talbot manuscript of *c.* 1700, preserved in the library of Christ Church College, Oxford (Music MS. 1187). From this document we learn that the French *Hautbois* was at that date barely forty years established, and Talbot's notes contain valuable comments and measurements. The new instrument was made in three parts with tenon-and-socket joints, not, it is true, an entirely fresh form of construction, but one which about that period was rapidly proving its advantages in the hands of both flute and bassoon makers. There were six finger-holes arranged in two groups of three, the middle pair being duplicated for 'half-notes'; below these were a pair of small closed keys right and left handed; below these again came a single large jointed key standing open. The bell joint was longer than absolutely required to sound the lowest note and was pierced about half-way up by two more holes permanently open. The reed projected clear of the top of the instrument, so that the player was quite free to lip as much or little of it as required. The compass of the treble instrument was from $c'$ to $c'''$ with all half tones, the second octave being produced by a greater lip pressure, which elicited the second harmonic (sometimes only approximately) of the note fingered. All these features, or their equivalent, with the possible exception of the doubled fourth hole, are to be found in succeeding instruments right up to the present day, though they do not all invariably occur together.

In the description of wind instruments with side-holes, the term 'primary scale' is one we often encounter. It has long been customary to take this scale to be the one sounded by opening in succession the six holes controlled by the first three fingers of each hand, beginning with the lowest. Notes sounded by holes placed above or below this group are regarded as belonging to extensions of the primary scale. The convention seems reasonable enough, since on the simplest form of tube no more than six holes are required to produce the diatonic intervals in an octave. The lowest note sounds from the open end of the tube, and its second harmonic completes the octave. On the primitive oboe, then, the primary scale would be that provided by the open finger-holes, and the notes produced by the keys would belong to a downward extension. This scale began on d', as also on the contemporary transverse flutes, and the 'less' and 'great' keys added d#' and c' respectively. On modern oboes the same applies, only the lower keywork has been amplified to extend the compass downward by semitones to b♭, or even to a.

In spite of the general acceptance of this principle, at least one present-day writer[3] has rejected it in favour of a theory which postulates a seven-hole primary scale for all woodwinds. A good deal of ingenious discussion has been brought forward in support, though much of it savours of special pleading and many of the arguments adduced seem to be derived from a much more advanced and self-conscious music than that known when the oboe made its debut. The seven-hole theory is by no means accepted generally, and as far as description is concerned in these pages, there seems to be no reason to abandon the older and perfectly serviceable system.

From the foregoing we can derive a short list of features which we may regard as definitive of the early true oboe, viz.:—

1. Three-part jointed construction.
2. The duplicated third and sometimes fourth holes.
3. The jointed 'great key' covering the lowest hole.
4. The duplicated 'less keys'.
5. The bell with open holes in the waist.
6. The reed mounted clear of the upper joint.

7. A compass of c′ to c‴, two octaves, with all intervening half-tones.

In the above and all subsequent descriptions the following common conventions have been observed: the blowing end of any instrument is regarded as the *top* or *upper* end; all holes are numbered from the top downward; *right* and *left* are defined from the player's viewpoint; likewise *front* or *upper surface* is the side away from the player, and the *back* or *underside* is that nearest him while playing.

It may be noticed that so far I have carefully avoided using the word 'chromatic'. This is because nowadays many of us, have taken our conception of chromaticism from the rigidly defined equal temperament of the piano. In the case of woodwind instruments, however, the intervals between adjacent notes are to some extent under the control of the player, for reasons to be explained later in the chapter 'Acoustics'. This facility had to be cultivated particularly in playing the older instruments, where special fingerings were required to obtain twelve notes to the octave. There were only eight holes available for the purpose, and no doubt some of the peculiarities of the bore were devised to aid flexibility. Later on the development of key mechanism allowed the provision of a separate hole for each semitone in the first octave, but the player still retained control over the inflection of each note. Even today, when the twenty or more holes on an oboe are tuned basically to the intervals of equal temperament, the sensitive player is able to inflect as his ear dictates, and nowadays few instruments are more amenable to such use. It is a fallacy, albeit a common one, that a woodwind player's notes are rigidly 'made for him' by his instrument.

From quite early times wind players have recognised the value of a flexible intonation which elsewhere is found only in the unfretted strings. La Riche's tablature for the oboe, quoted by Talbot, goes so far as to show enharmonic distinctions between $g^{\sharp\prime\prime}$ and $a^{b\prime\prime}$, and between $f^{\sharp\prime\prime}$ and $g^{b\prime\prime}$ with different fingerings for each. Unfortunately, writers have not always been so percipient, and the pages of musical criticism are marred by such ill-considered statements as Dr. Burney's that 'it is natural for these instruments to be out of tune'. Dr. Burney, it seems, must have heard some very poor or careless players. Or perhaps he encountered only desperately bad instruments, for of course, if an oboe or any other woodwind is grossly ill-made, the best performer in the world will be unable to force it into tune. The point is that, as used of old woodwinds, the term *chromatic* implies the presence of semitones but says nothing about *temperament*.

## ETYMOLOGY

The word OBOE has an interesting derivation. Its modern English spelling seems to have reached us through the Italian, in which tongue it makes a reasonable phonetic rendering of the French *Hautbois*—literally *High Wood*—though the word here seems to imply 'strong' or 'powerful' rather than 'high-pitched'. In passing from written Italian to spoken English the final 'e' became suppressed, as is common with such words, leaving us with the pronunciation ōbō. The old English forms 'hautboy' and 'hoboy' are obviously more direct corruptions of the French word and indicate in their last syllable a pronunciation which was occasionally used in England until within living memory.

It may be interesting to note here that the word 'hautbois' has also passed into English in circumstances quite unconnected with music. In Norfolk, some seven miles north-east of Norwich, lie the villages of Great and Little Hautbois, both undoubtedly named many years ago on account of an obvious feature of the landscape. The second case occurs in the realm of horticulture. One of the parent strains incorporated in the highly-cultivated garden strawberry of today is the Hautbois Strawberry (*Fragaria moschata*), a native of Central Europe. This plant is said to owe its name to its habit of bearing fruit on a stem standing high above the leaves. Although greatly inferior to the modern hybrids, the Hautbois Strawberry was at one time a popular fruit in England, and London street vendors could be heard calling, 'Fine ripe Hautboys!'

To return to our musical instrument, in Germany two forms of the word are recognised: *hoboe* and *oboe*. In both the final 'e' is sounded, though not heavily accented, the major stress falling on the second 'o'. Both pronunciations appear to come from the French direct, and some German etymologists regard the initial 'h' as a sign of vulgar usage at some stage in the transition. The term *oboisten* was for a long period applied in Germany to military bandsmen in general, regardless of their particular instruments, a custom which clearly shows the importance attached to the oboe in early military music.

The matter of terminology is one which has given no little trouble in the literature of musical instruments. Certain words have at different times and among different people acquired special shades of meaning which can be most confusing, and at the present time some international agreement among scholars is most desirable. Until about the year 1500 the names of European reed instruments in general seem to have been derived more or less directly from the Latin *calamus* (a reed), whence the old French *chalemie* and *chalemelle*; English *shalme* and *shawm*; Italian *cialamella*; Spanish *chirimia*; and German *schalmey*.

In the latter part of the 16th century and onward both in France and England the smaller double reeds were regularly referred to by some form of the word 'hautbois'.[4] After the middle of the 17th century, however, custom began to reserve this name for the particular instrument which now bears it. The restriction is generally maintained in English-speaking countries today, though modern French and German writers have shown a tendency to revert to a wide usage as well as a strict one.

Thus we sometimes find *hoboe* or *hautbois* signifying double-reed instruments both primitive and modern, European or Exotic. In English texts this is nowadays rare. Usually the older instruments are called *shawms* or *waits*,[5] while related extra-European types are given Proper names or are referred to by description. It is a useful convention which makes for clarity, and I have observed it in these pages. For simplicity in a small book I have also regarded the true oboes as a single group, though, as noted above, subdivisions would be called for in a fully systematic classification. The matter has been treated in great detail by Bessaraboff, though even he has found difficulty with ambiguous naming.[6]

[1] Theobald Boehm himself wrote to Mr. Broadwood of London in August 1871. '. . . I could not match Nicholson in power of tone, wherefore I set to work to remodel my flute. Had I not heard him, probably the Boehm flute would never have been made.'

[2] Very little of the vast quantity of flute music published during this period can be regarded as important. The social and musical needs of the time were for the majority of people met by the 'Brilliant Fantasia' or 'Variations on Popular Airs'.

[3] E. Halfpenny in *Proc. Roy. Mus. Ass.*, 75th session, 1948–49, and Grove's *Dictionary of Music and Musicians*, London, 5th edn.

[4] As far as we know, the first written use of the word in English occurs in a letter from Robert Laneham describing the entertainment provided for Queen Elizabeth I at Kenilworth Castle in 1575. He says, 'This pageaunt was clozd up with a delectable harmony of Hautbois Shalmz

Cornets, and such oother looud muzik'. The juxtaposition of 'hautbois' and 'shalmz' can, however, hardly be taken to indicate any distinction (except perhaps of size) between the two instruments at that period.

[5] 'Wait' as an instrument is an abbreviation of 'wait-pipe'. It derives basically from the German *wacht* = 'watch', for the early town musicians in Europe were in the first place watchmen rather than minstrels, and their instruments were provided either for sounding the alarum or to give periodic proof of their vigilance.

[6] N. Bessaraboff, *Ancient European Musical Instruments*. Harvard University Press, 1941. Introductory section.

# CHAPTER 2

# *Reeds*

'THE nerve-centre of the oboe lies in its reed, and in the bore is its soul.' So wrote Adam Carse in his book *Musical Wind Instruments*, and in that sentence he gave us perhaps the best appreciation we have so far of a connection which is both intimate and extremely delicate. The acoustician might be satisfied by the plain statement that this is the relationship of tone-generator to resonator, and to him it implies a host of complications. The player is, however, not often a scientist as well. He knows that, broadly, the *kind* of tone he produces is due in the first place to his reed, but that its subtlety is largely influenced by the bore of the instrument.* He knows, too, that the one must be most delicately adjusted to the other so that both may work well together, yet as a rule he finds words inadequate to express what he senses so surely.

The twin-bladed cane reed is a familiar object—so familiar, indeed, that it has furnished the common-usage name for both the oboe and the bassoon families: 'the double-reed group'. As no consistent account of these instruments can be given without frequent reference to reeds, it will be useful to deal with these at once before passing on to other matters; to discuss their structure, materials, and what they are required to do. The whole subject is a big one, but here we need consider in detail only those reeds which are taken directly between the player's lips. In bagpipes and certain obsolete instruments, similar reeds are used isolated in wind-chambers, but these do not come within our province and will need only passing notice.

## HISTORY

The lineage of the double reed goes back to remote antiquity, though its story, as we have it now, is far from continuous. We know that it was in use among some of the oldest artistic civilisations of which we possess records, and indeed it may well have been known to primitive man. It is in essence a simple thing, and

* But see also Chapter 12, p. 147.

its discovery would entail no more than pinching the end of a ripe straw between the finger and thumb, as country children sometimes do today to make a 'squeaker'.

In the Cairo museum are preserved numerous cylindrical Egyptian pipes dating from the 18th dynasty (1400–1300 years B.C.), some of which show clearly the remains of double-reeds. Examples of the ancient Greek *aulos*, sometimes sounded with a double-reed, are still extant, and traces of the Roman *tibiae*, again double-reed instruments, are found wherever Roman civilisation extended. In Oriental countries today the double-reed is used with instruments that have probably not changed in form in a thousand years—there is, for instance, evidence in Sanskrit musical writings —and it is almost certain that from the East it found its way into Western Europe. The time and manner of that migration are, however, uncertain. It has often been assumed that it occurred at the time of the Crusades, and certainly through the Holy Wars of the 12th and 13th centuries Europeans gained closer knowledge of Eastern arts and customs than ever before. Yet, when all our information is sifted, it becomes clear that the use of the double-reed was known in England, France, Spain, and Germany many centuries earlier. The evidence has been admirably discussed by that great scholar Canon F. W. Galpin in Chapter 9 of his *Old English Instruments of Music* and elsewhere.

To the peculiar climatic conditions of parts of Egypt and neighbouring countries we owe the actual preservation of ancient instruments with at least fragments of their reeds, but in the West the case is very different. Here very few musical instruments of any sort have been preserved that can be dated earlier than the 16th century, and most of our information comes from pictorial or literary sources. Such evidence calls for much care and experience in its interpretation. The oldest European books devoted entirely to musical instruments did not appear until the early 16th century, and the most informative of them over a hundred years after that.[1] Even within the period of the true oboes there are large gaps in our knowledge which can only be filled by conjecture. Of the changes which affected the body of the instrument during that time we have ample evidence; regarding the associated reed we have very little. The oldest undoubted oboe reeds we possess today go back no farther than the later years of the 18th century. This is not surprising when we remember how delicate the apparatus is and how perishable in use. The wonder is that any have survived at all, and in this light the preservation of the Egyptian specimens seems almost miraculous.

The somewhat crude woodcuts in the early books indicate that the reeds known to the writers were, compared with modern types, rather broad in relation to their length, and of the 'wedge' shape we now associate mainly with the bassoon. Such reeds were also used with the first oboes, and the measurements noted by Dr. Talbot *c.* 1700 show that in their dimensions they differed little from those used with the contemporary shawms. Some important

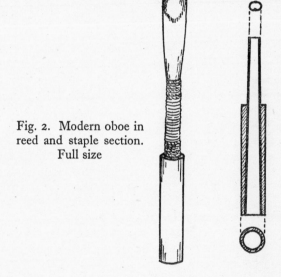

Fig. 2. Modern oboe in reed and staple section. Full size

though damaged specimens in the Pitt-Rivers Museum in Oxford can be dated by association at *c.* 1770, and these indicate a maximum width of some 9·5 mm., though the blades when complete seem to have been rather shorter than Talbot's average. Further evidence is provided by a reed-case, probably of the mid-18th century, belonging to Mr. Edgar Hunt of Chesham Bois. This has slots that will accommodate reeds about 10 mm. wide. A curiously broad Italian reed is depicted in the first edition of Grove's *Dictionary of Music*. This dates from 1823, by which time, in France at least, a much narrower type was already in favour. In England the broad reed seems to have persisted longer than anywhere else,[2] and was certainly used by some players as late as the

1840s. At the time of writing, a number of workers in this country
are trying to recreate the 18th-century reed for use with surviving
antique oboes, and no doubt their experiments will bring to light
much useful information.

STRUCTURE

The usual oboe reed today consists of two slips of 'cane' of suitable curvature and between 0·20 and 0·50 mm. thick[3] shaped as
in the accompanying drawing.

This shows an average modern example to full scale, but both
the size and shape of the blades are subject to some variation,
according to the needs or taste of the player. The blades are firmly
bound with thread to the narrow end of the conical brass staple,
which, in order to accommodate them better, is slightly flattened.
The blades themselves lie closely in contact along their edges. At
their free ends they present a narrow elliptical opening, and here
they are scraped down to feather edge for about 7 mm. According
to the quality of the original material and the character of the
'scrape', a reed may be responsive or unyielding ; excellent throughout the compass of the instrument or altogether useless. In order
that they may match in character, as far as possible, each pair of
blades is made from a single piece of cane. To do this a section of the
stem about 11 mm. in diameter and cut from between two knots is
taken. The French call this raw material a 'canon'. The canon is
split long ways into three, or occasionally four, sections, and a
piece is roughly shaped and cut just long enough to make the two
blades. It is then evenly gouged on the inside to the required thickness and in such a way as to preserve the siliceous outer skin.
Formerly this was done entirely by hand and eye, but since the
mid-19th century a small plane or 'router' with a curved blade
sliding on steel guides has been employed, and this does the work
very easily and accurately. The gouged cane is then nicked and
scraped a little exactly in the middle and folded over a metal shape,
which also forms a guide for trimming the taper. The folded slip is
next fitted to the staple and firmly bound on with thread. At one
time staples were frequently provided with a small metal collar
which helped to support the root of the blade, but this is not essential, and seems to have gone out of fashion in recent years. Next the
fold itself is cut away, thus separating the two blades and forming
the elliptical mouth. A thin steel tongue or 'plaque' is gently inserted in this as a support and the feather edge is developed by

scraping with a keen knife. This last is the most critical part of the operation, though all of it calls for a great deal of practice.

The above is no more than a sketch of the process of reed-making, and much has necessarily been omitted. Moreover, every maker has his own personal secrets and preferences. Most workers, for instance, soak the cane at various stages, while a few prefer to keep it almost dry all the time. Readers desiring more information will find excellent articles in Barret's *Oboe Tutor* and in that of Louis Bas, as well as invaluable advice in Evelyn Rothwell's *Oboe Technique*. No written instructions, however, will replace the teaching of an expert, which is really essential to a beginner.

The ability to make his own reeds was formerly regarded as an indispensable item of every oboist's technique. Nowadays this is no longer so, and the greater part of those used are supplied by a highly developed specialist industry. Indeed, in England in the past year or so a patent process has been introduced which virtually does away with most of the hand work described in the previous paragraph. By this method slips of cane sufficient only for single blades, and already gouged and shaped by machinery, are mounted in batches on a rotating mandrel. This then moves automatically beneath a diamond-faced cutting tool in such a way that every blade receives an identical feather edge. This appears to be the nearest approach to mass production applicable to oboe reeds, and were it not for the natural variation in the raw cane it would offer absolute uniformity throughout every batch. Even with such advantages as this, however, many players still prefer to buy their canes partly finished and carry out the final stages for themselves. In any case, the player must be able to *scrape* his own reeds, for this is the only way to adjust them to his individual lip and to his instrument. Upon the scrape depends the whole character of a reed, as well as whether it will play in tune when attached to a given oboe. The personal factor, too, is vitally important, and a pair of players, playing on identical instruments and producing as nearly as possible matched tone, may, on account of differences in lips, teeth, etc., require markedly different reeds.[4]

There is an anecdote told by the late Edward Buttar concerning the celebrated player Dubrucq which is well known among oboists, but which I may be excused for repeating, since it shows not only the care taken over their reeds by the older generation, but also the extraordinary skill they sometimes attained. Dubrucq had a summer engagement in an orchestra at Eastbourne. He left in the middle of the season to take another appointment and was succeeded by E. W. Davies. He met Davies on handing over and said, 'Have you any decent reeds to play on?' Davies replied that he had some about as good as he could make them. Dubrucq inspected these and said, 'I cannot let you go into the orchestra with such stuff as this.' He produced a knife, with which he touched each one here and there and replaced them *without blowing on them either before or after the magic touch*. 'Those reeds,' said Davies to Buttar, 'were the best I ever had.' This story, I think, also sheds an interesting light on two well-known personalities, for Davies, though the younger man, was even then no mean artist, and in later years rose to high esteem in his profession.

The process outlined above applies also to the making of reeds for the larger oboes, though these, instead of having staples, are usually mounted on quite small brass tubes which fit on to the end of the metal crook. (See Plate I and also Chapter 'The Larger Oboes'.) Occasionally no metal tube at all is incorporated in the reed, and the socket end is formed by notching the roots of the blades longways so that they will themselves, when bound with wire and strong thread, form a sort of tube. This is how bassoon reeds are usually constructed, and certain makers, Italian in particular, favour the same thing for the smaller version as well.

Before leaving our general description of double reeds, two more points require notice. In order that there shall be no leakage of air along the edges of the blades, some makers wrap them to about half-way with a layer of gold-beater's skin. Others place a turn of strong, thin wire around the blades, twisting the ends together. This certainly prevents the blades from separating, but its greatest service is to provide through its stiffness a minute control over the shape of the opening. Many reeds tend to soften in use and close up entirely, and the loop of wire, by pressing on the edges, can often correct this. The wire is an essential feature of all larger modern reeds, and some players find it useful on small ones as well.

Concerning the tone of the wedge-shaped oboe reed some scholars have made ill-judged and rather derogatory assertions. These, I feel sure, are due to inadequate appreciation of the general circumstances of 17th- and 18th-century music. The question is surely one of purpose, and it is unfair to compare the old and the modern type without reference to the sort of instrument to which each is properly allied. The user of a modern oboe expects his reed to respond to a wide range of sharply defined frequencies and to give a sound rich in upper partial tones. He works within a framework of equal temperament and has, indeed requires, only a moderate degree of control over intonation. Even so, there are many conductors today who deplore the convention of taking the tuning A from so sensitive an instrument, and many oboists who, if possible, will avoid the responsibility. (See Chapter 'Acoustics'.)

The older player, of necessity, used a simpler oboe with a smaller compass, and at a time when the temperament of scales was by no means stable. To him freedom of intonation was necessary to an extent that nowadays would be almost unthinkable.[5] Until about 1750 his instrument had a comparatively large bore and deeply undercut finger-holes which contributed to his freedom, and it so happened that the sort of reed that accorded best with that kind of tube was, by modern standards, very broad. We know nowadays that the wider the blades of a reed are in relation to the bore of an instrument the less prominent will be the upper partials. Hence we may deduce that the older players produced a broader and less incisive tone than is usual today, but we are not entitled to regard this as a defect. In passing, we may note that the chanter reeds of both the Northumbrian Small-Pipes and the Irish Uillean pipes are usually 11 mm. wide at the mouth and upward. The tone of both these instruments, though powerful and somewhat 'buzzing', is much warmer and has less 'edge' than that of the oboe.

As the blades of the oboe reed have changed with the passing years, so also has the staple. Today this is a very carefully made conical tube which forms a perfect extension of the main bore of the instrument. A modern oboe whose intervals have been closely adjusted during manufacture may well be put hopelessly out of tune by the use of a staple of a different make. This evidently was not the case with earlier instruments, whose tuning was intentionally marginal.

The actual advent of the staple is difficult to date for lack of evidence, but it was certainly known in connection with the shawms and before the true oboes appeared. Its presence is generally regarded as a diagnostic feature of the latter instrument, but we must note here that it has sometimes been dropped. Many of the old oboes were made much shorter than their nominal sounding length at the pitch of their time,[6] thus implying the use of either a supplementary crook or a very long staple. The average staple recorded by Talbot was about 64 mm. long, as against 34·5 mm. for a recent example. On the other hand Diderot's *Encyclopedie* of 1767

illustrates only a plain reed, without any sort of metal tube incorporated, which plugs directly into the top joint. A number of
French oboes of this period appear to have been intended for use
with such reeds, for they are *longer* over-all than average by just
about the dimensions of a staple. These seem, however, to be less
common than the shorter type.

Modern staples are made from solid brazed tube drawn to shape
over a tapered mandrel, or, in the latest patent process, are built
up by electro-deposition. The latter type offer the advantages of
absolute uniformity between one example and the next and a
mirror-like smoothness in the bore. The earlier ones were simply
rolled up out of sheet metal, and the seam was made airtight by
extending the thread lapping which fastened on the blades. More
thread was then wound on to form a sort of cigar-shaped plug.
This apparently crude construction was in fact very useful, for it
permitted some little adjustment to the diameter of the end. On
instruments with a tapered socket this in turn regulated the depth
to which the reed could be pushed home and provided a species of
tuning adjustment which is still sometimes employed in bag-pipe
chanters.[7] The majority of present-day oboes are built with a
plain cylindrical socket for the reed and a distinct 'shoulder' where
this meets the main bore. The staples made for these are served
with a layer of cork, which makes a very firm and airtight joint.
Even with this construction some tuning can of course be effected
by pulling the reed out, but only at the cost of breaking the smooth
continuity of the bore. This again did not seem to matter so much
with the more simple and wider-bored instruments. In recent
years some reed makers, I am informed, have provided a small
screw adjustment built into the body of the staple itself. This
does not seem to have been welcomed by the majority of players,
and indeed appears to have the same disadvantage as the German
tuning sockets to be noticed later in Chapter 5.

### THE 'CANE'

To the horror of many botanists, the substance from which oboe
and clarinet reeds are now made has for long been called simply,
and without qualification, *cane*, and no doubt it will continue to be
so as long as naturally occurring vegetable stems are employed. It
is useful, indeed essential, to have some such general name, but it
is rather unfortunate that in English we should have adopted one
which is apt to be misleading. In technology the term *cane* is

applied, on account of their shape, to many different objects, some of them not vegetable at all. To very many of us also the word has become practically synonymous with *bamboo*. The material of choice for reed-making is *Arundo donax*, sometimes also called *A. sativa*. This is botanically a *reed* and not, in spite of the assertions of some prominent wind-players, a *bamboo*. The two are in fact only distantly related within the great family of Grasses, which embraces thousands of species. It is one of the curiosities of our language that the name *reed* has become detached from the material and transferred to the product, and thereafter extended to include almost all laminar vibrating bodies.

*Arundo donax*, the largest of the grasses found in Europe, is a handsome plant with tall jointed stems largely enveloped by long, narrow, glaucous leaves which spring from the joints. It is indigenous to certain tropical countries, but is hardy, and transplants so well that it has for centuries been virtually a native of the Mediterranean coasts of France and Spain, where its many uses have made it an article of considerable commerce. It is also grown, mainly for ornament, in the milder parts of the south of England. Under tropical conditions this plant attains an enormous size, but in a temperate Continental climate its growth is limited to between 7 and 12 feet. It is these moderate-sized stems that are used by the reed-maker, and their cultivation has become a specialised industry in the Doubs and Var départéments of France, especially the latter, whence all the best material comes. The business is almost entirely centred on the town of Fréjus, whose immediate neighbourhood supplies the most choice *rozeaux*. In this area the soil is a micaceous and siliceous alluvium, not rich in the general agricultural sense, but with water always available 2 or 3 feet below the surface. In addition, there may be traces of rare elements in the soil—many growers confidently assert that there are—but if so they have not been fully identified.

The stems are cut when still green, stripped of their protecting leaves and gathered into conical stacks and left to season in a cool, dry place outdoors. During the seasoning, which usually takes two years but may last up to four, selected stems are carefully watched and are turned at intervals, as they develop a rich golden-yellow colour with various degrees of mottling. The maturing of the cane calls for much judgment on the part of the grower, and to him the colour of the ripening stem will indicate its probable future quality. Mottling is not usually regarded as a fault, and indeed some reed-

C

makers prefer mottled cane, but any remaining greenness will almost certainly prove fatal. When considered ready, the canes are sawn into convenient lengths and are sorted according to diameter into lots suited to make into larger or smaller reeds.

In the years following the two World Wars the supply of French cane was very badly curtailed, for the reed-beds were largely destroyed by the enemy and the necessarily long seasoning period for new-grown stems made recovery a very slow matter for the industry. To the despair of players, much immature cane found its way on to the market, and various substitute materials were tried out. In view of all this, it may be asked why a supply has not been sought from tropical cane cut when still comparatively small. The answer is that the idea has been tried, but with little success, the reason being apparently that tropical cane, even when small enough in diameter, has already become too coarse-fibred for the purpose. The art of growing cane for reed-making seems to lie in harvesting the plant at the right degree of *immaturity*, and the Var climate, constantly sunny yet tempered by the dry and cold *mistral*, contributes to this very markedly. Recently some interesting attempts have been made to cultivate suitable strains of *A. donax* in southern England, but it is still too early to assess results. Some ten years ago a small quantity was discovered growing wild in Bermuda, and samples showed this fortuitous growth to be of a particularly fine quality. It does not appear, however, to have been commercially exploited as yet.

The exact period when *A. donax* became universally accepted as the best material for musical reeds is difficult to determine, and I do not think that such information as I have been able to gather as yet justifies a definite statement. Over two thousand years ago the Greek *auletes* obtained cane for his double reeds from the shores of Lake Copais in Bœotia or from a lake in Phrygia, and this may well have been *A. donax*, though we have no means of knowing for certain. We do know, however, that even at this remote period a system of harvesting and seasoning quite as exacting as that of the modern French grower was employed. Nowadays the reed grows abundantly in that area, though the soil is a pure limestone one and bears little resemblance chemically to the alluvium of the Var. Very much later, in the 16th century, we find literary references to the musical use of a substance called in German 'meerrohr', which is, with some justification, thought to be *A. donax* again.[8]

In modern times there is much indirect evidence of at least a century of deliberate attention to the needs of the musician. For instance, there are today in France two cane-growers whose records show beyond question that with them cultivation for musical use has been a family speciality for four generations. It is reasonable to suppose that the reed came into use in different places at different times and in those countries where it grows naturally before others. We know that before an organized music industry began to supply all wants, wind players of necessity made their own reeds and sought for suitable material wherever it could be found. The Northumbrian bag-pipe makers, for instance, often made single reeds from the stems of the native elder or 'bour tree' with the pith burnt out. These reeds served for the drones and also on occasion for the chanters as well. Double reeds which can be kept dry in use may also be made of slips of various other British woods, even pine. Both Northumbrian and Scottish pipers also make their reeds of what has long been known as 'Spanish Cane'. This is a coarse-fibred variety of *A. donax* found, as its name indicates, in Spain and not specially cultivated. It is brought into England nowadays for making certain types of fishing-rods and in the form of flower-baskets, especially those used by the growers of mimosa. More than one oboe-player in recent days has made usable reeds from a bit of cane picked up casually in Covent Garden market, and it was to the flower and vegetable merchants that the old bag-pipers looked for their regular supply. This dependence on an apparently unrelated trade has a curious parallel in the violin world, for at one time bow-makers regularly secured the best Pernambuco wood in the shape of discarded barrel staves from the tobacco importers.

### ALTERNATIVES TO THE DOUBLE-REED

Near the beginning of this section I alluded to the traditional association of the double-reed with narrow conical tubes—the oboes and bassoons of today and the shawms and curtalls of an earlier age. So far we have accepted this without comment, but we cannot close the chapter without reference to some efforts directed to eliminating this form of tone-generator altogether and to replacing it with something more consistently reliable. An obvious approach to the problem is to adapt a clarinet-type mouthpiece with a single flat beating reed. The beating reed is much simpler to make than the gouged double blade and, though cane is usually preferred, it need not be of vegetable material at all. Metal and certain synthetic substances, all of them far less variable than cane, have been found suitable. In consequence, such a mouthpiece, if perfected, would seem to offer considerable advantages.

In creating the saxophone over a century ago, Adolph Sax combined the 'beak' mouthpiece with a conical tube of wide bore, and apparently without much difficulty. The problem of uniting it satisfactorily with so narrow a tube as that of the oboe is, however, much greater, and has been the subject of many experiments. One of the earliest successes was achieved about 1830 by the Scottish bandmaster William Meikle when he brought out his newly invented 'Caledonica', a name subsequently altered to 'Alto-Fagotto'. This extremely interesting instrument was improved in design by George Wood, the well-known London maker, and well-preserved specimens show it to have been both simple and practical. There appears, indeed, to be no good reason for its short life except, perhaps, that it appeared at the time when 'flute fever' was rampant in this country. Almost certainly it was easier to manipulate than either the contemporary clarinet or bassoon and its early eclipse is one of the puzzles of musical history.

In outward appearance the alto-fagotto was not unlike a shortened bassoon with a rather flaring bell and a short metal crook bent at right angles. Its bore, though about the same as that of the bassoon at the end of the crook, widened more rapidly, and it was furnished with a long, slender mouthpiece of clarinet type. In spite of the existence of an adequate number of specimens in both public and private collections and the survival of instruction books in the libraries of the British Museum and Cambridge University, no obsolete instrument has been so mishandled by historians as the alto-fagotto. Against evidence, it has been repeatedly described as a double reed, and in exhibition catalogues it has even been re-christened 'Dulcian' and 'Tenoroon'. The confusion seems to have had its first roots in some rather inaccurate memories of the celebrated clarinettist Henry Lazarus, who played on one of Meikle's instruments as a boy and then, at the age of seventy or more, passed on his recollections. In 1932 the whole matter was meticulously reviewed by the late F. G. Rendall in the pages of *Musical Times*, and in 1934 by L. G. Langwill in *Musical Progress and Mail*. Thus, at long last, both Meikle and his invention received their due.[9]

In association with the bassoon, single-reed mouthpieces have been successfully used on a number of occasions. Some musicians in church gallery orchestras in England certainly employed them in the early part of last century, though with what tonal effect we do not know for certain. A Belgian patent granted to the elder Sax in 1842 illustrates, in addition to other improvements to the bassoon of his day, a small apparatus of this type. As regards the oboe, however, there is little evidence earlier than the beginning of the 1900s.

An interesting idea which appears never to have progressed beyond the drawing-board was patented in France in 1856 by a certain Mons. Bornibus, together with the manufacturer Gustave

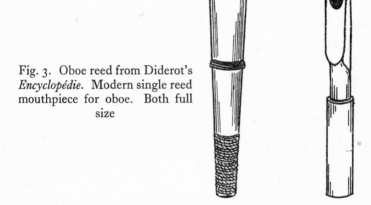

Fig. 3. Oboe reed from Diderot's *Encyclopédie*. Modern single reed mouthpiece for oboe. Both full size

Besson. The apparatus, which went by the rather portentous name of *Neorgane*, consisted of a beak mouthpiece with two opposed tables or 'lays' for flat reeds, one on either side of it, and both communicating with a central sound chamber. This generator was to be applied not only to normal reed instruments, but was expected to replace the cup mouthpieces of the brass as well. So far I have failed to discover any account of the Neorgane in practical use, but the description suggests fascinating speculations. Did it ever work at all?, and what would happen if, on tonguing a note, the two reeds should elect to beat in opposition of phase with each other?

Some time before 1890, Heckel, the celebrated bassoon-maker of Biebrich-am-Rhein, devised a beak mouthpiece for the bassoon which was to be made of ebonite or silver and fitted with either a cane or a metal blade. This, it seems, was not designed for continuous playing, but was intended as a sort of 'test piece'. Its form and materials were chosen so as to be as stable as possible, thus providing the player with a 'standard' generator to which he could adjust and tune the body of his instrument without relying on orthodox reeds, which might themselves be unexpectedly 'off colour'. The idea has since been abandoned as a result of modern research into the effect of different types of tone generator on the very complex harmonic array of the bassoon. About twenty years ago some fairly satisfactory miniature mouthpieces were marketed, particularly in America, and enjoyed a passing vogue among danceband players, presumably on account of the facility they seemed to offer in 'doubling' instruments. At the time of writing, too, at least one American firm is offering beautifully made metal mouth-pieces for both oboe and bassoon and claims that well-known instrumentalists are using them without appreciable loss of characteristic tone. At present it is too soon to speak of the success or otherwise of this venture—comparative tone analyses would be interesting—but it seems likely that the majority of oboe-players will adhere for a long time to the traditional reed in which they are convinced the true character of their instrument lies.

[1] Virdung, 1511. Agricola, 1528. Praetorius, 1618–19.

[2] Except Austria and Germany, where special conditions prevailed, which are discussed in a later chapter.

[3] The writers of instruction books appear reluctant to commit themselves on figures. The actual thickness of gouged cane varies greatly with its hardness and with the individual views of the reed-maker.

[4] M. M. Porter, L.D.S.Eng., 'Dental Aspects of Orchestral Wind Instrument Playing', *British Dental Journal*, London, Vol. XCIII, No. 3, pp. 66–73, and 'Dental Factors Adversely Influencing the Playing of Wind Instruments', *ibid.*, Vol. XCV, No. 7.

[5] 'He seems to possess a happy and peculiar faculty of tempering a continued tone to different basses according to their several relations.'— Charles Burney writing of Carlo Besozzi, *The Present State of Music in Germany*, 1773, Vol. II, p. 45. See also Freillon Poncein as paraphrased by E. Halfpenny. *Galpin Society Journal*, VI, 1953, p. 30.

[6] Disregarding the extra length below the vent-holes in the bell.

[7] W. L. Manson, *The Highland Bagpipe*, Paisley, 1901, pp. 378–9.

[8] E. Bossert, *Wurtembergische Viertlejahrshefte f. Landesgeschichte*, 1900, p. 276.

[9] F. G. Rendall, 'The Saxophone before Sax', *Musical Times*, London, Dec. 1st, 1932, pp. 1077 *et seq.*

L. G. Langwill, 'The Alto-Fagotto—misnamed Tenoroon—its Original, the Caledonica and their Inventor', *Musical Progress and Mail*, London, April 1934, pp. 165–6, where the original and the improved instruments are illustrated.

# CHAPTER 3

# The Precursors and the Advent of the Oboe

OUR knowledge of wind instruments in Europe between the end of the Roman era and the mid-Renaissance is derived almost entirely from literature, pictures, and sculpture. To quote again from Adam Carse,

> 'The occurrence of the names of wind instruments in the records and literature of the Middle Ages or contemporary pictorial or carved representations of such, do little more than establish the existence of certain types at more or less vague periods.'

Such sources assure us of the continuity of basic principles (i.e. the double reed), but they provide little or no technical information. It is not until the early 16th century, whence both actual instruments and specialised writings about them survive, that we can begin to speak with some certainty.[1]

Towards the middle of the 4th century the Roman Theatre, owing to its moral laxity, fell under the ban of the Church, and for nearly eleven hundred years the secular drama in Europe lapsed. Under Roman civilisation the theatre had been the principal home of music, but now its cultivation came into the exclusive care of the monastic houses. In the ritual of the early Church vocal music alone was permitted, for instrumental playing bore the stigma of its association with the stage. Instrumental music might indeed have disappeared entirely but for the fact that, after the suppression of the theatre, many musicians took to a wandering life, playing and singing as opportunity offered. It is due to them that knowledge of instruments and their techniques was preserved to be developed in turn through the Minstrels of different periods and social standing—the knightly troubadours and their jongleurs, the solid and respectable Brotherhoods of Town Musicians, and the exclusive Guilds of Trumpeters. The inter-relation of these various classes and the laws affecting them form a fascinating chapter of social history. As regards the Church, after some three hundred years a change of opinion occurred, and by the middle of the 7th century instrumental music had become acceptable. Of all instruments, the organ, formerly the accompaniment of gladiatorial displays, was regarded as a fitting support for choral worship.

With the dawn of the 16th century we pass from indirect to direct evidence, and encounter at the same time an era of surprising richness. As Dr. Alexander Buchner has pointed out,[2] no period either before or since the Renaissance has produced so great a variety of instrumental types. Many of these are today obsolete, in spite, or perhaps because, of the high development of our present music. Probably they had already reached the limit that their construction permitted and were not susceptible to further technical improvement. Among the woodwinds, two families then flourishing—the cornetts and the mirlitons[3]—have passed quite out of use and in Europe have no modern representatives at all, if we except such mere toys as the 'kazoo'. Of other families certain features have survived, though in smaller instrumental groups, or in specialised instruments which are seldom admitted into the orchestra.

It is evident from many sources that the double reed was highly developed in the 16th and 17th centuries and was employed in a number of different ways. Among the mouth-blown instruments it was either placed in an isolated wind-chamber (Fr. *capsule*; Gr. *windkapsel*) with a blow-hole at the end or in the side, or it was taken directly into the player's mouth. Moreover, both methods of blowing were associated with either cylindrical or conical tubes. We find therefore four main classes of double reed instruments in use at the time:—

1. Cylindrical with enclosed reed.
2. Conical with enclosed reed.
3. Cylindrical with lipped reed.
4. Conical with lipped reed.

The fourth of these classes contains the curtals, primitive bassoon types, and the straight-tubed pommers and shawms *sensu stricto*, and it is among these that we must seek the first ancestor of the oboe. We should note that some Germanic writers regard the second class as shawms also, and indeed the two types may well have sprung from a common stock. Many believe also that the folded tube of the curtals arose in an attempt to make the unwieldy bass Pommers more portable, though some authorities are by no means convinced about this.

It would be pleasant here to describe in detail the many double reeds known at the beginning of the 17th century, for this was clearly their peak period, and they offer some attractive problems to the musical detective. That is, however, beyond the scope of this book, and readers are invited to consult the general bibliography. The following table of varieties mentioned by Praetorius (as the fullest writer of the time) may serve for quick reference, if we bear in mind that the information we have from different sources is not always consistent, and that there are today no known specimens of certain types. In cases of doubtful identity I have adopted Kinsky's interpretation of the evidence.[4]

The shawm played a major part in European music from the 13th to the late 17th century, and, though it is clear that double-reed pipes were known in western Europe long before the beginning of that period, it is most probable that this particular form of instrument reached us from the East during the Middle Ages. In the Turkish *zurnah*, the *zamr* of Egypt, and allied reed pipes used today in various eastern Mediterranean countries we find preserved the early Islamic prototype of the shawm, and though this differs in certain details from its Western descendant it is essentially the same instrument. From the literature of the later Crusades we know that the *zurnah* was widely used, together with trumpets and drums, in the large military establishments of the Saracen princes and the practice was subsequently copied, albeit on a smaller scale, in the West.[5]

Canon Galpin has observed that the shawm does not appear to be one of the instruments which an accomplished jongleur of the early 13th century was expected to play, but in the mid-century it was well established in the quasi-military town bands. Siena, for instance, in 1252 employed three trumpets, one *cialamella*, and one drum—a very typical group at the time.[6] Well before the year 1500 trumpet-and-shawm bands had risen to great importance at the big ducal courts; for example, that of Burgundy, whose domestic accounts record the purchase of 'bombardes à clef' in 1423 and 'teneurs à clef' in 1439.[7] A glance at European social history suggests that in the first instance we may owe our refined and gentle oboe not so much to fresh cultural influences from the East as to the desire of Western princes to emulate the pomp and circumstance of the Orient.

So far as is known at present, the oldest captioned illustration of the shawm appears in the Sloane MS. 3908 (British Museum) of

| | Praetorian Name | Equivalents | |
|---|---|---|---|
| | | English | German |
| 1 | Pommer | Waits<br>Shawm and var. | Bombart and var. |
| | Schalmey | Bumbarde<br>Hoboye and var. | Bomhart<br>Pumhart |
| 2 | Fagott<br>Dolcian<br>Kortholt (generic) | Curtal and var. | Fagotten<br>Dulzian |
| 3 | Sordun | — | — |
| 4 | Kortholt (proper<br>    name)<br>Kort *instrument* | — | — |
| 5 | Doppioni | — | — |
| 6 | Rackett<br>Ranket | Sausage Bassoon | Wurstfagott<br>Faustfagott |
| 7 | Krumbhorn | Crumhorn<br>Cromorne | Krumhorn |
| 8 | Schryari | — | Schreierpfeiffen |
| 9 | Bassanello | — | — |
| 10 | 'Nicolo' | — | Rauschpfeiffe<br>    (Burkmair 1518) |
| 11 | Cornamusa | — | Dolzaina?<br>    (Kinsky) |
| 12 | Sackpfeif | Bagpipe | Dudelsack<br>Bock<br>Dudey, etc. |

| French | Italian | Characteristics |
|---|---|---|
| Hautbois<br>Haulxbois<br>Bombarde<br>Chalumeau | Piffero<br>Bombarde and<br>[var. | Straight conical bore—lipped reed. |
| Basson | Fagotto | Doubled conical bore—lipped reed.<br>A. Bell open ⎫<br>B. Bell muted⎭ in Germany. |
| Courtaut<br>Courtaud<br>Sourdine | Sordone | Doubled cylindrical bore (twice)—lipped reed. |
| Courtaut?<br>(Mersenne<br>1636) | — | Doubled cylindrical bore—muted—lipped reed. |
| — | — | Mentioned without description in Zacconi and Praetorius. |
| Cervelas<br>Cervelat (Mersenne) | Racketto | Ninefold cylindrical bore—lipped reed. (Bore slightly conical in late types.) |
| Cromorne<br>Tournebout | Cromorne | Bent cylindrical bore—enclosed reed. |
| — | Schryari | Mentioned by Praetorius only—enclosed reed. (Presumably inverted conical bore.) |
| — | — | Straight cylindrical bore—lipped reed. |
| Hautbois de<br>Poitou (Mersenne 1636) | — | Straight conical bore—enclosed reed. (Virtually obsolete in Praetorius' day, except perhaps the basset.) |
| Douchaine?<br>Douceine? | Dulzaina? | Straight cylindrical bore—muted—keyless—enclosed reed. |
| Cornamuse<br>Musette<br>Biniou | Surdelina<br>Cornamusa<br>Zampogna<br>Piva | A. Mouth-blown ⎫<br>B. Bellows-blown⎭ enclosed reeds. |

the early 14th century, while the earliest written account of it is given briefly by Tinctoris, *c.* 1486.[8] Thereafter more particular information is furnished by successive specialist writers up to Praetorius, by whose time a complete family of different sizes from high treble to double bass had developed. The shawm appears to be the first European wind instrument to have undergone so full an evolution, though, unlike the cornett, it was not regarded as chromatically complete.

### *The Shawm Family* (after Praetorius—1618)

| German usage | English and French | Compass |
|---|---|---|
| Klein Discant Schalmey | — | $a'-e'''$ |
| Discant Schalmey | Treble (*dessus*) | $d'-b''$ ($d'''$) |
| Alt Pommer | Tenor (*taille*) | $g-d''$ |
| Tenor Pommer | — | $c-g'$ |
| Basset Pommer | — | $G-g'$ |
| Bass Pommer | Bass (*basse*) | $C-c'$ |
| Gross Bass Pommer | — | Variable |

*N.B.* The last three were provided with *four* keys which extended the lower compass.

Authentic specimens, corresponding in detail to each of the seven sizes known to Praetorius, can be found in one or other of the European museum collections. In considering these, however, we must remember that this author evidently knew best the instruments of Germany, and contemporary usage in both France and England appears to have been less extravagant. From the first, shawms belonged to the category of the 'Loud Music', whether employed indoors or in the open air, and, although capable of forming an harmonic group or 'whole consort' by themselves, they were early combined with wind of other sorts. For instance, at the Duke of Burgundy's wedding in 1480 a motet was performed on three *schalmayes* and *trompette saicquebotte* (trombone).[9] There is some evidence also of the trial of these instruments in company with the strings of the 'Still Music' group—fiddle, harp, and lute—but their pungent tone would hardly seem to recommend them here. With the appreciation of more subtly blended consorts of strings, cornetts, trombones, and organs which marked the close of the Elizabethan Age, the shawms declined somewhat in dignity and, in general, became limited to the less refined grades of musical service—town bands and outdoor Court ceremonial—and remained so for the last century of their active life. The shawms evidently served also as signal instruments in cases where no trumpets were available.[10]

The characteristic structure of the shawms is simple and easily recognised. The body (except in one late variety) was all in one piece, with little external ornament, cylindrical or slightly tapered in outline, and expanded at the end into a trumpet-like bell. Internally the tube was regularly conical for some four-fifths of its length, below which it flared in a fairly smooth curve. The bore generally was rather wider in proportion to its length than in the modern oboe and the expansion of the cone was more rapid. Six finger-holes, in two groups of three situated in the upper half of the body, gave a primary scale of an octave, and a seventh hole set below these carried the compass one tone downward. There was in the European shawms no thumb-hole, as is usually found in similar Oriental instruments. On the smaller shawms the finger-holes were fairly evenly spaced, but, with increasing length, the grouping became progressively more marked. Theoretical placing was easy with the small Discant, only about 49 cms. long, or even with the Alt Pommer (76 cm.), but beyond this size the limited stretch of the hand made a well-proportioned lay-out impossible. This unavoidable feature, only slightly mitigated by boring the holes diagonally through the thickness of the tube wall, must have given rise to considerable tuning problems, but we have no reason to suppose that shawm-players did not find practical solutions, or that they were any less sensitive in the matter of intonation than were the early oboists. (See Chapters 2, p. 15, and 9, p. 123.) Like certain instruments even at the present day, the shawm was at its best in a limited number of keys, and no doubt these were to some extent dictated by the compromise spacing adopted for the finger-holes.[11] (Praetorius recommends that where treble shawms are used the music should be transposed from the customary C or F into G, which was the best scale on these instruments.)

On the smaller shawms the seventh hole, stopped by the little finger, was regularly duplicated, and placed to the side out of line with the other six, since, in their day and until well on in the life of the true oboe, musicians suited their own convenience as to which hand was placed above the other. The unused hole was plugged, usually with wax. From the tenor pommer downward, the seventh hole was single and was controlled by an open-standing key which had a bifurcated touchpiece to accommodate either right- or left-handed players. In the list quoted above from Praetorius it has been pointed out that the largest pommers, basset, bass, and gross bass, each had a further extension of three tones to the lower range. Three more holes, each with a key, provided this, and one of them again was 'fishtailed' for either hand. The remaining two keys were placed at the back, where the lower thumb could work them. All these keys were protected from damage by perforated wooden barrels (Fr. *fontanelles*; Gr. *schutzkapseln*) surrounding the body of the instrument.

Among the several remarkable features of the shawm group the most noticeable is probably the extreme length of the tube beyond

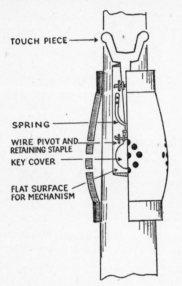

TOUCH PIECE ⟶

SPRING

WIRE PIVOT AND
RETAINING STAPLE

KEY COVER

FLAT SURFACE
FOR MECHANISM

Fig. 4. The *Fontanelle* in elevation and half-section to show early type of key-mechanism beneath

what is necessary to sound the lowest nominal note. Nearly half the total length seems at first sight to be redundant, but its function as a resonating chamber (see Chapter 'Acoustics') was probably most important from the tonal point of view. As with the true oboes later on, the excess length of the tube was compensated by a group of from two to six permanently open holes in its lower part. At one time a rather ridiculous though ingenious theory was advanced that these holes, on the bass instruments at least, could be closed by the player's knees, thus providing even deeper tones. In fact the idea is entirely without support.

Before leaving the body of the shawm and passing on to other matters we should perhaps notice a special type which flourished in

Germany and the Netherlands from the late 1600s till after 1710·
Known as the 'Deutsche Schalmey', it was more slender and
elegant than the earlier form, more ornamental externally, and
usually built in two sections with a tenon-and-socket joint near the
middle. Only trebles and tenors appear to have been made on this
model, and the former had the peculiarity that no key seems ever to
have been fitted to them. Quite a number of examples are known
both in museums and in private collections, and in every case the

Fig. 5. Reed, staple, and pirouette
in section. The drawing is purely
diagrammatic for the pirouette was
made in a great variety of shapes
according to the fancy of the instrument makers

seventh hole is without means of closure, although a fontanelle is
regularly there. These instruments were employed in particular in
military music, and the trebles were usually tuned a major third
lower than the older trebles observing the same standard of pitch.

The last peculiarity of the shawm which requires special notice
here is the blowing apparatus, and this is so characteristic as to be a
diagnostic feature of the group. It consisted of three separate
parts: the staple, the 'pirouette', and the reed itself. The staple
was a tapered metal tube which was inserted in the top of the main
bore and from which, in the treble size, it projected some 3 cms.
Upon this was impaled the pirouette (Dr. Talbot's word is 'fliew'),

a turned wooden piece bored down the middle and shaped like an inverted bell. A small hollow was cut in the face of the pirouette so as to leave the tip of the staple clear, and this carried the reed.

This arrangement was evidently designed to guide and support the lips in loud and sustained playing and was probably an improvement on an ancient Eastern prototype. In discussing it, however, some reputable scholars have fallen into error. The Oriental equivalent of the pirouette is a flat metal disc, often a coin with a hole in the middle, and it is the custom for the musician to press his lips firmly against this while taking the entire reed into the cavity of the mouth. The mouth then becomes simply a windchamber, and there is little or no control over the behaviour of the reed. From the mere presence of the pirouette it has been argued that the shawm-player had likewise no control over the reed. It is here, however, that the subtlety of the apparatus appears. The hollowed face permitted the base of the reed to be set in quite deeply so that in use the blades lay between the player's lips. Thus, while still supported, the lips could to some extent exercise control. It was on account of this facility that the compass of the shawms could be carried upwards beyond the first octave and was not limited, in Praetorius' own words, to 'as many tones as there were holes'. We do not know for certain what material was used for the *zurnah* reeds of Saracen days, but today a soft rush or maizestraw is employed. Such reeds close up very easily and will not speak clearly if touched at all by the lips, while, on the other hand, hard material such as *Arundo donax* must be firmly held if it is not to give just a wild squawk. It is generally supposed that *A. donax* or something very similar was used with European shawms as long ago as the 16th century, and recently some very interesting theories have been advanced concerning the relation between the characteristics of early reeds and the pirouettes used with them.[12] At the moment, however, these ideas must be taken with some reserve, for they lack any experimental proof. The technique of the pirouette is to be seen at the present day among the Sardana musicians of northern Catalonia, whose instruments, the tiple and tenora, though fitted with modern key-work, retain the three features which are generally regarded as definitive of the Praetorian shawm—viz. one-piece body and trumpet-like bell;* characteristic

---

* For the sake of lightness and balance the bell section of the modern Tenora is sometimes made of metal, but it is not detachable and the join is usually a permanent one.

relative proportions in the bore, quite unlike those of the oboe; and the hollowed-out pirouette itself.[13]

A further feature that may be of evolutionary importance has recently been stressed by Josef Marx,[14] who points out that we have today neither specimens nor pictures of the bass or gross bass pommers with the pirouette attached. These instruments were respectively some 244 and 304 cms. long and were most unwieldy. They were, however, made a little more portable by making the top 25 cms. or so in the form of a tapered metal S-crook, and this, like the staple of the shorter instruments, carried the reed. We may, of course, assume that because reeds and pirouettes were detachable and easily lost, none of the bass size has survived; but the crooks, too, were detachable, and these we have. Besides, the basset pommer was also a crooked instrument, and in Praetorius' woodcut it is clearly shown with a pirouette on the same page as the bass without one. On another page the gross bass is figured, and this, too, shows only a simple reed. The matter can hardly have been merely one of carelessness on the part of the engraver, and we can only conclude that by 1618 these two monster instruments were being played without the pirouette. They may have matched the other members of the family in earlier years, but we have, so far, no means of telling. It may be significant, however, that the folded bassoons, which seem never to have required a pirouette (and which were unknown to Virdung in 1511), had by Praetorius' day become well established as bass instruments and were already ousting the larger Pommers even in the sphere of outdoor music.

The foregoing, though of necessity greatly compressed, is, I believe, a fair outline of what we now know about the shawm in Western Europe, its arrival, rise, and decline, and its status in the middle of the 17th century. This was a time of fresh influences in many directions, particularly in the Latin countries. In Italy the first seeds of opera were sprouting, while, in France particularly, instrumental music was being organised with imagination and a thoughtful regard for special purposes. Instrumental requirements were changing and the time was evidently ripe for new resources.

Before 1625 the outdoor music of Louis XIII consisted of two treble shawms, two cornetts, four tenor shawms, two trombones, and two bass shawms, while about the same time, in London, James I had a similar though smaller band. Unfortunately the composition of the latter is not accurately known. At the opulent Court of

D

Louis XIV—'le Roi Soleil'—(1642–1715) musical organisation reached its highest state and musicians could find employment in several different spheres: the Chapel, the Chamber Music, and above all in the 'Grande Ecurie'—the large band administered by the Master of the Great Stables of the King. Nowhere else in Europe was there so large a body of musicians whose service was so secure, so remunerative, or carried such social advantages. Appointments were eagerly sought and, when granted, were hereditary and could be bequeathed by will. With such rewards in view the highest standard of contemporary musicianship was expected and secured. The period is so well documented that we can feel almost a personal acquaintanceship with the Philidors, the Hotteterres, the Chédevilles, and many other celebrated musical families whose different generations served French Royalty in the 17th and 18th centuries.[15]

The music of the Grande Ecurie itself was divided into five corps: (1) the Trumpets; (2) the Fifes and Drums; (3) the Violins, Shawms, Sackbuts, and Cornetts; (4) the Krumhorns and Trumpets Marine; (5) the Hautbois and Musettes de Poitou. Such an organisation could obviously provide both the rigidly traditional music required by certain aspects of Court ceremonial and the more ephemeral entertainment music, as well as being at the same time a nursery for up-to-date experiment. In three of its departments woodwind virtuosi were sure of a welcome, and it was upon these men that the autocratic Lully was to draw for the wind players required in his entertainments in the years following 1654. There is little doubt that this irascible innovator provided the stimulus that gave birth about this time to a new voice, the true oboe.

Among the men of the Grande Ecurie were some notable instrument-makers, in particular the Hotteterre family, who are generally credited with introducing the transverse flute into France, and, in the light of some interesting musical deductions recently published by Josef Marx,[16] it seems quite probable that the eldest of these, Jean Hotteterre I (in conjunction perhaps with Michel Philidor), originated the new instrument. This would have been a year or two before 1660, a date which accords well with Talbot's statement already quoted in our descriptive section. Probably this is as near as we shall ever get to the root of the matter, unless some hitherto unsuspected document of the time should some day come to light.

The next ten years or so we can well imagine as a period of research and practical improvement at the hands of the French Court

instrument-makers, and then we arrive at a most significant date—
1671. This was the year of Cambert's opera 'Pomone', which is
usually cited as the first work in which the oboe as such was speci-
fied in the orchestration. In fact it seems that Lully may have
given his men opportunities to present the new instrument in
public before this time; but thereafter it became prominent.[17]
Soon we hear of it in the hands of, not only the younger Hotteterres and the Philidors, but also of Descoteaux and Philbert, the
recorder players, and the bagpipers Brunet, Destouches, and
Piesche, father and son. The musicians of the Grande Ecurie were
always at least 'double-handed', and once the oboe was established
they were expected to add it to their other accomplishments.

In England during this time instrumental music had suffered at
least a partial eclipse. The leaders of the Commonwealth had little
time for what they supposed frivolities, and at the Restoration
things began again where they had left off in 1643–4 with the old-
fashioned shawms, recorders, sackbuts, and cornetts. In 1674,
however, a great event occurred. Cambert, who had established
himself over here two years earlier, was commissioned to supervise
the great masque of 'Calisto' by John Crowne and Nicholas
Staggins. The latter was one of a long line of Royal musicians who
specialised in the old English 'hoboye' or 'waits'. For his masque
Staggins was authorised to employ a certain number of foreign
musicians, including the French oboe players Paisible, de Bresmes,
Guiton, and Boutet.[18] We can hardly doubt that these men used
the new French instrument, for there would have been no point in
importing shawms which were readily available from many sources
at home, and of the four, Paisible is known to have been a virtuoso
on the French hautboy and to have been closely under the influence
of the first generation of oboists in France. Like Cambert, he spent
the rest of his life in England and entered the King's service.

Was the production of 'Calisto', then, the first public appearance
of the true oboe in England? We cannot be sure, but it seems
likely indeed.[19] As the following details show, the instrument
'caught on' extremely rapidly, and its rising vogue here is typical
of what took place simultaneously on the Continent. In 1676 it was
well enough known to be the subject of a topical jest in Etheredge's
'Man of Mode'; in 1678 it was adopted in Army circles, and three
years later Purcell made a first trial of it in the score of his 'Swifter
Isis'. Thereafter, from 1690 till his death, he used it regularly in
most of his larger music. The form of oboe which Purcell knew is

depicted in the well-known drawing in Randle Holme's *Academy of Armory* of 1688.[20] Finally, as if to round off the apprentice period, in 1695 there was published in London *The Sprightly Companion*, which contains the first known printed tutor for the instrument. The true oboe had made its debut.[21]

---

[1] Sebastian Virdung, *Musica Getutscht*, Basel, 1511. Reprint, Berlin, 1882 (facsimile), Kassel, 1931 (facsimile).

Martin Agricola, *Musica Instrumentalis deudsch*, Wittemberg, 1528–32–42–45 ; Reprint, Leipzig, 1896 (facsimile).

Zacconi, *Prattica di Musica*, Venice, 1596.

Michael Praetorius, *Syntagma Musicum*, Wolfenbuttel, 1618–19. Reprint, Berlin, 1884, Kassel, 1929 (facsimile).

Marin Mersenne, *Harmonie Universelle*, Paris, 1636.

[2] Alexander Buchner, *Extinct Wood Wind Instruments of the 16th Century*, National Museum of Prague, Vol. VII, Historia No. 2, 1952.

[3] Wigley and McGregor's *Flauto di Voce*, c. 1810, employed the characteristic sympathetic vibrating membrane, but was in other respects a flute like the Chinese ti-tzu, and in no sense a mirliton. The Indian nyastaranga employs the true mirliton principle.

[4] We must be careful in reading and translating these early names. Even contemporary writers used variants on the same word to indicate quite different instruments. Also such a name as Dulzian (a bassoon type) is easily confused with dulzaina, which probably represented a capsuled instrument of soft tone. See Buchner and also Kinsky. The latter's study of instruments with enclosed double-reeds, *Doppelrohrblatteninstrumente mit Windkapsel*, is an invaluable reference work.

[5] In the course of the last few years workers in the Conservatoire of Ankarah have reconstructed from literary sources certain authentic Turkish military music of the 14th century. This music is proscribed by the Government for public performance, but a few private recordings exist which clearly reveal the importance of the *zurnah* in this context.

[6] Vessella, *La Banda*, 1939.

[7] Jeanne Marix, *Histoire de la Musique et des Musiciens de la cour de Bourgogne sous le règne de Philippe le Bon*, Strasbourg, 1939.

[8] Johannes de Tinctoris, *De inventione et usu Musicae*, c. 1486, edited by K. Weinmann, Regensburg, 1917.

[9] Olivier de la Manche, *Memoires*, Vol. III, p. 152.

[10] A. C. Baines. Article 'Shawm' in *Grove's Dictionary of Music*, London, 5th Edn. This is an excellent survey of the vicissitudes of the Shawm family, and well documented. See also *Archaeologica*, Vol. XXIII, London, 1831, p. 44. From a petition of Richard Traughton, Bailiff of South Witham, Lincs., to the Privy Council 1553 :—

> 'And so we wente to the market crosse in the hearying of the countrie people and solemply w[th] the noise of shawmes iij seuall times blowen w[th] distyncyion. Afterwerd on commanded of men kepe sylence and here the Quene's proclamacyon.'

[11] Baines, *op. cit.*, states that on specimens of the Bass Pommer tested the cross-fingered accidentals are remarkably good and the tone in general free and pleasing.

[12] Josef Marx, 'The Tone of the Baroque Oboe', *Galpin Society Journal*, No. 4, London, 1951, pp. 7 *et seq.*

[13] A. C. Baines, 'The Shawms of the Sardana Coblas', *Galpin Society Journal*, No. 5, London, 1952, pp. 9 *et seq.*

P. Bromse, *Flote, Schalmeien, und Sackpfeiffen der Sudslaviens*, Brno, 1937.

[14] Josef Marx, *op. cit.*, p. 8.

[15] The most important studies of these men are to be found in the following:—

J. Ecorcheville, 'Quelques documents sur la Musique de la Grande Ecurie du Roi' in *S.I.M.G.*, Vol. II, pp. 608 *et seq.*

E. Thoinan, 'Les Hotteterre et les Chédeville' and 'Les Philidor', in *La France Musicale*, 1894 and 1867–8.

[16] Josef Marx, *op. cit.*, p. 12.

[17] *Op. cit.*, p. 14 and note 24, p. 18. There seems to be no doubt that Bechler and Rahm are mistaken in claiming Benevoli's 'Salzburg' Mass of 1628 as the first orchestral score to include the true oboe.

[18] H. C. de la Fontaine, *The King's Music*, London, Novello and Co., 1909, pp. 281–90.

[19] E. Halfpenny, 'The English Debut of the French Hautboy', monthly *Musical Record*, London, July 1949, pp. 149 *et seq.*

[20] Harleian, MSS., Brit. Mus. 2034, f. 207. Note that although the 'brass keys' are mentioned, only the great C key appears in the drawing.

[21] Before the close of the 17th century two more instruction books and a printed tablature had appeared in England. They are well discussed by Halfpenny in *Galpin Society Journal*, No. VI, 1953, pp. 24–5.

# CHAPTER 4

# The Oboe in the 18th Century

THE history of the oboe, as I have already said in the Introduction, is continuous, although naturally it falls into phases. Divisions, though in the strict sense artificial, are nevertheless helpful in maintaining a clear picture of the whole. Thus the year 1700 may usefully be regarded as the beginning of the second stage, for the following reasons. At this date the oboe had passed its experimental period. On the civilian side the more advanced composers had already come to accept it as the only possible soprano reed instrument, while its adoption by the Horse Grenadiers in 1678 proves that it had been found equally fit for more robust service. 'The greatest Heroes of the Age', wrote J. B. in 1695 '(who sometimes despise Strung-Instruments) are infinitely pleased with This for its brave and sprightly Tone.' By about 1715, in this country, town bands had finally discarded the instruments known as 'waits' and were using the new 'hautboy', though perhaps in a not particularly refined way.[1] 1700 marks also the publication of the first French instruction book, that of Freillon Poncein, and this was followed by a dozen or so more in different countries during the next sixty years. The best known are:—

1. Hotteterre, *Principes de la Flûte Traversière*, Paris, 1707, 1710. Containing instructions for the hautbois as a supplement to the main text.
2. *The Modern Musick Master* (Prelleur), London, 1738.
3. Eisel, *Musikus Autodidaktos*, Erfurt, 1738.
4. *The Compleat Tutor, c.* 1750 ⎫ (Probably derived from No. 2
5. *The Muses' Delight*, 1754 ⎭ above.)
6. Minguet Y Yrol, *Reglas, y Advertencias Generales que ensenan el modo de taner todos los instrumentos mejores* . . ., Madrid, 1754.

Finally, Dr. Talbot's invaluable notes and measurements were made, if not actually in 1700, within a year or two of that date.

It has become the custom in musical text-books to look upon the oboe as merely a development of the shawm, and to say that each

member of that family 'became' in time the corresponding
modern instrument. Such statements have given rise to much misunderstanding, for they are only true to a limited extent. The
situation was in fact not nearly so simple as the text-book writers
suggest. Allowing that both instruments were based on the principle of the double reed allied to an un-bent conical tube, and that
the originator of the oboe, whoever he may have been, had before
him the example of the shawm, we may certainly say that the latter
was physically the parent instrument. Between the two, however,
were great differences of construction, method of playing, and
musical purpose. The oboe was not just a refined version of the
earlier instrument, but was something called into being by
changing taste and growing musical demands which the shawm
could not adequately meet. It has recently been pointed out also
that the earliest oboes, in the refinement of their construction and
ornament at least, appear to owe more to the highly developed bagpipes of the French Court musicians than to any shawm. The new
instrument surpassed the old in having a compass of two complete
octaves and all semitones within it. Its tone, dynamic range, and
agility were evidently superior. In *The Sprightly Companion*, once
more, we find such phrases as 'Inimitable charming sweetness—
Majestical and Stately and not much Inferiour to the Trumpet',
and again, 'with a good Reed it goes as easie and soft as the Flute'.
As in the case of the viol and violin, the two types existed side by
side for some long time, each performing a quite distinct musical
function. It was only near the beginning of the 18th century that
the more versatile oboe, by successfully taking over most of the
remaining duties of the shawm, finally gave the *coup de grace* to an
instrument that was already in general decline.

The second phase of the oboe, which lasted for some ninety
years, may conveniently be labelled the 'two-and-three-key' period.
During the whole of that time the instrument underwent no radical
change, though improvements were made fairly continuously. The
oboe that served Bach and Handel, Haydn and Mozart, and even
the young Beethoven, was essentially the same as that which first
reached England, we believe, in the hands of the Frenchman
Paisible and his colleagues. It was the instrument which replaced
the shawms and cornetts of Louis XIII's 'Douze Grands Hautbois
du Roi'[2] and which is depicted in Tardieu's engraving of that élite
corps as they appeared at the coronation of Louis XV in 1722.[3]

In the orchestra of the 18th century the oboe was at first

employed somewhat tentatively, often merely as a *ripieno* instrument, together with the strings to which it gave a telling pungency. Even the works of Bach are full of examples of this sort of writing, though it is evident that as early as his Weimar period he regarded it as a valuable soloist. A well-balanced orchestra of this time, according to Quantz, would consist of Strings 4, 4, 2, 2, 2, two flutes, two oboes, two bassoons, together with horns as required.[4] Before the end of the century the two oboes had attained the status of fully independent voices able to sustain simple harmonic writing by themselves.

Though a great advance on any former reed instrument, the oboe was still really fluent in a few keys only. The demand for twelve notes in the octave with no more than eight holes available resulted in a fingering technique which became more difficult with every remove from the natural key of the instrument, three sharps and three flats being the practical limit. There is, however, no evidence that 18th-century composers found the oboe less perfect than their other woodwinds. Players whose livelihood depended on it mastered its shortcomings to the best of their personal skill and appear to have accepted its limitations as they (sometimes) did their working conditions—with resignation. Most professional musicians in the 18th century undoubtedly had a hard and ill-rewarded life even when admitted to polite society, but we may hope that not many had the experience recorded by Congreve. In a letter to a friend he wrote: 'The Hautboys who played to us last night had their breath froze in their instruments till it dripped of the end of 'em in icicles, by god this is true.'

The above, then, was the state of the oboe for a very considerable time, and before the last years of the century we find only one suggestion of any attempt at mechanical improvement. This appears in some manuscript addenda made by Walther to the first edition of his *Lexikon* of 1732, and refers to work done by Hoffmann of Rastenburg, though clearly there has been misunderstanding or mis-translation by later scholars. As a result some wholly untenable statements have been made and repeated by successive writers until almost the present day. This is a great pity, and we ought to admit that, lacking further information, we cannot properly interpret Walther's notes. If Hoffmann did really make some improvement to the oboe of his time, it remains so far one of the unsolved mysteries of musicology.[5] (See also *Gerhard Hoffmann*, Chapter 14, p. 161.) Prior to Hoffmann, the flautist Quantz is sometimes credited with adding to the oboe a low $c\sharp$ key, which, however, did not prove acceptable to contemporary players. This statement is to be found in Sandford Terry's book on Bach's orchestra, but his authority seems dubious.

The oboes of the 18th century all conform in general to the description given on p. 3, but when we compare a large number of examples, we quickly see that there was over the years a great deal of variation, and of more than a minor character. We can, in fact, recognise several distinct types, though we shall be wise if we do not try to classify them too rigidly. In all comparative work, too, we must make allowance for the differences between, say, French, English, and German taste in ornament at any given time, which applies as much to instrument-making as to any other branch of art. Before passing on to describe fingering, then, it may be well to consider in more detail the instruments themselves, since many of their peculiarities are directly concerned with this matter.

In the first place, comparison of these instruments and the known working dates of some of their makers shows that they fall naturally into two groups: the two-keyed and the three-keyed. Though it seems odd at first sight, the three-keyed are nearly always the older; indeed, we find that few oboes of the sort were made after about 1750. Rather before that date the two-keyed oboe became the common type, and it was still occasionally being made sixty or seventy years later when up-to-date instruments were well advanced in the third stage of development. The situation, in fact, contains no paradox; both varieties of the instrument were musically the same, the only difference being in the way in which they could be held. The three-keyed type followed the tradition of shawm and recorder, whose players could please themselves as to which hand lay uppermost, while the disappearance of the left-hand duplicate small key $c$. 1750 merely shows that about that time the modern convention of 'left over right' had become accepted. The list on p. 42 of oboe-makers with approximate dates according to Lyndesay G. Langwill may be useful to students of the period.[6]

From these columns it will be seen that our information concerning individual makers varies greatly. In some cases dates of birth and death are both known; in others only the working period, or even a single significant date.

Let us now look at the actual varieties of the 18th-century oboe,

| Early Group (Three Keys) | | Later Group (Two Keys) | |
|---|---|---|---|
| Anciuti, Milan | 1722–40 | Cahusac, T., London | c. 1755–98 |
| Denner, I. C., Nurnberg | 1655–1707 | Delusse, J., Paris | 1763– |
| Denner, I. (jun.) Nurn- | | Delusse, C., Paris | 1783–89 |
| berg | 1735 | Goulding, G., London | c. 1784–99 |
| Haka, R., Amsterdam | 1645–1709 | Grenser, C. A., Dresden | 1727–1800 |
| Hotteterre, Paris | c. 1700 | Grenser, J. H., Dresden | 1764–1813 |
| Kinigsperger, A. | ? | Grundmann, J. F., Dres- | |
| Knikker, J. van de, Til- | | den | 1727–1800 |
| burg | 1731–1815 | Klenig, ? | ? |
| Lehner, Switzerland | ? | Kusder, London | c. 1762–82 |
| Liebel, Joh. G., Adorf | c. 1798 | Lot, T., Paris | c. 1770 |
| Lindner, L., Augsburg | ? | Milhouse, W., Newark | c. 1763–89 |
| Lott, D., France | ? | Milhouse, W., London | 1789–1813 |
| Richters, Netherlands | ? | Prudent, T., Paris | c. 1770 |
| Rijkel, C., Amsterdam | 1667–1705 | Rottenburgh, J-H-J., | |
| Schlegel, Ch., Basle | c. 1713 | Brussels | 1672–1765 |
| Stanesby, T. (sen.), | | Rottenburgh, G. A., | |
| London | 1734 | Brussels | 1709–90 |
| Walch, G., Berchtes- | | Schlegel, C., Basel | 1763–92 |
| gaden | c. 1660 | Stanesby, T. (jun.), | |
| | | London | 1692–1754 |

as far as we can differentiate them. The first has sometimes been termed the 'baroque' type and, overlapping the turn of the century, is almost certainly the sort of instrument that Purcell knew. Probably it represented the original form developed in France by the first experimenters. Undoubted 17th-century oboes are today extremely rare, but a few survive which clearly belong to the same group as the earliest 18th-century examples. In general appearance these instruments were robust in outline, of good proportion, and with much ornamental turning of almost architectural precision. At the top of the upper joint there appeared a graceful baluster, while the socket of the middle joint swelled out to complement this. Both these thickenings served to strengthen the tube at points where splitting might occur in use. Below the finger-holes on the mid-joint a heavy raised ring of square section was slotted to provide the mountings of the duplicate small keys and the fish-tail touchpiece of the 'great' key. Still lower, another ring, this time of curved section, carried the head of the great key, and the joint ended with yet another moulding. The socket of the bell usually followed the profile of the middle one. The 'waist' of the bell was almost truly cylindrical and was defined by two rather prominent raised rings, one above and one below the 'tuning holes'. Below this again came a marked flare terminated by an inflated and cushion-like lip which was invariably undercut inside to a depth of 3 or 4 mm., probably with the idea of checking the progress of any split which might occur at this point. The possible acoustic properties of the inner rim so formed are discussed in the appropriate chapter. On the richer examples plain wooden mould-ing were sometimes supplemented by ivory mounts; but, on the whole, these were less usual with the oboe than with other con-temporary instruments. Occasionally carved decoration was applied, with fluted or gadroon edges and, very rarely, inlaid work. In the majority of instruments of this type both the third and fourth finger-holes were doubled, but quite early specimens are known in which the third only was so treated. The bore of these instruments was, as a rule, large in comparison with modern standards. For the keys sheet metal, brass or silver, was invariably used, and the springs were attached to the body and pressed up-wards against the under-side of the touchpiece.

The above general characteristics are common to all the earliest oboes, but in detail the oldest surviving English instruments (1700–40) show distinct differences from contemporary foreign examples. The baluster at the top of the Continental baroque oboe almost always ended in a funnel-shaped expansion which both Carse and Sachs regard[7] as a vestige of the detachable pirouette of the shawm. This view is not without support, for in the Boers Collection of the Rijks Museum, Amsterdam (now in the Gemeerte Museum, The Hague), is an early specimen by Coenraad Rijkel (*b.* 1667, *d.* 1705) on which the 'funnel' is hollowed out in a manner which certainly recalls the separate pirouette. Later foreign instru-ments do not show this hollow, but the pirouette *profile* seems to have lasted until nearly the mid-century before it became gradually reduced to a more cylindrical form.[8] For some reason, as yet un-explained, no known English instrument shows this feature, and here the baluster usually ended in a finial rather like an empty cotton reel. As regards the bell, Continental oboes seem to have retained the almost trumpet-like flare (again reminiscent of the shawms) only until about the end of the 17th century, after which the curve, and likewise the lip, became much less pronounced. In England this feature persisted for at least another forty years, and the more moderate bell does not seem to have been adopted before the whole style of the instrument had changed. The French haut-bois, we suspect, came to England in almost its original form, and this conservative country seems to have found no good reason to

A           B           C

Fig. 6. Bell and Baluster profiles of three typical early oboes
    compared

A. Continental, *c.* 1690 by Rykel, Amsterdam. The bell strongly
    flared and the top finial of pirouette form

B. English, late 17th to early 18th century by Stanesby senior.
    Bell strongly flared, finial of 'cotton reel' shape

C. Continental, contemporary with B, by J. C. Denner, Nurn-
    berg. Bell already much compressed but the finial still
    reminiscent of the pirouette

alter it for many years. Finally, in England, the small keys were invariably of a dumb-bell shape with small cross spurs, a form rare on the Continent, where square heads with round or fiddle-shaped touchpieces were usual.

Towards 1750 the elaborate and finely balanced baroque oboe gave place to a much simplified version in which beauty of form was subordinated to the plain and practical. Almost all ornament was suppressed, and the sockets and baluster, which had formerly been the turner's joy, became merely functional. In many cases the heavy rings which supported the keys were reduced as far as possible, leaving only rather ugly 'block' mountings for the pivot wires. It is, of course, not to be thought that so radical a change occurred suddenly, and museum specimens exist which show various degrees of simplification. Instruments of this model are known with both three and two keys, which seems to identify them as a link between the two main 18th-century groups. The great majority of such oboes known today were made in France; in England they were apparently not common, and soon yielded to an even more severe type which seems to belong to this country alone. Here the upper joint is completely straight, and is strengthened at the top by an ivory or metal ring. In spite of the extremely plain lines of these instruments, their general appearance is more pleasing than that of the former type, largely due to the better proportions of the sockets, emphasised by an occasional discreet ornamental ring or thread. These oboes come exclusively into the two-keyed group, though in the matter of the mountings some of them show a curious reversion to earlier fashions. Some had only minimal 'block' mountings, others retained the front half of the mounting ring, while on yet others the rings were left entire and completely surrounded the body.

There has been much discussion as to the *raison d'être* of this special group of English oboes. Some have suggested that they were designed particularly for military service, but there is little or no evidence, and no really satisfactory conclusion has been reached. It is to be noted that the bore is definitely narrower than that of the baroque or French transition types, and these instruments seem to be tuned rather flatter when compared length for length. The pitch of antique instruments is, however, a matter on which little can be said with safety, so many factors are involved. Some oboes are known to have been furnished with alternative upper joints of different length, and unless we possess all of these in any given case, we are liable to be deceived. Moreover, tube-length is not a really safe guide unless considered in relation to the other proportions of the bore. A modern reed, too, is almost certain to be useless for testing. Some recent experimenters have succeeded in reconstructing what we believe the 18th-century reed to have been, and if, with one of these reproductions, an instrument sounds reasonably 'in tune with itself', we may perhaps apply pitch measurement with some confidence. A great deal, however, remains to be done in this direction, and there is scope for much detailed work.

The comparative abundance today of French oboes of the second variety suggests that, on the Continent, after the baroque period, there may have been as much as a decade of stability, but very soon another transition was on the way. We know from actual dated specimens that by 1780, in Germany, and probably in France too, the simple oboe had reached its final shape with a return to a modified form of the baroque profile. This reversion to an older style is another matter which has not, so far, been explained, but we may note that it coincided with a further narrowing of the bore and an upward trend in the pitch of woodwind instruments in general. In England this last change seems to have occurred rather later than elsewhere, and it appears more spectacular because of the intervention of the very plain straight model. From this time on most developments in this country lagged slightly behind those of the Continent.

In comparison with the baroque instrument, these oboes of the early Classical period are frequently less satisfying in their outlines. Sometimes they attained great refinement, but quite as often their curves appear ill-balanced and aggressive. The tubes were usually slender, but the sockets were stout and heavily moulded, and the formerly elegant baluster became shortened and thickened to a form often described as like an inverted onion. At this period the bell showed much variation in detail, though in a representative group we can clearly differentiate a French and a German style, and this is the first sign we have of a national divergence which in the next century led to two completely separate lines of development. Taking them in order from the socket downwards, the most consistent features of these bells are, first, a heavy moulding like that of the mid-joint; next, a single raised ring *above* the tuning-holes; third, a smooth flare, simple or slightly pear-shaped, terminated by another raised ring; and finally, a second shorter flare or a straight cone leading to an inflated lip. The inside and outside profiles were no longer related to each other; the cylindrical portion about the tuning-holes had disappeared; and the walls became progressively thicker towards the mouth. The inner rim to the latter was, however, preserved. Further characteristics of these instruments were the duplication of both third and fourth holes and the revival of heavy encircling key-mounts. The keys themselves were almost invariably of silver, and only in the rarest of cases were there more than two. The fish-tail touchpiece was, however, retained, and for the first time the heads of both keys assumed an octagonal form. Such was the general appearance of the latest simple oboe, the instrument which even before the end of the 18th century was already receiving a few additional keys at the hands of such enterprising German makers as Grenser and Grundmann. In the third stage of development it was to become very fully mechanised indeed.

FINGERING

In its basic fingering the simple oboe followed the system common to all European side-hole instruments from very early times, among them the shawm. Lifting in succession the first three fingers of each hand produced nominally a diatonic scale exactly as in the instruments of the Middle Ages, and, since the moderate length of the tube created no physical problems in spacing, the holes *could* have been accurately tuned for this purpose alone. The oboe was, however, required from the outset to be at home in a number of keys.[9] Simple fork-fingering could provide some of the necessary semitones, but others could not be obtained without some adjustment to the actual primary holes. The result was a certain degree of compromise, with ambiguous tunings, for which the player was expected to compensate with both lip and finger, as the key of the music dictated. It may be that the oboe with its 'cane' reed, was at first less amenable to blowing sharp or flat than, say, the contemporary transverse flute, and so the makers turned their attention to another member of the coupled system, the tube, and devised special refinements to that. Such are the twin holes which did not appear on other instruments till very much later.[10] There is a great deal of evidence to show that early oboe-players were much concerned with enharmonic distinctions, probably because they often found themselves associated with strings in 'mixed consort'. One of Banister's special claims for the hautboy was that 'it is the best wind instrument for use with the violin on account of its pitch', and a very similar statement appears in Talbot.

In text-books and museum catalogues it is often said that the layout of the finger-holes on the simple oboe followed the pattern of its forerunners—i.e. two evenly spaced groups of three with a wider space between. This is, however, only partially true. As a rule the division into two groups is obvious, though often the space between the third and fourth holes is little greater than between any other pair. Within the groups themselves the spacing is sometimes far from even, particularly in cases where the fourth hole is not doubled. (See Plate II, No. 5 which, in its mid-joint, almost anticipates 19th-century practice, though, of course, without the vent-key for $f\sharp$.) In the great majority of examples the upper three holes were much smaller than those of the lower set, and often they were pierced obliquely; Nos. 1 and 2 slanted upward towards the bore, while the twin No. 3 sloped the other way. More rarely the fourth hole also was bored upwards. No doubt all these subtleties were connected to some extent with the systems of tuning used by different makers, but the oft-repeated assertion that the oblique piercing of holes was adopted in an attempt to reach the bore at more nearly correct acoustical positions is open to question. This device was evidently necessary and the assertion true in the case of long-tubed instruments with thick walls—e.g. bassoon (see Plate VIII, No. 3), but on the comparatively short treble oboe the advantage gained can hardly have been important. Also we may well ask what were the 'acoustically correct' positions for finger-holes in an instrument which depended so much on compromise throughout its entire compass? Comparative measurements seem to show a connection between oblique boring, when present, and the diameter of individual holes, and this in turn suggests that it had more effect on tone-colour than on deliberate tuning. This matter is discussed at some length in Chapter 9.

The scale of the two or three-keyed oboe begins on $c'$ sounded with all holes and the 'great key' closed. On the evidence of the later 18th-century tutors $c\sharp'$ is often described as altogether missing, but in fact in early days it was a recognised note and was produced by the rather uncertain process of half closing the lowest key. It has been observed that on some of the oldest surviving instruments the touch of this key lies rather closer to the body than on later examples, and it has been suggested that this was intended to ease a difficult piece of fingering. On the other hand, with the rather malleable sheet metal of those days, we can hardly be certain that these keys have reached us in their original state. After *c.* 1730 this note definitely vanished from the published tablatures and did not reappear until a special *c*♯ key was provided many years later. The next note, *d'*, was sounded with the little finger lifted and the great key fully open. Until about the mid-century this fingering, with a 'tighter' lip to force the octave harmonic, served for *d''* also. Thereafter the flute fingering for this note (with the first hole open) was commonly in use. *e*♭' and its octave both sounded from their own hole normally kept closed by the 'less' key. Hole No. 6 gave the *e*♮ in both octaves. The *f'* was regularly sounded as a 'forked' note with hole No. 5 open and No. 6 below it closed. No. 5 without the fork fingering gave a nominal *f*♯, but on most instruments it was rather flat, and its utility depended to some extent on the context of the music. This was because the hole had to be tuned in the first place to give a good clear forked *f*♮ for which there was no possible alternative. The twin hole, No. 4, provided an alternative *f*♯ if one side only were opened, or a *g* in both octaves if both were uncovered. Several alternatives for *f*♯ are found in different instruction books, and indeed this seems to have been one of the more controversial notes. In early charts it is sometimes shown fingered as the forked *f'* with the hole above half closed; at other times it appears as a forked *g'* flattened by closing the hole No. 5 or even 5+6. Some of the oldest known oboes had only a single *g* hole placed rather high and very convenient for half stopping on the diagonal. A similar arrangement, but with even spacing, was followed in the undecorated English instruments of 1760–90. In these cases, however, the *f*♯ hole No. 5 was somewhat enlarged, which brought the note better into tune, though it introduced the need to steady the forked *f*♮ by opening the *e*♭ key. Nearly all charts show different fingerings for the *f*♯ in the two octaves.

On the upper half of the instrument hole No. 3 was invariably doubled, and for some reason remained so long after key mechanism made this redundant. Opening one half gave *a*♭ in each octave and full opening *a*♮. An enharmonic *g*♯, produced by fingering *a* and closing hole No. 4 to flatten it, was also recognised. Occasionally some tablatures reverse the naming of these two fingerings. Hole No. 2 gave *b'* and *b''*, and a fork with Nos. 1 and 3 closed the corresponding *b*♭s. An alternative *b*♭'' of late date was provided

E

by 1 and 2 closed, 3 open, 4, 5, and 6 closed. Although the old fingering charts seldom mention the fact, notes sounded by short lengths of tube on the upper joint were frequently steadied by closing one or more holes lower down, the actual ones employed often depending on the idiosyncrasy of the individual instrument. For example, the next note—middle c''—was nominally produced by closing hole No. 2 only, but in practice 4, 5, and 6 were usually closed also. In passing notes and in shakes c'' could also be sounded by stopping the third hole only. Middle c#'' was regularly

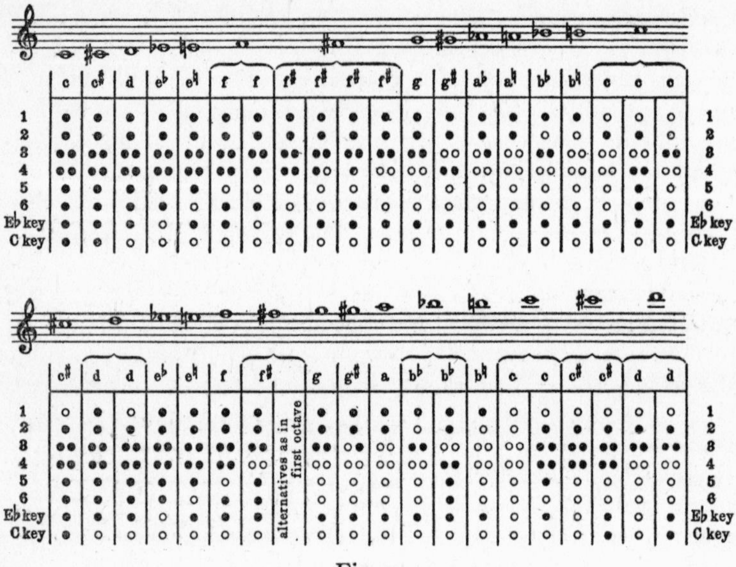

Fig. 7

made with the first hole only open, all others, including the keys, being closed. The original top note of the instrument, c''' was, till about 1750, produced with all holes open, but later, when it was discovered that a very satisfactory d''' could be obtained as the third harmonic of g', a new c''' and a c#''' also came into use. This d''' was fingered with holes 2 and 3 stopped, aided by opening the eb key or closing the c key, whichever suited a given instrument best. c#''' was fingered as d''', but flattened by closing hole No. 4 as well, while for c''' only Nos. 1, 6, and the great key remained open. As an alternative this latter note could be fingered as c'' 'pinched' and vented with the eb key.

It is not to be supposed that all these fingerings worked equally well with any one instrument, but the number of alternatives, since most of them had their own shades of intonation, makes it clear that a dexterous player on the two-keyed oboe had a very considerable control over inflection, more, indeed, than the average modern oboist may ever be called upon to exercise. The chart on page 50 is not an authentic 18th-century one, but is compiled from various sources in such a way as to place alternative fingerings side by side for quick comparison. The usual symbols for open, stopped, and half-stopped holes are employed, and, where a particular fingering applies only to instruments with a single fourth hole, this is indicated.

[1] The records of the Waits of the City of Edinburgh mention explicitly the 'French hautboyes' as early as 1696, and show that these then replaced the cornetts formerly used by this band.

[2] J. Ecorcheville, 'Quelques Documents sur la Musique de la Grande Écurie du Roi', *S.I.M.G.*, II.

[3] E. Thoinan, 'Les Hotteterre et les Chédeville' in *La France Musicale*, 1894.

[4] See Carse, *The Orchestra in the 18th Century*, W. Heffer, Cambridge, 1940, p. 31.

[5] Adam Carse, *Musical Wind Instruments*, London, 1939, pp. 133-4.

[6] Lyndesay G. Langwill, *A List of Wood-wind and Brass Instrument-makers and Inventors*, Edinburgh, 1941 (and six supplements), privately issued. An invaluable reference work, the result of many years' study and collation of data from sources of all kinds, comprising some 3,000 names.

[7] Curt Sachs, *The History of Musical Instruments*, London (J. M. Dent), 1942.

[8] In discussing Freillon Poncein's tutor, Ecorcheville has stated, in spite of the written instructions which clearly refer to a free-blown reed, that the instrument depicted is not a true oboe and has a pirouette. I am unable to agree. Freillon Poncein's cuts form part of his fingering chart and for clarity he omitted the keys, indicating instead the holes they covered. In other respects his illustrations agree in detail with typical late 17th-century oboes. The finial at the top has the pirouette profile, but there is no reason to suppose that it was detachable. The identical feature is clearly to be seen in Randle Holme's sketch. Harl. 2034, f. 207b (British Museum).

[9] We should remember that when the oboe first appeared, mean-tone temperament for keyboard instruments was well on the way to complete acceptance in Europe. The range of three degrees sharp and flat of C major, within which oboe fingering was reasonably easy, covered all the good keys of that system.

[10] As early as 1726 Quantz added to the flute a duplicate hole and key for $e^b$ as distinct from $d^\sharp$, but, except in Germany, the device was generally ignored.

# CHAPTER 5

# The Oboe in the 19th Century

THE previous two centuries having seen the advent of the true oboe and its acceptance as the leading reed instrument of the early Classical orchestra, the 19th marks approximately the period of its improvement and refinement. This third stage was one in which empirical growth gave place to organised development at the hands of skilled craftsmen and distinguished artists in the service of an ever more exacting music, and the result was one of the most delicate and expressive of all orchestral voices. Such refinement had, of course, been potential in the instrument from the beginning and was inherent in the principle of unsupported control of the reed between the lips, a fundamental distinction between the oboe and the shawm families. The 19th century was also the period during which two distinct lines of growth became evident, each of which culminated in a highly organised instrument with its own particular virtues.

In the last years of the previous century the transverse flute seems for a while to have outstripped the other woodwind, for by about 1700 flute-players were regularly using four keys, three of them supplying semitones not available on the simple instrument save by means of fork-fingerings. The oboe did not generally possess such keys for nearly another twenty years, in spite of the experimental work of C. A. Grenser and Grundmann in Dresden some time before 1800. Grundmann made a practice of marking his products with the year of manufacture and a device of crossed swords similar to the well-known Dresden porcelain mark. Oboes of his dated 1781, 1793, and 1797 which were formerly preserved in the Berlin Hochschule and Hamburg collections show a selection of keys which did not become part of the routine equipment for some considerable time. Among these we find the octave key, but, as the instruments bear 'saddle' mountings, which may indicate additions, as well as the more primitive 'blocks', we cannot take them as conclusive evidence that the 'speaker' was applied to the oboe in the 18th century. In musical collections today we find much evidence that cherished instruments were repeatedly modernised by successive owners. (Plate III, No. 2.)

Even so, mechanical improvements came to the oboe at first somewhat irregularly. The many surviving examples prove that the Two-keyed instrument was still being made probably as late as 1820, and there is evidence to show that it was not regarded even then as very imperfect. In considering this point, however, we must remember the law of supply and demand. Composers have always shown a tendency to write up to, and beyond, the capacity of their most skilful performers, who have in turn made ever-increasing demands on the instrument-maker. On the other hand, the conservatism of some players has no doubt tended to retard the adoption of mechanical improvements originated by the more imaginative makers. It may well be that at the beginning of the 19th century the oboe was not so much behind in development, as that the demands of both amateur and professional musicians had forced the transverse flute ahead at a time when that instrument was extremely popular. Certainly the 'forked' semitones of the eighteenth century one-keyed flute were less easy to bring into tune than were those of the contemporary oboe. It is difficult to account otherwise for one family of instruments not equalling another when the same manufacturing skill was available to both.

It is today almost impossible to date accurately the advent of the first additional keys, though careful comparison of instruments whose individual histories are known, or whose makers' working period is recorded, provides very fair indication. In this matter 18th- and 19th-century trade directories have proved invaluable, as well as such private collections of trade cards as that of Sir Ambrose Heal. It seems probable that the so-called 'speaker' or octave key came early. Many old two- and three-keyed oboes are known to which later keys have been carefully added, and not infrequently the speaker is the sole addition, showing the value that was placed upon it. Some examples show additional keys which are clearly of different dates, and amongst these the speaker is nearly always the oldest in style.

During the first quarter of the 19th century six further keys began to appear more generally; probably in the following order:—

1. A closed $g\sharp$ key for the left little finger, supplementing but not replacing the doubled hole No. 3 which survived at least until 1865.

2. A vent-key for the right little finger which covered a hole almost mid-way between Nos. 4 and 5. This greatly improved the intonation of the $f^\sharp$ with the normal fingering. A similar key is often found on contemporary clarinets, and it remained in use on both instruments till superseded about 1840 by the now universal open-standing key controlled by two rings surrounding the two holes immediately below, Nos. 5 and 6. This is the so-called 'spectacle' or 'brille', almost certainly borrowed from Boehm's flute mechanism of 1830.

3. The low $c^\sharp$. The rather dubious fingering for this note which died out *c.* 1730 has been mentioned in the previous chapter. In the 1800s a special key for this note alone came into use, and was usually allotted to the right little finger. Some authorities aver that with the coming of this key the old fishtail touchpiece of the $c^\natural$ key disappeared. This, however, is too general a statement, for at least two English instruments are known to the writer which carry both the fishtail and the $c^\natural$ key as part of their original equipment, and there must have been many more similar. One of these is an unusual specimen by the celebrated Milhouse of London (who flourished from 1798 to 1838), and has three keys only—the $c^\natural$, a $d^\sharp$ for the right little finger and a long $c^\sharp$—in this case carried right up to the *left* little finger. This latter key is engraved 'W. Parke, inventor'—possibly William Parke of *Musical Memoirs* fame, himself a well-known oboist. Unfortunately the key is of an exceptional type, and Parke's claim to its invention sheds no light on the origin of the more usual right-hand one. The sounding of $c^\sharp$ on this instrument required the use of both little fingers, one to open the $c^\sharp$ and the other to close the $c^\natural$. With the more common allocation of both these keys to the right hand only some device is needed to make a single pressure open one and close the other simultaneously to sound $c^\sharp$, as well as allowing the $c^\natural$ key to be closed independently when required for the bell note. Many ingenious arrangements have at different times been evolved for this purpose. (Plate IV, No. 1.)

A second English oboe with both fishtail and low $c^\sharp$ keys is preserved in the National Museum in Dublin. This was produced by Bilton of London (1826–56), who was a prolific maker especially of military band instruments. In most respects similar to the 9-keyed German oboe, this instrument has a right-hand $c\sharp$ overlapping the $c\natural$ in the common manner of the time, but the latter key retains the fishtail touchpiece.

On an oboe by Gerhard Hartmann of Hamburg, made about the middle of the century, the long *left-hand $c\sharp$*, is the only one provided, but in this case it automatically closes the $c\natural$ by means of an intervening lever. Numerous other German and Austrian oboes of rather later date are furnished with both right- and left-handed $c\sharp$ keys, though purely as alternatives and with no sort of interconnection. From such examples as these it is evident that the most convenient disposition of the $c\sharp$ key was in doubt for some years after its first appearance.

4. A closed $f\natural$ key set across the lower joint as in the contemporary flute was, in all probability, the next to arrive, although there is some slight evidence that this may have preceded the $f\sharp$ vent key mentioned above (No. 2).

5. A closed $b\flat$ on the upper joint, worked either by the left thumb or the right forefinger, and later on by both as alternatives.

6. A closed upper $c\natural$ allocated to either the right forefinger or to the left ring finger. The choice of position for this key also seems to have remained open for some time after the disposition of the others had become fairly settled, for both arrangements are found on oboes made at least as late as 1850.

Finally, during the period 1800–25, a very long-shanked key was developed which covered a hole in the bell in the place formerly occupied by one of the 'tuning holes'. This added a semitone to the compass, the bell note now becoming $b\natural$. The duty of closing this key, at first given to the left thumb, was eventually transferred to the left little finger also. The second air hole in the bell is often supposed to have disappeared at this stage from all but German style oboes, but in fact certain French makers, among them the elder Triébert of Paris (1810–48), retained them for some time longer.

To summarise thus far—an up-to-date and fully equipped oboe such as Beethoven might have known in his last years would be pierced with fifteen note-holes and one speaker, ten of them controlled by keys, and the instrument would be fully chromatic from low $b\natural$ without fork-fingering being essential. Simpler instruments with as few as two keys would not, however, be regarded at the time as completely obsolete, though their limited upper range would count against them. At that time advanced players with the newest instruments had already extended their compass to $f'''$ and even to $a'''$. The practice of fork-fingering did not die out with the completion of full chromatic key-work, and indeed it remains today as an important part of all woodwind technique.

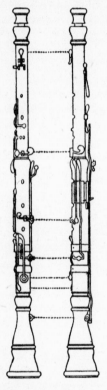

Fig. 8. Sellner's 13-keyed oboe. Redrawn from his tutor of 1852

Probably the most advanced instruments that remain to us from this period are those made according to the ideas of Josef Sellner, a notable performer who, between 1811 and 1817, had played under Weber in Prague, and who was later a member of the Court orchestra in Vienna. He added extra levers to the $bb$, $f\natural$, and $d\sharp$ keys, and thus evolved what is generally termed 'Sellner's thirteen-keyed Oboe'. For this instrument he published in 1825 a tutor which enjoyed considerable success, and was subsequently translated into both French and Italian. The original Sellner oboes were produced by the celebrated Viennese flute-maker Stephan Koch, but very shortly other makers of repute both in Austria and in Germany began to build instruments on this model, and for a while the initiative in making improvements seems to have remained in these countries. The fifteen, or at most sixteen, note-holes required by the Koch-Sellner design, and their relative placing along the tube, remain virtually unchanged on typical German and Austrian style oboes at the present day.

## THE RISE OF THE FRENCH OBOE

In spite of the apparent ascendency of the Vienna oboe in the second decade of the 19th century, it was just at this time that the French instrument began an independent existence. It has been suggested that the tendency of the oboe to develop along national lines may already have been established by the late 18th century. Subtle differences between typical instruments by such makers as T. Lot or C. Delusse of Paris on the one hand, and the Grensers or Grundmann of Dresden on the other, might perhaps be taken to show that even then the French were cultivating a sensitive and refined tone, while German[1] taste was already favouring warmth and robustness. There is material here for interesting speculation.

By about 1820, however, the picture had become quite clear. Two entirely different ideals of oboe tone were being pursued in Europe and two corresponding types of instrument were developing. In the French oboe the upper bore was beginning to get appreciably narrower, although both types still kept many essentially 18th-century features in common, among them the heavy inner rim to the bell, the 'step' at the top of the bell joint, and the characteristic exterior turning as interpreted by the taste in ornament of the two nations. By the end of another twenty-five years the French instrument had lost all of these, while the German type retains some even today.

At this point it will be useful to glance for a moment at the conditions under which music and the arts in general were to develop in France during the rest of the 19th century. Unlike most of the German-speaking part of Europe, which, until 1871, still remained a conglomeration of more or less independent sovereign states in which patronage of the arts depended largely on the tastes of individual rulers, France was a large country with State academies of arts and sciences, some inherited from pre-Revolutionary times and preserved by successive Governments. The effect of such a system on the development of music was very marked. In 1793 the Paris Conservatoire had been founded, providing at once a centre of advanced teaching whose eminent professors attracted the most promising talent from all over the country. Naturally such an institution also stimulated the various trades associated with the practice of music in the capital, among them the manufacture of instruments.[2] Because of this we find the records of the early 1800s full of references to small artist-manufacturers in Paris and its neighbourhood, some of whom were also teachers. Many of these firms concentrated on one particular kind of instrument, yet there is no sign that they had difficulty in finding an adequate market for their output. Their market was in fact on their own doorstep. The smaller and widely distributed art centres of Germany do not seem to have afforded opportunities for such close specialisation. (See Appendix I.) In France centralisation was fully established, and though this no doubt restricted the field of employment for the average musician by keeping competition intense and standards very high, it had obvious advantages for the musical manufacturer. The position is very well reviewed by Adam Carse in Chapter 4 of his book *The Orchestra from Beethoven to Berlioz*.

From the beginning the Faculty at the Paris Conservatoire included a Chair of Oboe-playing, which in the course of time has become influential throughout Europe and beyond. Curiously enough, the influence of the first two professors was, in France itself, decidedly reactionary. The first of them—Sallantin, a distinguished player from the Opéra who held the position until 1813 —is known to have used the old two-keyed instrument with the addition only of the low $b\natural$ and $f\sharp$ keys. Vogt, Sallantin's pupil and successor at the Conservatoire from 1813 to 1853, also favoured this simple instrument. Writing in his MSS. 'Méthode' some time after 1813, he speaks specifically of 'our oboes which have only four keys', and compares them with the contemporary nine-keyed German oboes, much to the disadvantage of the latter. Vogt argued strongly against multiplicity of keys on the grounds that they were liable to leakage, and also that they tended to endanger the close stopping of adjacent finger-holes. It seems that both these eminent teachers valued such keys as they did adopt mainly as aids to improved intonation.[3]

The conservatism of Sallantin and Vogt was, however, by no means unchallenged in Paris, and younger players were already awakening to the advantages of well-constructed additional keys. Pre-eminent among these was Vogt's pupil, Henri Brod (1799–1839). At the age of twelve, Brod was accepted as an oboe pupil at the Conservatoire, and by 1819 had already achieved distinction. In that year he occupied an oboe desk at the Opéra, playing second to his former professor.

Early in his professional life Brod became dissatisfied with four keys only and set himself to devise improvements to his instrument. It is probable that in this he was associated with the maker Guillaume Triébert, for in Part I of a 'Méthode' published c. 1835 he stated that Triébert's oboes were then the best available, and he illustrates an eight-keyed instrument which was, no doubt, that maker's model of the day. The engraving shows the keys carried in brass 'saddles' screwed to the tube, and not in wooden blocks derived from the substance of the tube itself. This, of course, enabled the external profile to be cleaned up, but the instrument itself remained little more than a slender version of the current Vienna oboe.

In the same year, having acquired tools and equipment which were formerly the property of the younger Delusse,[4] Brod himself set up as a maker, and remained in business until his death early in 1839. During his few remaining years Brod made some notable improvements to several members of the oboe family. He used metal 'pillar' mounts for all his keys, thereby further smoothing out the profile of the instrument (although he kept the baluster at the top), and he adopted shallow metal cups for the key-pads, an improvement which was not to be found on Triébert's earlier instruments. Brod's oboes are probably the most slender that have ever been made, and their keywork, though delicate, was completely practical. Valuable information about much of Brod's work is to be found in the second volume of his Tutor published rather later than the first. In this he claimed to have devised the 'half-hole' plate for the left forefinger as a result of the trouble some of his pupils had experienced in accurately half closing the upper c♯ hole. Half closing, or rather half opening this hole to encourage the production of certain upper harmonics became an essential point of technique soon after the compass was extended beyond c''', and very shortly it was found to have advantages in the lower octaves as well. The mechanism is to be found in one form or other on almost every oboe today. Illustrations in Volume II show also an improved oboe, a new straight-bodied *cor anglais* with a small recurved crook of bassoon type—termed by Brod '*cor anglais moderne*'—and a baritone oboe bent back on itself by means of a doubly bored joint rather like the boot of a small bassoon. A set of reed-making tools, including a machine for the accurate gouging of cane, was also shown. All these inventions and improvements were entered at the Paris Exhibition of 1839, where they received high praise. It is sad to think that Brod died at the early age of forty and before the reports of the exhibition jury could be published.

Of a number of 'artistes-ouvriers' who entered the musical instrument field between 1830 and 1840, Brod, combining fine workmanship with musical skill and appreciation of the player's needs, probably contributed more than any of his immediate contemporaries to the advancement of the oboe in France. As in the case of so many pioneers, the originality of some of his work was in later years called in question, and historians have differed as to the justice of some of his claims. Fétis, writing in 1855, specifically mentions the half-hole plate, which he attributes to Frédéric Triébert, second of the remarkable dynasty of oboe specialists in whose hands the French instrument reached its final form.[5]

## THE TRIÉBERT FAMILY AND THEIR WORK

That the founder of the firm whose researches brought the French oboe to its highest perfection should have been by birth a German seems at first sight somewhat paradoxical. It is, in fact, not so, for Guillaume Triébert, though born at Horndorf in Hesse, removed to Paris when quite young and spent his whole working life in the city. It is recorded that he first worked in a cabinet-maker's, but soon abandoned that trade to enter the workshop of the flute-maker Winnen. His formative years were therefore spent entirely under French influence. In 1811 he applied for and was granted the privileges of French citizenship.

In 1810 (just a year before Brod's entry into the Conservatoire) Guillaume Triébert opened his own business, which he continued to direct until his death in 1848. Thereafter his sons Charles-Louis and Frédéric, both professional oboists, assumed control of the firm, which continued for another thirty years. Charles-Louis (1810–76) took always a minor part in the direction of the factory, the work of a virtuoso performer occupying the greater part of his time. He had gained the first prize for oboe-playing at the Conservatoire in 1829 at the age of nineteen. On the other hand, Frédéric (born in 1813) is known to have given up professional playing after 1846 in order to devote all his time to research and manufacture. On his death in 1878 the firm's equipment passed into other hands, and in 1881 was bought, together with the right to use the Triébert trade mark, by the house of Gautrot.[6] The tradition of the firm was, however, maintained by the admirable workman François Lorée, who had been foreman since 1867 and who set up for himself on the death of his employer. In 1881 he was fortunate in securing the contracts to the Conservatoire and National Schools of Music which had formerly been held by the Triéberts. By Lorée's son the modern French oboe in its most admired form was finally perfected, and fine examples of his work command high prices among players even today.

Under the Triébert régime the oboe underwent carefully considered development, in every phase of which the taste of fine performers went hand in hand with mechanical skill of a high order. Between 1840 and 1880 the instrument was completely re-formed in all its parts, particular attention being given to the proportions of the bore and to the relative sizes and placing of the note-holes. A reed rather narrower and lighter than used formerly was found to favour the French ideal of tone, and this in turn called for extremely subtle adjustments to the diameter and expansion of the interior cone, or rather series of cones.[7] At this period the Triéberts abandoned the inner rim to the bell, though some other French makers retained it for at least another thirty years. At the same time mechanical facilities were continuously improved, and advantage was taken of all the most up-to-date ideas available. The axles perfected by Boehm for his flute of 1832 were very soon put to numerous uses; pillars screwed directly into the wall of the tube were adopted for all keys; and the outline of the upper joint finally smoothed out, leaving only the small and elegant finial which is used by all makers today.

A typical French oboe of 1840 or a little before shows the following equipment: $c$, $c^\sharp$, and $d^\sharp$ keys, all on separate levers operated by the right little finger; low $b^\natural$ and duplicate $d^\sharp$ with long levers for the left little finger; a cross $f^\natural$ on the lower joint, and the old $f^\sharp$ lever replaced by a vent key attached to a 'spectacle'. (Although undoubtedly originated by Boehm, this is included in Sax's Belgian clarinet patent of 1840.) A cross $g^\sharp$ for the left little finger supplements the double hole No. 3, the upper $c$ overlaps the $b^\flat$ so that both keys open together for the former note; a 'half-hole' plate is fitted to the upper $c^\sharp$ hole and an octave 'speaker' is operated by the left thumb. The most important work of the Triéberts in the matter of keys may be regarded as based on this instrument, and their first development of it (called by them 'Système 3') showed

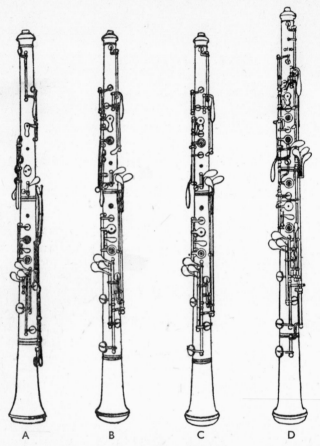

Fig. 9. A. Typical French oboe, c. 1840.
B, C, and D. Triébert's Systèmes Nos. 4, 5 and 6

only two changes, viz. the use of axles instead of levers for the right little finger and the provision of a second octave key (used from *a* above the stave upwards) opened by the knuckle of the left index finger. An instrument of this model is known to have been used as late as 1865.

Oboe Système 4 appeared about the time of Guillaume Trié-

bert's death and was often called 'Système Charles Triébert', after
the elder son, who advocated its use at the Conservatoire. A. M.-R.
Barret, another pupil of Vogt, who made a great name for himself
as solo oboe at Covent Garden from 1829 onwards, adopted this
system with the addition of a low $bb$ key and made it the basis for
the first edition of his celebrated Tutor published in 1850. This
model had a ring for the left-hand second finger associated with a
duplicate hole supplying a 'forked' $c$, and also a special key for the
$c$-$d$ trill which was impossible on Système 3. In addition, the long
keys on the left were replaced by a single axle with a double or
'butterfly' touch, which, when moved one way, closed the low $b\natural$
and when moved the other way opened the $d\sharp$. The connections
for the latter called for extreme nicety of construction. It is worth
noting that French illustrations of this oboe show a single hole only
for $a\natural$, third finger left hand, but the rather poor drawing in Barret's
Tutor indicates that he still favoured the double hole as an alternative to the $g\sharp$ key. Moreover, his long keys for the left hand are
all on separate axles.

Système A4 followed the general lines of 4, with the addition of
a perforated plate and pad instead of a ring for the right middle
finger. This had the effect of greatly improving the $d$ in the third
octave, and has since become part of the routine equipment of all
French-style instruments. Oboes of this type are still extensively
used in military service, where comparative simplicity and robustness are highly desirable.

In spite of the enormous advantages which had been conferred
upon players by the above-mentioned instruments, there still remained at this time one rather marked disability. The movement of
the right hand from the normal fingerings of $bb$ and $c\natural$ in the middle
and upper registers to the holes of the lower joint was extremely
awkward in certain passages. This difficulty was brilliantly overcome on oboe Système 5 by the device next to be described.

The holes for the $bb$ and $c\natural$ are transferred from the side to the
front of the tube, and each is provided with a small cross-key, both
being independently pivoted on the same axle. Attached to the $c\natural$
key is a ring surrounding the $b\natural$ hole, and to the $bb$ key a touchpiece
for the right forefinger. These keys are both lightly sprung to
stand open, and their tails are bent so that they overlap, the $c$ on
top of the $bb$. Both key-tails together engage with one end of a
rather stronger needle spring clamped at the other end to an extension of a pivoted plate placed under the left thumb. The effect is

that when the oboe is held in the normal manner, the pressure of the thumb transmitted by the plate and associated spring holds the keys closed against the bias of their own springs—but a pressure

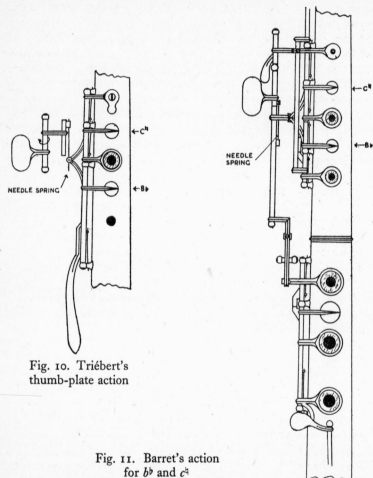

Fig. 10. Triébert's
thumb-plate action

Fig. 11. Barret's action
for *b*♭ and *c*♮

of the right forefinger sufficient to overcome the plate spring allows one or both keys to fly open, depending on whether or not the left middle finger is holding down the ring. Thus the notes *b*♭ and *c*♮ can be made either by the orthodox fingering, or by a simple release of the left thumb in passages where the right hand is not readily available. At first sight this action would appear to be delicate and difficult to adjust, but in practice, as constructed by good crafts-men, it seems quite satisfactory. It is in fact used today by many leading professional players who cannot afford to risk anything that may be liable to sudden failure. A minor but distinct advantage is also gained by the transfer of the covered holes to a part of the tube which is usually more free of condensed moisture (Fig. 10).

The above mechanism is nowadays frequently called the 'Barret action', though apparently with rather doubtful justice. It would probably be better to reserve the name for a slightly different application of the principle which was in fact used by Barret in the special key system which he launched about 1860, almost at the same time that Système 5 appeared. In the preface to the second edition of his Tutor, introducing the new oboe, Barret commends highly both the skill and ingenuity of F. Triébert, to whom he en-trusted its manufacture. The two men are known to have been associated for some long time, but on examination there appears no evidence that Barret had any hand in devising the first thumb-plate and open $b^b$ and $c^{\natural}$ keys. The elements of that arrangement are described in a patent granted to Triébert in 1849, and in the same document the perforated plate for the third octave $d$ is men-tioned. Barret's name does not appear at all in the specification, as it does in some later Triébert patents, and he did not adopt the high $d$ plate for his own instrument. It should be mentioned that the same mechanical principles, though realised in a rather different manner, were used in some of the excellent English instru-ments made by Alfred Morton. The firm of Alfred Morton and Sons (1872–83) later adopted the standard French mechanism.

A later addition to the Système 5 was a low $b^b$ key for the left little finger. Such a key had exceptionally been fitted since Brod's time, and it now became part of the routine equipment.

While discussing the thumb-plate, two unusual specimens of Triébert's work which are preserved in an English private collec-tion are perhaps worth mention. On one—a boxwood oboe on the general lines of Système 4—a simple thumb-plate without any intermediate spring controls open-standing $b^b$ and $c^{\natural}$ keys, as an alternative to the ordinary side keys, which are also provided (Plate V, No. 2). On the other—a *cor anglais* which also conforms in general to Système 4—the plate, through an intermediate lever, closes the normal $c^{\natural}$ key, which is sprung to stand open, though the $b^b$ is un-affected and is a closed key as usual. These instruments are prob-ably typical of the experimental stages through which Triébert's

F

ideas passed before being finally embodied in one or other of the Systèmes, or they may have been designed to meet the requirements of particular players. The evidence of single examples must always be accepted with some reserve.

## BARRET'S IMPROVEMENTS

Before passing on to the last of the Triébert models we must notice an important instrument which they made in the 1860s, although it did not properly belong to the main stream of their work. This was the full Barret system oboe, which had for some time a considerable vogue, especially in England, where its designer, Appolon Marie-Rose Barret, was for many years much admired both as performer and teacher. Beginning, we may presume, with the simple oboe advocated by his own teacher Vogt, Barret advanced to more and more complex instruments. In 1837 he is known to have possessed one of Brod's oboes with ten or eleven keys, while by 1850, when he published the first edition of his *Complete Method*, his equipment amounted to fourteen. In the course of the next twelve years Barret's experiments progressed much further, and in 1862, with his second edition, he introduced what was virtually a new instrument. Writing in his introductory preface, he outlined the objects of his new design as follows:

> "The principal object I have attained have been to procure the same fingering for each octave from *c* below to the upper *c* . . . to have more perfect shakes on each note, some of which were before impossible; to do away with the half-hole. . . . Besides all these improvements acquired by the instrument, it also possesses a greater facility of slurring, especially from the high to the low notes and vice versa, this was formerly impracticable but now by slight modification of the fingering and a new combination of the octave keys it is as easy as to slur as from *e* to *g*."

The means by which these desiderata were more or less satisfactorily achieved were extremely ingenious. On the matter of practical construction, F. Triébert had been called in consultation, and although it is believed that he did not altogether approve of some of the details, his firm undertook to manufacture the instrument.

The main features of the Barret oboe are probably best reviewed by taking them one by one from the top of the instrument downwards. Thus we find:

1. The two octave keys were both arranged to open when released by a movement of the left thumb, the selection of which one actually did so at any given moment being governed by a ring for the left third finger. This resulted in an automatic change-over of octave keys in passing from *g♯* to *a* in the second register, and undoubtedly eased slurring to a great extent. A duplicate touchpiece occupied the position of the former independent second speaker.

2. Barret's reference to 'doing away with the half-hole' is rather obscure. The evidence of surviving instruments suggests that he objected to the rolling or sliding movement of the left forefinger which is necessary to open partially the upper *c♯* hole, and that he distrusted the ordinary plate. An oboe made by Brod and engraved with Barret's name and the date 1837, possessed by the late Mr. F. G. Rendall of London, showed no sign of any half-hole device, although it was made at a time when Brod's mechanism, and probably Triébert's also, were available if desired. In other respects this much-worn instrument has been brought up to date (probably by F. Triébert), so it seems fair to assume that the half-hole plate was omitted at Barret's express wish. The half-open *c♯* hole is, however, essential in all modern fingering systems, and in the drawing in the second edition of his Method, Barret showed a pierced plate covering the hole and apparently linked to a small extra touchpiece for the left thumb, as well as to the ring which governed the automatic octaves. By this device the half-hole also operated automatically for all normal fingerings without any shifting of the left forefinger. In certain exceptional circumstances, however, the thumb could take over. This method of controlling the half-hole was also used by Alfred Morton and Sons on some of their full Barret-system oboes, although details of the other key-work differed from that of the 'Triébert-Barret'. It should be noted that some French illustrations of the Barret oboe of rather late date show a normal pattern of half-hole without the thumb-touch, and the same is found on a baritone oboe marked 'Triébert' and 'Barret à Londres' in the Rudall Carte collection.

3. The most important feature of the instrument is probably the arrangement used to control the upper *b♭* and *c♮* keys. As in Triébert's patent of 1849, these are sprung open and are closed by a thumb-plate, but the counter pressure which

releases them is not applied by a touch-piece at the side.
Instead, any finger of the right hand serves for this by simply
dropping in its normal position, the right-hand rings etc.
being linked with the upper-joint mechanism by a light lever.
In order that the $b\flat$ may not operate when not wanted, the
ring for the left third finger (attached to the 'automatic'
octave), is provided with a lug which holds that key down
until the $a\natural$ hole is opened. This, it is submitted, is the only
mechanism to which Barret's name should properly be
applied (Fig. 11). In the 'Conservatoire' oboe, which appeared a little later, a rather similar action was adopted, but
this was originally operated by the right forefinger only, and
has no thumb-plate. It is therefore distinct from the true
Barret action. An interesting version of the mechanism is
found on a large B$\flat$ oboe marked 'Triébert' and 'Barret à
Londres' in the Rudall Carte collection. This instrument
corresponds exactly to Barret's 1862 illustration as far as the
lower joint is concerned, but the three right-hand rings and
the thumb-plate operate on the normal side keys for $b\flat$ and
$c\natural$, and no holes for these notes are provided on the top of the
tube. Unfortunately, the key-work is so damaged that it is
difficult to determine the arrangement of the leverages used.
This example probably represents a stage in the experiments
that led to the final Barret action. Again there is no half-hole
plate.

4. The position at the side of the upper joint formerly occupied
by the $c\natural$ key was now taken up by a duplicate touch-piece for
the $g\sharp$, and a ring given to the right forefinger was arranged
with a projection which overlapped the cup of that key. This
could close the key when pressed down without the need to
release the left little finger, thus giving an easy trill on $f\sharp$-$g\sharp$.
Under the name of 'articulated $g$ sharp' this action is in constant
use at the present time on both the oboe and the clarinet.

5. Various other trills throughout the compass of the instrument
were obtained by the addition of duplicate touches.

## TRIÉBERT—THE LAST PHASE AND SUCCESSORS

We come finally to Triébert's last design. It seems that many
players in the 1870s, as today, disliked the use of the left thumb to
close the $b\flat$ and $c\natural$ keys, and Triébert set himself to the task of providing some other arrangement. A similar device to Barret's was

adopted, with this difference, that the right forefinger alone was used to operate these keys, the thumb-plate being abolished (Fig. 12). Some players claim a secondary advantage for this mechanism in that the closing of the $g^{\natural}$ hole, which occurs every time it is used, has the effect of steadying the $b^{\flat}$-$c^{\natural}$. In addition, the articulated $g^{\sharp}$ with alternative touches was incorporated, as well as the low $b^{\flat}$ key and an improved form of automatic octave patented in 1872.

These were the principal features which, with one or two

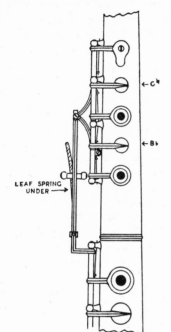

LEAF SPRING
UNDER →

Fig. 12. 'Conservatoire' action for $b^{\flat}$ and $c^{\natural}$

additional facilities, characterised Système 6 at the time of Triébert's death. Work did not stop, however, and the elder Lorée continued to experiment, shortly producing Système A6, in which any of the first *three* fingers of the right hand could operate the $b^{\flat}$-$c^{\natural}$ mechanism. The eminent player Georges Gillet had considerable influence on Lorée's work, and in 1882 he secured the adoption of Système A6 in his oboe class at the Conservatoire. From that date this type of French oboe without thumb-plate has been universally termed the 'Conservatoire' model, although a distinction is sometimes made between 6 and A6 by calling the latter the 'Gillet System'. Under Gillet's influence also F. Lorée produced a Conservatoire oboe with perforated cover-plates to the finger-holes in place of rings, and this was finally perfected by his son in 1906. A considerable number of outstanding players favour this model, which first figured in the Lorée catalogue as No. 6 bis and is nowadays listed as standard by many good makers.

At the end of the Triébert period a few defects still remained in the scale of the oboe, most of which have since been remedied. These mainly concern trills in different registers, and call only for passing notice. One more serious matter, however, requires detailed mention. The $f^{\natural}$ produced by the cross key for the right third finger has always been an excellent note. The same note sounded by the forked fingering is often appreciably flat. This is due to a slight re-positioning of hole No. 5, which has come about over the years in connection with the tuning of certain other notes. Even when in tune the forked note is often dull and 'stuffy' in quality. The common expedient of opening the $e^{b}$ key immediately below is not good, since it tends to over-correct the fault and to destroy the tone as well as occupying the little finger, which may immediately be required for some other duty. On the oboe d'amore and cor anglais, with their more widely spaced holes, the position is even worse, and it has long been the custom to remedy the trouble by the provision of a small vent-hole which opens automatically with the raising of the right middle finger. Unfortunately, on the shorter tube of the oboe, this device is not so generally satisfactory, since the hole falls at a point where it tends to upset the tuning of several other notes. For this reason French oboists in general have rejected the help of the $f^{\natural}$ vent, preferring to leave correction of the forked note to the skill of the individual player. The problem has also been dealt with by furnishing the cross $f^{\natural}$ key with a second lever controlled by the left little finger—the so-called 'long $f$'—but this mechanism has not proved universally popular. It was not till 1907 that M. Bonnet succeeded in designing a mechanism which would open only for the forked $f^{\natural}$ and not when the middle finger was raised for any other purpose. Thus it is only some forty-five years since the last major weakness was removed.

Surveying the progress of the French oboe between 1820 and 1910, the story seems to be one of ever-increasing mechanical complication, but this is really only part of the truth, for tone has always been regarded as of first importance. As the mechanism has been added piece by piece, so has the bore required adjustment. At the present time this most vital part of the instrument conforms in general to the proportions adopted by the best opinion of over half a century ago, but in its details many modifications have been made, some of them so subtle as to be revealed only by the micrometer.

## THE OBOE ON THE BOEHM SYSTEM

The dominant position taken by the Triéberts in developing the French oboe must not blind us to the existence of other reputable makers in the mid-19th century, some of whom turned out first-class instruments of the accepted types, although they could not legitimately reproduce many of the Triébert improvements, which were heavily protected by patents. Distinguished among these was Louis Auguste Buffet (active 1831–67), whose name is perhaps best remembered today for his work on the clarinet. His contribution to the oboe was mainly in the application of the Boehm mechanism.

In 1832 Theobald Boehm of Munich introduced to the musical world a new and revolutionary type of cone flute. This was designed on the rational—though apparently at the time startling—principle that in making wind instruments with side-holes, the number, size, and position of these holes should be established first, the means of controlling them being left to second place. Accordingly, Boehm determined by experiment that a flute to meet his exacting requirements as a professional musician would need in all fourteen holes, but that no more than eight fingers and one thumb could be used to open and close them. In addition some of the holes must fall beyond the reach of the unaided fingers. Boehm also found that ideally most of the holes should be bigger than could be easily covered by the finger. On this point, however, he at first compromised by making the holes as big as practicable and placing them higher up on the tube than theory indicated. Later on, in his cylinder flute of 1847, he managed to avoid this compromise altogether.

Having designed the tube of his flute, Boehm's next problem was the provision of appropriate mechanism, and in this he proved his genius. For the sake of clear, unveiled tone, he decided on a system in which all keys except one stood open when at rest, and by attaching the cups to longitudinal axles which also carried rings surrounding four of the finger-holes, he enabled the available digits to operate them all as required.[8] In spite of its many good features, Boehm's flute did not immediately succeed, and it was nearly ten years before the conservatism of players began to yield

at all generally to its manifest advantages. The benefits of the
ring mechanism were, however, quickly recognised by instrument-
makers, and as this was not, as far as we can tell, patented, it soon
found a number of applications. One of the first of these was to
render automatic the $f$# vent-key on oboes and clarinets.

Once the initial prejudice against the new flute had been to some
extent overcome, Boehm's mechanism and its underlying principles found a rapidly growing appreciation, and before 1840
several workers were seeking to apply them more or less completely to other instruments. We know that Boehm himself either
supervised the design or actually made such key-work for both
oboe and bassoon.[9] It was, however, Buffet who did most in this
direction. In carrying out the designs of Victor Côche for a modified Boehm flute, Buffet acquired much skill and experience in the
making and fitting of ring-keys, and at the exhibition of 1839 he
showed a clarinet so equipped. In 1844 a patent was granted to
Buffet for a ring-keyed clarinet embodying the revolutionary ideas
of Klosé (then professor of the clarinet at the Conservatoire), and
at the same time protection was granted for an oboe on the same
lines. (Plate V, No. 5). The strict propriety of applying Boehm's
name without qualification to these instruments has been much
debated, for, as Adam Carse has pointed out, Boehm's *system* is one
thing and the *key-work* he devised to carry it out is another. In re-
modelling the clarinet Klosé only followed the Boehm theory in
part, though Buffet applied the mechanism more extensively. In
respect of the oboe, however, we have direct testimony from
Christopher Welch, who had it from Buffet himself, that Boehm
actually supplied a boring bit and dimensions for the holes. (Note 7
*ante.*) The first instruments made according to Boehm's directions
were eagerly taken up by A. J. Lavigne, a celebrated player resident in London from 1841 onward, and by the Paris oboist P. Soler.
The latter, according to Constant Pierre, was also in some way concerned in the actual production of the instrument. On its first
appearance the new oboe was of course regarded as quite un-
orthodox. Boehm's ideas on free tone production called for holes
much larger than customary at the time, and these, together with
the rather wide bore he favoured (4·35 mm. at the top compared
with 4·2 mm. as used by Brod or Triébert), resulted in a quality of
tone which must have been very different from that generally cultivated in France. Undeterred by this Lavigne, however, went even
further, and Buffet records that he insisted on having the holes in

his own instrument considerably larger than recommended. As a result he achieved a tremendously powerful tone of a quality that was by no means universally liked, though all agreed that his execution with the new key-work was amazing. In spite of criticism, Lavigne remained a staunch champion of the Buffet-Boehm oboe and continued to experiment and to remodel it until his death. The two strange-looking instruments illustrated in Plate V are thought to represent late developments of Lavigne's work. Both have plain cone bores without any suggestion of a bell, and both sound *a* below the stave as the lowest note. Though these instruments look ungainly and are heavy in the hand, they give remarkable facility in execution, the unusually high pillars allowing the key levers to be most delicately balanced. In both cases the tone is very powerful. It is unfortunate that the history of neither is known; both were found in general dealers' shops, one in London and one in the North. The more complex one has, however, been recognised by Mr. Montague George, who recalls that during his apprenticeship it was a frequent visitor for repairs to Messrs. Rudall Carte's workshop, where it was affectionately known as 'old spider-keys'. Recently, too, the writer has had the opportunity to examine certain of Lavigne's experimental oboe tubes which now belong to Messrs. Boosey and Hawkes, and one of these corresponds in almost every detail to this instrument.

Although the large and 'open' tone of the Boehm oboe has not usually commended itself in orchestral circles, in the field of military music the instrument seemed at one time to have a considerable future. The firm of Millereau, for instance, described it in their catalogue of 1874 as adopted by the Commission des Musiques de l'Armée, 'being very loud in tone'. It is nevertheless some time since it was abandoned by the French army in favour of the normal instrument. In the early 1870s there seems to have been a vogue for the Boehm oboe in Spain, where it is still to be found more often than elsewhere in Europe, and the well-known Madrid player E. Marzo wrote a tutor for it. As might have been expected, F. Triébert devoted some attention to it, although, according to Bleuzet, he found it defective alike in tuning and in tone. Triébert attempted both to reduce the size of the bore and to bring the fingering more into line with established practice. In both objects he was of course running contrary to the nature of the instrument as conceived by Boehm, and in neither did he achieve great success. A few military style oboes sold by the London flutemaker Wallis show an interesting feature which may have been an attempt to ameliorate the tone. These, which are obviously of good-class French manufacture, have a normal bore as far as the lowest finger-hole, below which the expansion is greatly reduced. The opening of the bell is so small as barely to admit the little finger. It is difficult to judge how, if at all, this affected the tone, but it undoubtedly resulted in a general flattening of pitch, for the total length of the tube is nearly 2 cm. less than in a regulation military oboe of the same date and to the same pitch standard.

In 1880 Lorée began to make a normal oboe with key-work adapted to Boehm fingering, and other makers have since followed suit. Today such instruments are listed by most leading makers, but their use is mainly confined to players whose work obliges them to change rapidly between flute and oboe, or oboe and saxophone. The latest development in this direction is the saxophone-fingered oboe, on which all holes are covered by finger-plates and all keys are shaped to feel as much like those of the saxophone as possible.

## THE GERMAN OBOE AFTER SELLNER

The foregoing three sections of this chapter have outlined the most interesting and important phases in the life of the French oboe and have carried its story as far as the first decade of the present century. We must now turn back some eighty years to follow the fortunes of the German instrument after it left the hands of Koch and Sellner. Here we do not find so spectacular a growth as in France, but rather a period of solid progress without startling innovations.

In the first place, the tone of the Sellner-type instrument (nearer in quality we may suspect to that of the mid-18th century oboe) was already favoured in Germany, with the result that makers found no need for basic changes in the size and shape of the bore. There is little doubt that in Germany from the early classical period onward the oboe has been valued quite as much for its ability to blend in an ensemble as for its qualities as an outstanding solo voice. Writing of the celebrated Mannheim orchestra in his *Ideen zu einer Aesthetik der Tonkonst*, the critic Schubart (1739–91) comments particularly on the homogeneity of the wind tone. At the present day the point will be clear indeed to any concert-goer who has had the good fortune to hear, say, the Beethoven Septet or the Schubert Octet, played by both the Vienna Philharmonic

Wind Ensemble and any first-rate group of English or French players. The comparison is not derogatory to either school of playing, but the blending quality of the actual instrument which Beethoven and Schubert knew—or rather its modern counterpart —certainly does impart a characteristic flavour to the music.

The tube, then, of the German oboe was to continue for a good many years without radical alteration. The bell remained wide and flaring, with a heavy inner rim, and a very pronounced 'step' where it met the middle joint. Sometimes there was also a step between upper and middle joints, though it was usually much smaller than in French instruments.[10] For some time there seems to have been little consistency of opinion on these matters or exchange of views between makers, possibly because of the geographical and political separation of the principal German musical centres. It is, how-ever, safe to say that well before 1900 leading German makers were united in the use of a smooth bore without steps, rather wider at the top than the French pattern (about 4·4 mm. as against the French average of 4·2 mm.) and with a slightly less rapid expansion. The inner curve of the bell now developed smoothly out of the main cone and finally contracted abruptly by some 8 mm. at the open end.

The key work of the German oboe during the fifty years after Sellner does not require much comment. On the whole, players remained content with the capabilities of the instrument as it left his hands, and the makers therefore concentrated on improving the existing mechanism. In one respect only does there seem to have been any dissatisfaction. The key for the low $b\natural$ given to the left thumb was undoubtedly disliked by many players, perhaps because the flexibility of so long a lever gave a sense of insecurity on that note, or perhaps because the thumb had already sufficient other duties. Uhlmann, like Koch, regularly made a most elegant version of the thumb key which was hinged to fold away when the instrument was packed in its case, but other makers very soon abandoned it and transferred the lever to the left little finger. This made for an altogether firmer and better-balanced key, more in keeping with the rest of the equipment. The old-fashioned wooden blocks for key pivots remained in favour for a long time after their demise in France, and they were regularly strengthened with metal lining. On the other hand, when the Germans at length adopted metal pillars, most of them did so in the best possible form, attaching them to anchor-plates screwed to the body of the tube. This excellent arrangement was used by Meyer of Hanover as early as 1860. By this time also the $f^\sharp$ with an axle and two rings for the right hand was regularly fitted. Except for this particular key, however, there seems to have been an abiding preference for simple levers for even the longest spans; a strange example of conservatism in the country which actually gave birth to the key-axle. Only during the last twenty years of the century, at the time when the outside of the tube was finally cleared of excrescences, did the axle come into extensive use.

The third and most important concern of German oboe-makers in the 19th century was that of tuning. It may well be that when Dr. Burney made his scathing comments, tuning was no better in Germany than elsewhere, but certainly by Sellner's time the matter was taken most seriously. Makers were expected to supply instruments that were of good general intonation, and perhaps some of the peculiarities of the bore already noted may have been concerned with this point. In the circumstances it is a little surprising to find that both the half-hole plate and the second octave key were rather late additions.

The adjustment of pitch also received much attention. The Koch–Sellner instrument included a tuning slide in the original design, and in Uhlmann's model this was adjusted by a fine pitched screw. Other makers seemed to have disliked the idea of introducing a cylindrical section in the bore, as is necessitated by any sort of telescopic slide, and these provided instead sets of two or three alternative upper joints of different lengths. The absence of any connection between the keys of the two joints made this a fairly simple matter. (Plate IV, No. 4.)

It has already been indicated that before the end of the century the heavy baluster at the top of the German oboe had in the main gone out of fashion. This feature will come up for discussion again in reference to the instrument of today, but as regards the period under review we may say in general that it ended with the German instrument as streamlined as the French one, though still heavier and more robust.

OTHER EUROPEAN COUNTRIES

To round off our account of the 19th-century oboe, its progress in Belgium, Italy, and Great Britain must be mentioned, though none of these countries contributed anything fundamental to its structure.

Belgium, although a small country, has, for her size, produced a most impressive list of instrument-makers since the middle of the

15th century. Many examples of their work are to be found in public collections and, of these, one of the finest in the world is the Musée Instrumental of the Brussels Conservatoire. According to the available records, the chief centres of the industry appear to have been Antwerp, Ghent, Malines, and, of course, Brussels, where in the period under review the most important makers were the elder Sax (Charles-Joseph), the Mahillons, Charles and his son Victor, and Eugène Albert and his family and successors.

In the last two centuries Belgian players and teachers have been no less distinguished, and a considerable number of them have become prominent in England and in America. M. Bleuzet, writing in 1927, refers in particular to Guillaume Guidé as one of the most outstanding oboists of his time. Guidé was professor in the Brussels Conservatoire from 1885 till his death during the First World War, having been also a director of the Théâtre Royale de la Monnaie, noted internationally for the excellence of its resident orchestra. In addition to Brussels, Belgium has important academies of music in Ghent, Liège, and elsewhere which, according to Bleuzet, have remained somewhat independent of Paris influence as regards the oboe. On the other hand, Constant Pierre stated in 1890 that the usual Belgian oboe was then based on Triébert Système No. 5.

Between 1800 and 1850 good oboes of the type usual in the rest of Europe were produced by Italian makers, notably Maino and Piana, both of Milan. In general, the tendency there was to follow French models, though Austrian influence was also felt. The excellent instruments by Miraz of Udine, for example, were definitely Austrian in style.

It will be recalled, too, that Sellner's Tutor was issued in Italian translation during the period when a considerable part of Italy was under Austrian rule. The position in Italy towards the end of the century is recorded by Constant Pierre in his account of the Paris Exhibition of 1889. At that time, he tells us, the ordinary French oboe (Triébert No. 5) was in common use, but that there were also two native systems peculiar respectively to the Conservatoire of Milan and to the St. Cecilia Conservatoire in Rome. The former had thirteen keys, but no rings, and the latter fourteen or fifteen. The same key-work was also applied to the cor anglais, and Pierre observes that the Milan instrument was still being built in the curved form which Paris had almost abandoned.

In England oboes of the early and mid-19th century tended to be no more than well made but unimaginative successors to the 18th-century types. As late as 1840 instruments were being built with no more than eight or nine keys, mostly by firms whose principal business was flute-making, and this at a time when both Barret and Lavigne were already established in London. The influence of these and other continental teachers soon grew powerful, however, and an increasing number of English players began to look to Paris for their instruments. To meet these conditions, British music houses began to import French oboes for sale under their own names, a practice which continued until comparatively recently.

Although English-made oboes of *c.* 1840 generally inclined more to the German than to the French pattern, the fully developed German instrument has never really taken root in this country. This might seem a little surprising, in view of the extravagant admiration accorded to German music and musicians in Victorian England, but the fact is that the brilliance of the French oboe professors in London put their chosen instrument beyond serious competition in this country. Perhaps also the geographical question mentioned earlier in this chapter had some effect. At the time communication with France was certainly easier than with Germany, while the large French music industry centralised in Paris was probably better able to supply export requirements in quantity. For the above reasons British oboe makers in general dropped out of the picture after about 1850, with, however, two notable exceptions. These were Alfred Morton of London, and John Sharpe of Pudsey, Yorkshire, and both were important outside the purely local field.

Morton (1827–98) began his career as an apprentice in Uhlmann's workshop in Vienna, where he completed his indentures in 1847. Thereafter he seems for a time to have abandoned the instrument trade, and there is reason to think that he was engaged in a branch of metal-working. Towards the last quarter of the century Morton resumed instrument-making in London, specialising in double reed instruments, and becoming the leading English maker of his time. With his background of Vienna training, Morton might have been expected to adhere to the Austrian type of oboe; in fact he did nothing of the sort. The test-piece he made at the end of his apprenticeship already showed some slight departure from accepted Vienna practice, while the magnificent instruments of his later London period were virtually French oboes. This does not mean that Morton was a mere copyist—he had far too independent a mind—but he did appreciate the Triébert principles and apply them. The proportions of his bore, however, were not always typically French, while his key work was frequently original in design as well as extremely efficient.

From 1872 Morton's sons became his partners, and during his life the new firm honourably maintained the reputation of its founder. During the later years of the partnership a considerable number of oboes and bassoons were made for the British Army, and many remained in use until the Service finally dropped the Old Philharmonic Pitch ($A=452.4$ vibrations per second) in 1929. Many symphony players had, of course, to abandon cherished instruments much earlier following the introduction of 'flat' pitch at the Queen's Hall in 1895, and its acceptance by the Philharmonic Society in the next year. Very few instruments built by the Mortons to low pitch are known, and the partners never seem to have got really into their stride working to the new standards. After the death of A. Morton in 1898 the firm gradually petered out and British oboe-making really came to an end for some time, though in that same year Morton's apprentice David Howell is recorded as having set up as a maker on his own account. He, too, seems to have disappeared from the scene some time before 1914.

John Sharpe, whose instruments at one time attracted a good deal of attention, was a contemporary of the Mortons, and his working period was approximately the last twenty years of the 19th century. Known as 'Oboe John', he is still remembered in his home town of Pudsey near Leeds as an instrumentalist and choir-singer, and as something of a 'character' as well. Being settled in Yorkshire, his fame might have remained purely local but for the fortunate circumstance that he was active at a time when orchestral music in the north of England had achieved international import-ance and could attract notable players away from London and send northern virtuosi southwards in exchange. In consequence a number of Sharpe's instruments found their way into London orchestras. Little is known of his earlier efforts (he is reputed to have started as an amateur maker and to have first interested him-self in the clarinet), but some indication is afforded by a note by Dr. Turpin in the *Musical Standard* for August 20th, 1881. The writer says:

"Some important improvements have lately been made in the construction of the oboe by Mr. Sharp (sic) of Pudsey, near Leeds. These not only give facilities for the better and more ready production of middle A flat and E flat by self-acting keys and levers but secure by its new key arrangements (5 in all being added) a better and more equal intonation throughout the compass of the instrument.''

Sharpe's later instruments combined a Boehm system lower joint with moderate-sized holes and a modified Barret-type upper. There appears to be much to recommend this idea, but in uniting the two, Sharpe incorporated certain automatic vent-keys of his own devising which required small 'floating' levers to reverse the motion. Examples still surviving show that they did not stand up well in use and were not very reliable mechanically. It is probably for this reason that an otherwise excellent instrument was ultimately abandoned by even the most ardent devotees of the Boehm oboe in this country. One of the last players of note to use a Sharpe oboe in England was the late W. H. Shepley, formerly a professor at the Royal College of Music, and though he, too, gave it up before the end of his professional career in favour of a more orthodox instrument, he was more than once heard to deplore having made the change.

[1] In this section 'Germany' is taken to mean German-speaking North-East Europe in general.

[2] It is not to be thought that French provincial standards necessarily declined with the foundation of the Conservatoire. Instruments as good as any made in Paris were produced in such centres as Lyons and St. Omer, though naturally the majority of workers were attracted to the capital. In Lyons, from 1808 on, the firms of Simiot, Muller, and Piatet et Benoit produced excellent instruments with features so characteristic as to form an easily recognised 'school'.

[3] Brod, in his *Méthode* (c. 1835), says that the low $b^{\natural}$ key had formerly been regarded only as a means of improving the low c. This it certainly does in the case of a Triébert oboe known to the writer, where a single tuning-hole only remains in the bell. This instrument, with all holes closed, gives a good $c^{\natural}$ as the lowest note, but with a relaxed lip gives also quite a passable $b^{\natural}$ with the same fingering. According to Constant Pierre, Cuvilier fils ainé, a maker of St. Omer, exhibited an oboe with a $b^{\natural}$ key useful as such as early as 1834.

[4] Christophe Delusse, Professor of the Flute and manufacturer of woodwind instruments. Records of him are unfortunately very far from complete, his known working period being only 1783–89. His oboes were much esteemed both for elegance and tone in the early years of the 19th century. Vide Constant Pierre, *Les Facteurs d'instruments de Musique*, Paris, 1893, pp. 102–3.

[5] A particularly ingenious form of half-hole action found on Brod's 'Cor anglais Moderne', c. 1835, occurs also on a baritone oboe marked 'Triébert' (author's collection), but which in other respects conforms to Brod's

illustration. It seems that collaboration between the two men is the most likely explanation. Triébert's standard half-hole key is quite different in construction.

[6] According to French commercial law, the acquisition of the goodwill of a business entitles the purchaser to use, if he wishes, the former owner's name and trade-mark. In consequence there are in France today certain large musical manufacturers who are legally entitled to brand their products with famous trade-marks which have come into their hands in this way. One at least has gone so far as to offer buyers of stock goods the choice of the name to be applied.

[7] At this remove of time fine measurements of 19th-century oboes are not altogether to be trusted. Actual corrosion during years of playing, as well as changes in the wood when out of use, must have affected the bore of many specimens. Nevertheless averages taken over a series of instruments do indicate the presence of a number of cones of different rates of expansion, and no doubt individual makers had their own jealously guarded formulae to which their bits and reamers were adjusted. For example, a fine and well-preserved oboe by Brod in the writer's collection shows a fairly rapid taper from the top to the region of the $c^{\#}$ hole, below which the cone becomes much more gentle, and, in addition, there are signs of other minor variations difficult to measure but clearly visible by reflected light. A contemporary specimen by Triébert has an identical bore at the top, which continues without appreciable change as far as the middle tenon. Below the tenon the bores of both instruments recommence with a sudden expansion in diameter of well over a millimetre. The pronounced 'step' so formed is a feature which seems to have become marked with French oboes of c. 1835. There is much less evidence of it in 18th-century examples, or with the earlier G. Triébert instruments, which still remain strongly 18th century in general character. This break in the continuity of the bore seems to have persisted in France at least until 1865, though by 1880 it had disappeared even from second-class instruments of old-fashioned type which were still sometimes made. There are signs of its return among the more modern French instruments of today. (See also Chapter 'Acoustics'.)

In interpreting the evidence of measurements, it must also be remembered that the process of final tuning often involved minor adjustments to the bore carried out by hand, with the result that we sometimes find differences between individual instruments from the same factory and bored with the same tools.

[8] For detailed description see Adam Carse, *Musical Wind Instruments*, London, 1939; also Christopher Welch, *History of the Boehm Flute*, London, 1892.

[9] As a young man Boehm worked as a goldsmith and jeweller, and flutes which he is known to have made himself show him to have been a most skilful mechanic. The case is parallel to that of Frédéric Triébert, who began as apprentice to an engraver, and thus gained a sureness of hand and eye that served him well in his later career as an instrument-maker.

[10] While conforming to the same basic proportions, the bores of German oboes made between 1840 and 1875 show a rather surprising diversity of detail. For example, some built by Uhlmann, a Vienna maker highly esteemed in the mid-century, are remarkable for having neither an inner bell-rim nor a step in the middle, while contemporary specimens by Bormann of Dresden show both features strongly developed. (See also Appendix I.)

G

# CHAPTER 6

# The Oboe Today

WITH the arrival of the Conservatoire oboe soon after 1880, many musicians felt that the last word had been spoken. That this was not in fact so became evident in a very few years. The truth is that the general perfection of the instrument now emphasised certain minor failings which had formerly been more or less disregarded. For example, the low $c$-$c\sharp$ trill was still missing, and a few notes were still consistently poorer than the rest. The definitely bad forked $f\natural$ and its final cure by M. Bonnet's mechanism in 1907 have already, for the sake of consistency, been noted in the previous chapter. During the next thirty years, then, the remaining problems were attacked one by one, and by 1910 nearly all were adequately solved.

At that time the player had four different and satisfactory systems to choose from, according to his tastes and circumstances. Both forms of the French instrument, 'thumb-plate' or 'Conservatoire', had reached a high degree of efficiency, and both had their confirmed supporters among the most eminent professionals. The German type, though by then often fitted with automatic octave keys, still remained less highly mechanised than the others, and many players found a virtue in its simplicity. Finally, for those to whom its special fingering was advantageous, the Boehm system oboe had also been greatly improved. Now it seemed for a while that the last word had indeed been spoken; but yet again time has shown that more changes were to come—not such spectacular changes, it is true, as in the previous century, but still changes of great musical importance. Much work has been done in the last forty years, some of it too recently for us to judge yet of its value, and this chapter must therefore record rather than evaluate.

In the present century the French oboe has progressed along two different lines: first, in the direction of a more powerful tone; and second, towards a still greater mechanical facility. Many modern players, in France especially, have felt that the later instruments by A. Lorée, while lacking nothing in refinement or intonation, were rather reticent in the lower register, and several makers have sought to improve this matter by once again re-designing the tube. The newest oboes now tend to show a slightly larger bore with fewer deviations from the true cone, the step at the middle joint which appeared on many Lorée instruments has been virtually abolished, and the upper joint is being made with considerably thicker walls. In addition, the tube is now often made rather longer than is absolutely necessary to produce the low $b^b$, the note being brought into tune by a small automatic vent-key on the side of the bell.[1] The purpose of the extra length is to steady certain of the upper notes and make them easier to attack, an effect which was first widely noticed with the introduction of the $b^b$ extension on Triébert Système 6. Certain of the extreme high notes are also rendered more certain by the provision of the third octave key. The whole instrument, in fact, while retaining its general character, is fast becoming adapted to an altogether more robust style of playing.

As regards keywork generally, there have been recently a number of most ingenious attempts to combine all the facilities of both major systems. The result has been the production of certain necessarily heavy and complicated instruments which are really not much in advance of Barret's last design. Amongst these the so-called 'Brussels Conservatoire' and 'Full Barret Conservatoire' models produced in England are notable. Many leading players regard such intricate keywork with some distrust, and the wise oboist is probably he who, having become familiar with one of the basic systems, adopts only those extra keys which he finds the most constant help. Certain notable players have, of course, devised 'systems' to meet their own ideas, of which we may perhaps mention in particular those of Charles Reynolds and of Stephen Whittaker. The former was peculiar mainly in the transfer of certain shake-keys to the opposite side of the body from the normal, while the feature of the latter was the sacrifice of the vent-key for the forked $f^{\natural}$ in favour of a mechanism which provided a very convenient $e^b$-$f^{\natural}$ passage which eased rapid playing in flat and extreme sharp keys.

In Great Britain there is today an influential school which holds that a limited number of facilities used with the assurance that comes of long practice are infinitely preferable to a mass of alternative keys which may become an embarrassment. Even 'automatic octaves' are eschewed by some of the older players and many use what is called a 'semi-automatic' mechanism which does no more than allow the thumb to remain on the touch of the first octave key while the second is operated as usual by the forefinger from $g^{\sharp}$ upwards. Naturally the style and make of instruments favoured by leading teachers have been adopted by their pupils, so that in certain areas we find a decided preference for one or another system. In America, for instance, the influence of Fernand Gillet has been profound, and the Lorée model with covered holes he favours is probably the most used. Following his lead, the artist-maker Laubin of Scarsdale, N.J., is producing examples of this type which are nowadays to be found in some of the most important orchestras in the Eastern States. On the western side of the country, round about Los Angeles, there is a marked preference for Cabart instruments with single-touch 'automatics', as a result of the widespread influence of De Buescher, the same who was a celebrated player in London at the beginning of the century. In Los Angeles also another maker, A. Lym, has recently come to the fore, and his instruments are at present enjoying considerable favour. It seems, therefore, that in the U.S.A. oboe-making flourishes at the present time.

In London in the early 1900s comparatively few oboes were made completely. As in other centres, the big instrument dealers there provided oboes, but the majority of them were imported from the Belgian firm of Mahillon or from France. The writer was once told by the late Sir Henry Wood that it was Mahillon who provided the pair of low-pitch oboi d'amore specially ordered for the Queen's Hall Orchestra, and it is known that Victor Mahillon himself spent some time in London advising certain prospective oboe-makers. He also provided two oboi d'amore with flared bells for the Dolmetsch concerts of ancient music. In spite of this, however, the deplorable custom of importing part-finished instruments (usually of the second class or worse) for marking and sale by London dealers persisted for some years. Then, between the wars, there occurred in London a revival which placed British oboes on a par with any of the world's best. This was achieved by the small Louis Musical Instrument Company under the managing direction of the celebrated clarinettist Charles Draper. This firm adhered to an excellent Lorée model. Within the last few years also another small London company, T. W. Howarth and Son, have produced a quantity of oboes of remarkable merit.

In France during the last ten years some change of loyalty seems to have occurred among the younger players, and today the most admired oboes are believed to be those of Marigaux, Riboutat, and Robert, all small firms producing rather heavy instruments in comparison with the Lorée types. The present owners of the Lorée mark do a very large export trade, and their instruments are popular, but the name no longer seems to carry the 'petit-spécialiste' connotation of former days.

The position of the German oboe today is curiously ambiguous. In Germany, after many years of exclusive loyalty to the Austrian style of instrument, a marked change of front occurred shortly after 1904. In that year Richard Strauss published his enlarged version of Berlioz's *Orchestration* and in the pages on the oboe he compared the current French and German styles of playing, greatly to the disadvantage of the latter. It was then, he said, 'thick and trumpet-like' and unyielding in the ensemble. Such an opinion from so weighty a source no doubt had great influence, and as a result we soon find the German music industry turning its attention to French models. Today such well-known German makers as Adler, Mollenhauer, and Heckel supply excellent conservatoire or thumb-plate oboes of their own manufacture. In an effort to determine accurately the period of the change, the writer consulted the late Herr W. H. Heckel, and was informed that by 1925 even that celebrated house found so little demand for oboes with the old German bore that they were obliged to begin working to French dimensions. To meet the changing conditions which then obtained in Germany, Heckel, with great cleverness, designed a number of different oboes combining French and German characteristics in varying degree. Just before the last war Heckel's catalogue illustrated no fewer than eleven types, ranging from the simple Vienna instrument to the fullest French models. With Herr Heckel's permission the catalogue drawing is reproduced here.

The last stronghold of the simple Austrian type oboe is Vienna, the city of its birth. There the leading players, notably those of the Philharmonic Orchestra, remain faithful to a fifteen-keyed instrument not much in advance of Sellner's model of a hundred and twenty years ago. The main additions are the 'brille' for the right hand $f^{\sharp}$, the second octave key, and the 'half-hole' plate. Occasionally this plate is duplicated by an entirely independent key, and the octaves are linked to operate automatically. Finally a 'helping-key' for the note $f'''$ is sometimes added, which corresponds more or less to the third octave key on recent French instruments. An arrangement has also been perfected by Heckel by which *three*

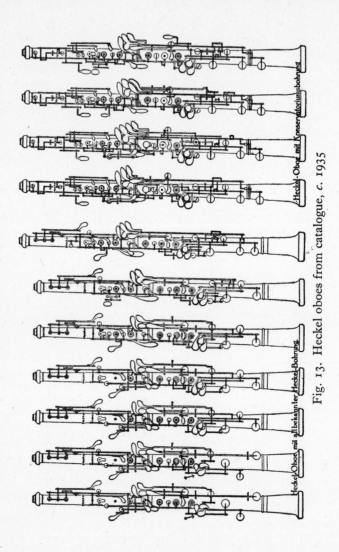

Fig. 13.  Heckel oboes from catalogue, c. 1935

speakers operate automatically with the use of only one touch-piece, a refinement which, as far as I am aware, no French maker has yet attempted. The low $b^\flat$ is not normally provided. Until a year or two ago, the small firm of Hermann Zuleger made the most favoured modern Vienna oboes, and he continued (as do his successors) to provide the thick inner rim and tuning-holes in the bell together with a pronounced 'step' at the bell joint. Most Vienna players hold that these features contribute much to the special quality of tone they cultivate. Unlike most other makers in German-speaking Europe, Zuleger persisted in retaining the heavy 18th-century baluster at the top of the upper joint, on the theory that a large mass of wood here makes the tube less susceptible to changes of temperature in its most sensitive region.

It is obvious that such a survey as the above can hardly be complete, and circumstances change from year to year.[2] World conditions have forced many makers into mergers and combines who nowadays handle the bulk of the instrument trade. The products of these large firms are often excellent, but even so the best esteemed instruments the world over still seem to come from the hands of the small specialist.

[1] Compare this with the long bell of the 18th-century oboe provided with permanently open 'tuning-holes'. See Chapter 'Acoustics', pp. 116, 117.

[2] In October 1953 it was reported that in Vienna instrument-making as a whole was in sad decline. At the time of writing there remained in the city only three woodwind makers: H. Zuleger's widow, Franz Koktan, and Josef Stecher. It is also credibly reported that in 1954 instruments bearing the name of Heckel, but without the full trade mark, are being unofficially produced outside Germany.

# CHAPTER 7

# The Larger Oboes and Exceptional Varieties

IT is probably true that today the larger oboes are more valued as individual 'tone-colour' instruments than as members of a homogeneous group. Group-writing for the oboe is of course frequently to be found in orchestral scores, but if maintained for long—as for instance by Elgar in certain of his works—the compactness of tone tends to cloy the modern ear. At the time when the true oboes appeared, the tonal solidity of the 'whole consort' had not entirely passed from favour, and no doubt the new instruments were at first treated by many composers as were the older families. Very soon, however, their greater fluency and fitness for 'broken music' brought them into a leading place in the rapidly developing art of the time. This was a style of music in which group-tone was replaced by more interesting combinations of solo voices with individual personalities.

ALTO (*Hautbois d'Amour, Oboe d'Amore, Oboe Luongo, Liebesoboe*)

The alto oboe pitched in A—a minor third below the type instrument—has, in the main, played a less important part in European music than any other member of the family, and, indeed, were it not for J. S. Bach it might be regarded as of little importance. Its first recorded appearance in an orchestral score comes in Telemann's 'Der Sieg der Schönheit' of 1722.[1] A few modern composers, notably Richard Strauss, Holbrooke, Holst and Ravel have used the instrument, but it is unlikely that they would have demanded it had it not already been in existence.

The origin of the alto is obscure, and it is often regarded as an off-shoot of the treble instrument built in a pitch more convenient for playing in sharp keys. It is probable that the oboe d'amore was originally taken as interchangeable with the treble when the *tessitura* of the music demanded, and this seems to be the way in which Bach usually regarded it. His writing for the d'amore shows a consistent tendency towards medium sharp keys, while such signatures are rare in contemporary parts for the C oboe. Conversely, Bach's choice of key may to some extent have been dictated by the instru-

ment in cases where he wished to exploit its characteristic tone—
more sombre than that of the treble, less weighty than that of the
tenor. Two oboi d'amore were available in the household of the
Prince of Anhalt-Cöthen, and at Leipzig, Bach employed one
regularly from 1723 onwards. As a rule he referred to it by the
French name of *hautbois d'amour*, but in the cantata No. 157 he
uses the term 'grand-oboe', which suggests, in this case at least, a
concern with pitch rather than with tone colour.

In structure the 18th-century alto oboe was merely an enlarge-
ment of the treble, usually with a small metal crook to carry the
reed. It is said that both flared and contracted bells were used,
though apparently the latter were the more common.[2] In present-
day collections early altos are very rare, and when examining those
we have we must beware of confusing them with trebles built to the
very low pitches of the time. In addition, the outer profile of the
bulb types is often curiously similar to that of the first ordinary
trebles. (Compare No. 1, Plate VIII with No. 5, Plate II.)
Towards the end of the century also we occasionally find what
appear externally to be normal flared bells with a thick cushion lip
and much ornamental turning, but which are spheroidal inside and
have quite a small opening at the end. Such a bell is to be seen on a
two-keyed cor anglais by Grundmann dated 1791 now in the Rushworth and Dreaper collection in Liverpool.

At this point we must consider briefly the history of the bulb or
'd'amore' bell in so far as we know it.

While positive evidence is still wanting, there are good grounds
for the conjecture that among the true oboes this began with the
tenor rather than with the alto. A number of bulbed tenors are preserved whose makers were certainly working between 1690 and
1710 and whose general features correspond closely with those of
ordinary oboes of *c*. 1700. This was twenty years or so before any
alto made its first tentative appearance in an orchestral score. In
addition, by 1700 the tenor was fairly well known in military circles,
and its comparative prominence recommends it as the more likely
subject for any experiment. In the following section two sug-
gestions are offered for the origin of the bulb-bell of the tenor, one
based on practical convenience, the other on economy of material;
but neither point seems to apply with much force in the case of the
alto, which was a reasonably small and compact instrument.

Probably in the 18th century, as later, the incurved bell was
credited with certain mysterious tonal virtues and was, because of

this, deliberately added to the smaller oboes. Occasionally even the treble instrument acquired it. Pursuing this idea, an attractive speculation has been advanced by Sandford Terry,[3] who suggests that the normal alto in A was modified by analogy with the viola d'amore and so took over the name. Once the name *d'amore* had been transferred to a particular oboe it became associated with the special feature of that instrument. Thus the bulb-bell became known as *pavillion d'amour* and *liebesfuss*, and hence we have the terms *d'amore*, *d'amour*, and *Liebes* applied to bulbed instruments in general be they of whatever parentage.

TENOR (*Tenor Hautboy, Haute-contre de Hautbois, Taille, Cor Anglais, Englisches Horn, Oboe da Caccia, Vox Humana. Sometimes erroneously Tenoroon*)

There is no doubt that instruments built a fourth or fifth lower in pitch than the treble were used before the end of the 17th century to complete the harmony of the oboes. Many historians have con-cluded that the tenor instrument developed more gradually than the treble, and in the sense that it seems to have taken longer to find recognition as an orchestral voice, this may be true. There is, however, no reason to suppose that it did not originate at the same time as the higher instrument, and, indeed, the most recent evi-dence suggests clearly that it did. Anthony Baines' re-examination of the Talbot manuscript has enabled us to date the advent of the oboe proper with some certainty.[4] Writing about the year 1700, Dr. James Talbot says specifically, 'The present Hautbois is not forty years old', and again under the same heading 'Tenor Haut-bois differs not from treble in shape'. We may therefore assume with some justice that the two instruments appeared almost together.

The Talbot manuscript gives in particular details and measure-ments of a tenor made by the celebrated Bressan which was prob-ably a true oboe, and not a shawm, although no mention is made of jointed construction. It is to be regretted that none of Bressan's oboes survives, though some of his recorders do, and show him to have been a fine workman. A further note of Talbot's refers to his having seen another tenor, this time by John Ashbury (*c.* 1690), which was made 'entire'—i.e. in one piece only. In spite of having this feature which characterises the shawms in general, the speci-men is carefully recorded by Talbot under the heading 'French hautbois', which seems to indicate that some at least of the instruments he knew in use were transition types. In quoting from Talbot we must bear in mind that his notes refer to instruments he examined in England, though much of his information was gathered from immigrant French players who after the Restoration found a welcome here. Concerning these two tenors it has been argued that since Talbot did not actually mention *joints* in the Bressan example, this instrument must necessarily have been made in one piece. To me it seems just as likely that his careful reference to the Ashbury specimen as 'entire' may indicate that, of the two, he regarded the Bressan as the more normal.[5] In this country very few oboes of any sort earlier than the 18th century are preserved, but in Continental museums there are sufficient to show clearly that the first tenors differed in construction very little from the trebles. On most of them the reed was carried by a small detachable metal crook, but it seems that sometimes the staple of the reed itself was long enough to make a separate crook unnecessary.[6]

As to the employment of the tenor oboe in its early stages, not a great deal is known. The first recorded reference to the instrument in an orchestral score is the often-quoted one in Purcell's 'Diocletian' (1691), but thereafter a number of respectable authorities seem to have remained ignorant of it. Neither Speer, Mattheson, Walther, Eisel, nor Majer make any reference to it, though, curiously enough, Walther did mention the oboe d'amore.[7] It might perhaps be argued that all of the above were German writers, and that in their time German experience did not extend to the larger hautbois of French origin. If, however, we accept this, how can we account for Bach's complaint to the Leipzig Council in 1730 that he had then no player for the Taille, or for his extensive use of the oboe da caccia between 1723 and 1740? It is to be noted that Bach appears to make a quite clear distinction between these two names for the tenor, though what special features he recognised under each we do not know.[8] Possibly it was only a distinction of usage—'Taille' for the tenor employed in harmony with other oboes, and 'da caccia' when used as a solo voice.

In the first years of the 18th century the most extensive use of the tenor oboe was in military service, and in many of the marches and flourishes included in the famous 'Collection Phillidor'[9] we find typical scoring for the instrument. Two trebles, a taille, and a basse de hautbois (bassoon) was the almost invariable combination for military use.

During the greater part of the 18th century the tenor oboe
exhibited a curious instability of form, the tube being anything
from completely straight to curved in a half-circle. Occasionally
also, near the end of the century, it was built in two straight sections joined by an angular 'knee'; 19th-century examples are also
known which have a straight tube doubled on itself near the bell.
In this peculiarity some authorities see a survival from military
days, and they regard the bending of the tube as evidence of an
attempt to make it more convenient for use under service conditions, especially on horse-back. In England the problem of compactness was evidently attacked in a different way with the introduction of a rather inelegant instrument called the 'vox humana'.[10]
In this the straight tube was retained, but was made in two pieces
only with no separate bell, while the proportionately rather long
crook was bent sharply at right angles. Thus the instrument would
be held canted to the side of the player with his hands quite close
to his body. At the open end a further economy was secured by
making the bell as a simple expansion of the main bore, with no
'step', very little flare, and no longer than was absolutely necessary
to sound the lowest note. By this treatment the instrument was
shortened a good deal, but the advantage of the typical 18th-
century bell as a resonator was sacrificed, and the tone was undoubtedly rather lacking in 'body'. The vox humana was known in
England from before 1750 till nearly the end of the century, and
quite a number of specimens are preserved in public and private
collections. A rare fingering chart for the instrument by Stanesby
junior, published by Longman, Lukey and Co., is to be found in
the Music Library of the British Museum.

While throughout the 18th century English makers seem to have
concentrated almost exclusively on straight tenors,[11] in the rest of
Europe these were fairly soon overtaken and supplanted in favour
by the curved types. Such were the instruments which came to be
known as *corno inglese*, *cor anglais*, and *Englisches horn*—names
whose origin has never been really satisfactorily determined. From
their first appearance these terms were regularly used by specialists,
so we cannot just pass them over on the basis that the layman tends
loosely to call any curved instrument a 'horn'. The tenor oboe is
obviously neither a horn nor of English origin. Probably the best
explanation is that *cor anglais* was at first a nick-name arising from
a fancied resemblance to a semi-circular hunting or forester's horn
said to have been common at one time in England. This suggestion

might be stretched to give also a rather far-fetched explanation of the earlier name *oboe da caccia* (hunting oboe), though for this there is also another possible derivation. In Zedler's *Universal Lexikon* of 1735 it is stated that reed instruments were for a time actually used in the chase. The idea is unthinkable in connection with hunting as we know it in England, but perhaps under the picturesque codes of Continental venery it is not so impossible. We do not know if the instruments referred to by Zedler were in fact capsuled shawms (*hautbois de Poitou*), or true oboes, but according to French usage the term *hautbois-de-chasse* would be applicable to either type if used in the hunting-field. This is an attractive theory, but unfortunately much more solid evidence is required before we can accept it as proven.

A second explanation of *cor anglais* and its Italian and German equivalents is that the words themselves are a corruption of *cor anglé*, meaning 'bent' or 'angled' horn. This is highly unlikely. Although it did at one time have a limited currency, mainly in connection with heraldry, the French word *anglé* has long been obsolete and the derivation in question was proposed only in the late 19th century. The actual name *cor anglais* occurs in the score of Gluck's 'Alceste' in 1767, while the Italian form, *corno inglese*, is even older, and is found in certain of Jomelli's works in 1741 and in Haydn's *divertimenti* of 1764. If *anglais* were indeed a corruption of *anglé*, surely we might expect to find *cor anglé* appearing at an earlier date than *cor anglais*, whereas there is no sign of this in musical literature. The whole matter has been described by one recent authority on French usage as 'one of those clever pieces of etymology constructed after the event, and fitting far too neatly to be true'. It is perhaps this very neatness which appeals to some modern lecturers who insist, with a fine show of assurance, in perpetuating what is almost certainly a fallacy.

The Continental tenor oboe, whether straight or curved, was a more elaborate instrument than the vox humana and was usually made in three sections with a separate bell joint and a small metal crook. Normal oboe features, such as 'air-holes' in the waist of the bell and twinned finger-holes, were regularly present. The bell itself was commonly of the pear shape nowadays characteristic of all the deeper oboes, though this was by no means universal. Tenors with an open bell have existed side by side with the commoner type right up to the present day. Sometimes, indeed, they have exhibited a widely flaring bell without even the inner rim of the early treble oboe. In trying to work out a consistent terminology, some scholars have reserved the term *da caccia* only for those with flared bells, while others have used it to signify all straight instruments (excepting perhaps the vox humana), regardless of the type of bell. Such distinctions seem to be entirely arbitrary and little justified by historical evidence.

Though the acoustic behaviour of the bulb-bell requires fuller investigation than it has yet received, there is no doubt at all that its effect on tone has been consistently exaggerated. Writers of text-books repeatedly mention the *liebesfuss* as 'reducing the harshness of the early oboe' and 'imparting a veiled quality to the sound', but if it does in fact modify the tone so markedly as some believe, surely it would have been an undesirable feature to apply to some instruments and not others in a group which—theoretically, at any rate—was tonally homogeneous. In advancing this argument we must of course recognise that in the mixed orchestra that was growing up in the first years of the 18th century complete families of each tone-colour were not necessarily called for in the way they had been formerly. Nevertheless it seems probable that, whatever its acoustic properties, the bulb-bell developed at first as a result of practical rather than æsthetic needs. One view is that for military use in early times it proved more convenient and less liable to damage than the open bell. Another is that it arose as a matter of economy in an effort to secure the resonating qualities of a flare with a less lavish expenditure of material. The large bells of some early tenors must have required huge pieces of flawless wood cut very much to waste.[12] This economy idea is offered entirely as a theory, without concrete evidence in support, but, curiously enough, it has recently been advanced quite independently by the well-known London oboist and consultant Horace Halstead in the course of a discussion on the difficulty of obtaining large and sound pieces of African Blackwood from logs which are nearly always twisted in growth and penetrated by 'shakes'. (See Chapter 'Materials and Manufacture'.)

In perusing the older musical dictionaries one cannot fail to remark the number of incompatible accounts one finds of the early tenor oboe. This is not altogether surprising, for the writers' personal experience may well have been limited to one or other of the several varieties. Unfortunately these accounts have been seized upon by book-learned musicologists of later days and combined and quoted in different ways without adequate reference either to surviving instruments or to practical players. In consequence, some quite extraordinary statements have been made. It has been alleged, for instance, that the only method of constructing a curved tube was to carve it out of plank-wood in two halves, and to glue and pin these together, as in the cornetts. From this it has been argued that the bores must necessarily have remained rough and ill-formed, with consequent bad effects on the tone, and from this again even so distinguished a scholar as Professor Sandford Terry[13] has concluded that the curved cor anglais proved unsatisfactory and was soon displaced by a return to the original straight form. In fact, there is ample evidence to prove fallacious all three stages of the argument. In the first place, museum specimens show that at least three different methods of construction were employed in the 18th and 19th centuries. Secondly, the bores of many built-up curved instruments are in fact quite as smooth (by reason of the way in which they were made) as those of the straight types, and their tone is demonstrably as good. Finally, the curved cor anglais was a favoured type in France at least until *c.* 1870, and in Italy considerably longer. As recently as 1900 an Italian oboist named Tromba was playing on a curved instrument at the Opera in London.[14]

In a recent study Josef Marx has advanced some very persuasive arguments as to the inventor of the true oboe. Some equally convincing work in regard to the originator of the curved cor anglais is badly needed. Unfortunately contemporary data are meagre in the extreme, and, unless hitherto unsuspected documents should some day be found, the position is likely to remain in doubt. On the evidence of Gerber (1792), Lavoix (1778), and Eitner (1899–1904), the idea of curving the tube is usually attributed to one Ferlendis, an oboist of Bergamo, who was established in Salzburg *c.* 1760. The matter has been examined by Miss Kathleen Schlesinger in the 11th edition of the *Encyclopædia Britannica* under OBOE and COR ANGLAIS, and her notes reveal at once the confusion that exists. There appear to have been two brothers Ferlendis, both oboe *virtuosi*, and they are reported as having appeared together in London in 1795. According to Eitner, the younger, Gioseffo, was born in 1755, so he can hardly have been the one who was active in Salzburg in 1760. French writers, including Lavoix, speak of *Jean* Ferlendis—in Italian *Giovanni*—from which we may suppose that this was the elder's name. On the other hand, Gerber refers the matter to a *Giuseppe* Ferlendis who was presumably

Eitner's *Gioseffo*. Finally, there is inconsistency between Miss Schlesinger's two articles. In the first she quotes the usual attribution to Jean Ferlendis, but in the second she refers it to 'Giovanni *or* Giuseppe', and observes that our information is inconclusive. Again we have a nice problem for the musical detective.

BASS (*Hautbois-Baryton, Basset Oboe, Bass Oboe*)

Unlike the oboe d'amore, which today is seldom employed except to reproduce at their proper pitch, the parts Bach wrote for it, the bass or baritone oboe, sounding one octave below the treble instrument in C, is of some considerable importance in its own right. Very little is known of its early history, but it seems quite clear that, although it stands in the same relation to the other oboes as did the bass pommer to the higher shawms, it was never employed as the regular bass to the oboe group. That function was usurped by the jointed bassoon, which in 17th century France was already referred to commonly as the *basse de hautbois*. Possibly the bass oboe arrived on the scene too late to compete with the bassoon for a place in the reformed orchestra, and in any case, with its long tube lacking any but the usual two keys, its intonation was probably more dubious even than that of the tenor. The earliest recorded specimen is one made by J. C. Denner (*c.* 1700), which before the war was preserved in Nurnberg. A facsimile, No. 958 in the Brussels Conservatoire, has been described in detail by Mahillon, and is reported by him to have a primary scale of *d* to *c'*.

A second important example, made by Charles Bizey, probably before 1750, is No. 494 in the Paris Conservatoire collection. This strange-looking instrument is shortened by doubling the tube back on itself below the *d* hole in the manner of the bassoon. From just below the *d*# hole the bore enters a sort of miniature bassoon 'boot', to emerge again in a small and rather conical bell. As usual, an 'air-hole' is present, though not placed in the bell itself, being instead nearly half-way down the boot. The *c*# key is of the typical 'fish-tail' shape. Two other bassoon-like features are a long, doubly bent crook, and two small 'wings' on the main tube, each accommodating a group of three finger-holes. In each group the outer two holes are pierced obliquely to meet the bore at considerably wider intervals than could be stretched by the fingers. Even so, the holes are grouped too closely for really good intonation.

Baritone oboes of English origin are excessively rare, but at least one example exists to prove that they were at one time made in this country. This instrument, formerly in the collection of the late Canon Galpin and how housed in the Museum of Fine Arts, Boston, Mass., can best be described as a baritone vox humana, for it has all the characteristics of that essentially English type. It has been fully examined and figured by Bessaraboff,[15] who dates it c. 1760, and it is also listed in Day's Catalogue of the Royal Military Exhibition, where it is called a basset-oboe. In addition, the Crosby Brown Collection in New York possesses a facsimile of an 18th-century English baritone, which, from Sachs' description, appears to be of a more normal type.

Before leaving the instruments of the 18th century we should notice a rather curious type which some historians have chosen to regard as an oboe, an identification which in the writer's opinion can only be accepted in its widest sense. This is generally called 'Basse de Musette' (Musetten-Bass, Basset Oboe), a name first bestowed by G. Chouquet in his 1875 catalogue of the Paris Conservatoire collection. Some sixteen examples are known today, as well as one or two facsimiles. All appear to be Swiss made, and from the date 1777 on one specimen we may assume that they derive from the last quarter of the 18th century.

In general appearance these basses de musette are similar to a large bass instrument illustrated in Borjon's *Traité de la Musette* (Lyon, 1672), save that their crooks are coiled in a large circle instead of a simple S-bend. The most notable characteristics are the surprising thinness of the tube walls and the extremely rapid taper of the bore, much more pronounced than that usual in any of the true oboes. The various recorded specimens show minor differences in construction and ornament, but all have one important feature in common—the seven note-holes are spaced more or less theoretically. By this arrangement only two holes, Nos. 2 and 5, can be directly stopped by the fingers, the others being covered by open-standing keys. The lowest key (hole No. 7) has a fish-tail touch.

Considerable experiment has been undertaken with some of these instruments, and when blown with a reed rather larger than that of the bassoon, W. Heckel pronounced their pitch to be B♭. Altenburgh,[16] however, considered that the pitch was C, on the basis that Church instruments (which many of these certainly were) were commonly built in 'Cammerton', one whole tone below the 'Chorton' of the contemporary organ. Their length of 127–132 cms. over all (just double the average oboe of the time with its reed

H

and staple) certainly supports the latter opinion. Altenburgh reports that the tone was relatively strong and full, in spite of the lightness and thinness of the wood.

From time to time efforts have been made to trace the maker of some of these instruments, and these have given rise to a curious misconception which has been often quoted. Certain examples bear on the lowest key the engraved initials I.IR., which Chouquet took to stand for J. J. Riedlocker, whom he claimed to be a Paris maker of the period. How Chouquet arrived at this conclusion is a mystery, and modern workers are extremely dubious about Riedlocker's existence.[17] Lyndesay Langwill's card index of wind-instrument makers of all countries and all ages reveals no such maker, and in any case his supposed initials would surely have been I.I.R., and not I.IR., as found on the instruments. Probably the letters stand for the name of some former owner, perhaps of wealth and position, who has not been identified. It is to be noted that the same initials appear on the keys of some bassoon-like instruments with spherical metal bells and pirouettes which are preserved at Berne, and which were almost certainly Church property. The variation that appears between individual specimens may well indicate the hands of several makers.

One last point remains in connection with the basse de musette, and it is a fundamental one. We have no written evidence as to how it was played, but two out of six specimens in the Berne Museum are preserved with pirouettes, and two examples in other collections have brass discs which probably once supported pirouettes fixed to the crook. It appears fairly certain, then, that they were sounded as were the shawms and should, in spite of their jointed construction, be regarded as an improved shawm type which survived in Switzerland for some fifty years after the parent family had passed out of general use.[18] They certainly cannot be classed with the true oboes any more than can Borjon's instrument of pre-1672.

THE 19TH CENTURY AND MODERN PERIOD

The larger oboes of the 19th century and later are most conveniently treated all together, for, after about 1800, the same influences affected all of them alike. Their development was parallel to that of the treble instrument, though not always so consistent or so complete.

The tenor oboe had attained its characteristic form with bulb-bell in the previous century, and it passed into the hands of the 19th-century workers as a most desirable but rather weakly relative of the oboe in C. Its length of tube called for fairly wide spacing of the holes, yet these had still to be kept within finger-reach. The result was usually rather poor intonation and, until Triébert's key mechanism had advanced sufficiently to solve this problem once and for all, little could be done to make the tenor fit for use in all keys at will. Attempts to bore the holes on a slant through the comparatively thin walls of the tube helped to some extent, but could hardly be carried far enough. From 1850, however, all difficulties with the placing of holes had virtually disappeared.

There remained at this time one thing which is rather surprising in view of the recognised initiative of the mid-century makers. It is the persistence in France, and especially in Italy, of the cor anglais with a curved body, although this must have involved tiresome and expensive techniques in building. One can only assume that once again the conservatism of players held up progress, for as early as 1839 Brod had produced a straight cor anglais of considerable merit, and had shown it at the Paris exhibition of that year. In Germany at this time the 'knee-shaped' cor anglais seems to have been much in favour, and such advanced makers as Uhlmann produced excellent models with all the refinements of their best oboes. From the middle of the 19th century onwards an ample number of specimens has come down to us, and these show clearly that by about 1850 the cor anglais had outgrown its former weakness and had become as efficient an instrument as any. It is obvious from comparison of many examples that makers at that time were again much preoccupied with the alleged tonal effect of the bulb-bell. The proportions adopted for it vary enormously, the actual orifice ranging from about 38 mm. diameter with F. Triébert to only 26 mm. in a fairly late cor anglais by A. Morton.

The foregoing remarks apply also in general to the oboe d'amore and to the bass oboe. Both of these, which had reached a fair degree of perfection by about 1760, seem after then to have suffered periodical eclipses. Koch,[19] who is incidentally our authority for the name *oboe luongo*, wrote in 1802 that the instrument was then very seldom used, and the Koch-Dommer 'Lexikon' of 1865 says that the oboe d'amore was difficult to play in tune and presumably fell into disuse for that reason. The most important revivals of the oboe d'amore took place in France at the hands of the maker Winnen about 1835 and again in 1889 under Lorée. A very successful d'amore with an open bell was also designed by Mahillon of Brussels in 1875, while about the same time the Mortons were making a bulbed instrument in London.

As regards the bass oboe the chief protagonist was again the firm of Triébert. Working to the order of Vogt about 1823 G. Triébert built an instrument which is now in the Paris Conservatoire collection (No. 335.) In shape this is not unlike the Bizey example described earlier save that it has a rather wide bulb-bell and eight keys instead of two. One key covers the lowest finger-hole which is fairly well placed, but the others are still too closely set and are bored on the oblique through thick projections of the wall. Somewhat similar instruments were made later by both Brod and F. Triébert though by their time key-work had removed the need for obliquely bored finger-holes. Curiously enough both these makers adhered to the principle of doubling back the bore inside a 'boot', and apparently it was left for Lorée in 1889 to re-design the instrument in the modern straight form. A very curious example of the doubled-back bass oboe with a *brass* bulb-bell, by Piatet and Benoit is in the John Parr collection at Sheffield.

At the present day both the oboe d'amore and the bass oboe can be regarded as tonally satisfactory. Both are constructed with all the facilities of modern key-work (except that the low $b^b$ key is usually omitted), and both are reliable in every way, though they are to be found as a rule only in the larger symphony orchestras. The bass oboe, moreover, is often replaced nowadays by the heckelphone, not always to the advantage of tonal balance.

### EXCEPTIONAL TYPES

To round off this chapter we must notice certain oboes, both large and small, which do not find a place in the normal orchestral group. To begin with, oboes in high D or $E^b$ are fairly well known, and they have been constructed in all the recognised key systems, including the Boehm. There is no doubt that many of these smaller varieties which have been produced at intervals during the last 150 years are no more than instrument-makers' improvements on the bucolic 'musette'. Some have even adhered to the musette fingering complete with a hole for the left thumb, and can only have been intended for rustic music. Others, however, are by definition true oboes. For instance, a small instrument illustrated in E. Marzo's Boehm System Tutor over the title 'Pastoral Oboe' shows every sign of being well designed and intended for serious music.

It is in continental military music that the high oboes have been chiefly employed and in the same surroundings we also occasionally find large instruments in B♭. Outside military circles B♭ oboes are rather rare and comparatively few old ones remain. One or two beautiful examples by F. Triébert are known, and as some of these are associated with non-military players, notably Barret during his London period, it is surmised that they were made for 19th-century performances of Bach's music. It is in Bach's scores that we find probably the most extensive orchestral use of the B♭ oboe, though its employment is recognised mainly by implication. While attached to the ducal court at Weimar (1708–17), Bach wrote numerous oboe parts requiring a compass beginning upon *b♭*, which, together with a tendency to flat key signatures, clearly indicates a B♭ instrument. Professor Terry, whose masterly analysis of Bach's scoring provides this information, goes so far as to postulate the existence also of a normal oboe in A to cover those cases where Bach demands that note in parts not specifically labelled 'oboe d'amore'. He seems, however, to have gone slightly astray in interpreting the entries in Mahillon's Brussels catalogue, which he cites in evidence, though we have other reasons to believe that such an instrument did at one time exist. Occasional descents to *g* in Bach's oboe parts are explained as errors due to the custom of treating the instrument, particularly the second desk, as a *ripieno* in unison with the violins. This is probably quite correct, and is supported by the appearance of corrections in some of Bach's scores, but in all matters of musical detection we must be very wary, especially as regards 18th-century compositions involving the organ. In Germany at that time organs were usually tuned to 'chorton' or 'cornett-ton', a whole tone or a minor third respectively above the 'hoher-cammerton' which—whatever its absolute value—was the customary pitch for concerted music. Unless we remember this we are liable to get very confused over the transpositions for other instruments.

In the modern orchestra the *B♮* of the baritone is accepted as the lower limit of true oboe tone, though from time to time a desire has been felt to carry it even lower. In the later years of the 18th century the celebrated Delusse devised a 'contrabass oboe' which now rests in the Paris collection and which, according to a musical almanac of 1784, was effectively used by the Opéra bassonist

Lemarchand for some six months. After this effort we hear no more of such an instrument for over a century. Then, writing in 1890, Constant Pierre presents the interesting information that Lorée, having introduced his new oboe d'amore and baritone the previous year, proposed to complete the family with a contrabass. This monster, had it ever been made, would have extended the range of the oboe down to $B,^\natural$ only a semitone above the normal bassoon. Pierre in his *La Facture Instrumentale* offers an interesting speculation as to its tone and future use. The project, however, seems to have been abandoned, possibly because there was insufficient demand among composers, who found that the long-established bassoon met all their needs in the 8-foot octave.

One other exceptional oboe requires mention here, and it is included, not because of its unusual range, but on account of its interesting theoretical construction. This is the instrument devised by Giorgi and Schaffner in 1881 and patented in France the next year. The inventors, proceeding somewhat on the lines adopted forty years earlier by Boehm, began by taking flute, oboe, and clarinet tubes of theoretical length. These they measured off for each note required according to the laws of physics, and at the divisions they placed a series of large rectangular holes of graduated size. Each hole was equipped with an appropriate cover and pad, and a complicated system of rods and bell-cranks brought them all under the control of the fingers. The fingering of all three instruments was intended to be identical, which might indeed have been of benefit, but the idea came into the field too late to compete with the other established systems. Whether the Giorgi–Schaffner flute had any advantages to offer over the Boehm instrument is difficult to judge, but as regards the oboe the system would seem to have been foredoomed. The admired 'closeness' of oboe tone depends very largely on the use of holes small in relation to the bore, and this is completely contrary to Schaffner's principle of virtually cutting off a theoretical length of tube for every note in the first octave of the scale. The objection is almost the same as that levelled at the earlier Boehm system oboes. A few Giorgi–Schaffner instruments are to be found in collections, but they remain nowadays merely as curiosities and monuments to a very considerable ingenuity.

[1] A possible claim to earlier employment by Bach has been disqualified by Sandford Terry on the grounds that the d'amore appears only in revisions of the works concerned made after 1722. *Bach's Orchestra*, O.U.P., London, 1932, p. 110.

[2] See Walther's description of a liebesoboe with an opening just large enough to admit a man's finger. *Musikalisches Lexikon*, Leipzig, 1732.

Globular bells are also occasionally found on certain Continental bassoon types, notably nine examples in the Berne Museum. See 'Basson d'amour', by L. G. Langwill, in *Grove's Dictionary of Music*, London, 5th edn.

[3] C. Sandford Terry, *op. cit.*, p. 107.

[4] *Galpin Society Journal*, Vol. I, London, 1948.

[5] E. Halfpenny in *Galpin Society Journal*, Vol. V, 1952, p. 18. I can find no justification for the idea that, once established, the tenor oboe for a time reverted to a more primitive form simply for lack of advanced orchestral parts to play.

[6] *Ibid.*, Vol. I, 1948, p. 24. Tenor oboe by Caleb Gedney in Boston Museum, England.

[7] Has this perhaps something to do with Walther's association with J. S. Bach in Weimar?

[8] C. Sandford Terry, *op. cit.*, pp. 99 and 103. Bach's practice in respect of any particular instrument must always be interpreted in the light of his current orchestral resources.

[9] André Danican (known as Philidor l'ainé), born *c.* 1647, died 1740, Court musician to Louis XIV. From 1684 he was musical librarian to the King, and compiled a large and famous collection of Court music, ranging from the time of Henri III to the end of the 17th century.

[10] French examples are known, but the type is almost exclusively English.

[11] A knee-shaped Tenor with bulb-bell by Milhouse of London (*c.* 1800) is exhibited at the Tower of London.

[12] Is this perhaps why certain bass recorders were provided with a pear-shaped foot joint instead of the (externally) flared ones seen on the higher instruments of a set? See, for example, the famous 'Chester' recorders by Peter Bressan (*c.* 1720), which are lavishly embellished with ivory.

[13] C. Sandford Terry, *op. cit.*, p. 103.

[14] I am indebted for this information to the late Mr. F. G. Rendall, who had it from the late Edward Buttar, a most reliable historian and amateur of the oboe.

[15] Bessaraboff, *Ancient European Musical Instruments*, Boston, Mass., 1949.

[16] W. Altenburgh. Article in *Zeitschrift fur Instrumentenbau* dealing with specimen No. 355 in the Paul de Wit collection, later No. 1352 in the Heyer collection, Leipzig.

[17] Lyndesay G. Langwill. Articles 'Basse de Musette' and 'Basson d'amour' in *Grove's Dictionary of Music*, London, 5th edn. The most diligent research into Paris directories etc. by R. Morley-Pegge has revealed no sign of a J. J. Riedlocker. A certain F. Riedlocker, born at Linz in 1753, is known to have made brass instruments in Paris from shortly before 1808 till 1832, but neither his working period nor his speciality tie up with the basse de musette.

[18] In Spain true shawms exist today in the Tenora and Tiple of northern Catalonia. See note 12, Chapter 3.

[19] Koch, *Musikalisches Lexikon*, Frankfurt (Offenbach), 1802.

# CHAPTER 8

# The Heckelphone

THE heckelphone is one of the most interesting of orchestral instruments and is probably unique in that, right from its introduction, it has been employed by influential composers without having to struggle for recognition or to compete with rival instruments. With a jointed tube, conical bore, and double reed entirely governed by the lip, the heckelphone is allied acoustically to the oboe, and indeed is often called an oboe, even by its makers. It is, however, better considered as an instrument *sui generis*, for the following reasons. The bore of the heckelphone is of proportions vastly different from those generally adhered to throughout the normal oboe group, and its origin and development were entirely independent. It was in fact designed from the beginning to meet a specific orchestral requirement, and it owes little or nothing to pre-existing types.

In 1877, on the death of J. A. Heckel, his well-known instrument-making business passed to his son, Wilhelm, who shortly afterwards concluded certain marked improvements to the German-style bassoon and contra-bassoon. The progress of these instruments roused much interest in German musical circles, and two years later, at the instance of Jahn, the Viennese Court conductor, Heckel, was summoned from his home at Biebrich-am-Rhein to Bayreuth. There he was presented to Wagner, who had many complimentary things to say about the new bassoons. Indeed, the great composer went so far as to say that he now regarded the bassoon as fully perfected, though he still felt a certain want among the woodwinds. This was a baritone voice among the double reeds which 'should combine the character of the oboe with the soft but powerful tone of the Alphorn'. Wagner's rather curious description fired the imagination of the young Heckel—he was only twenty-three at the time—and with the encouragement of other leading musicians he set himself to design such an instrument. This was of course nearly ten years before Lorée was ready to exhibit his perfected baritone oboe, and the existing versions of that instrument, representing merely a downward extension of the cor anglais with little power in the ensemble, did not commend themselves to Heckel. An altogether larger air column seemed to be necessary to produce the fullness and power he required. Nearly twenty-five years of calculation and experiment followed till, assisted latterly by his sons W. H. and August Heckel, he completed in 1904 the first model of the instrument which bears his name. In 1905 Richard Strauss introduced the heckelphone to the orchestral world with an important part in the score of his opera 'Salomé', and since then a number of other composers have used it extensively both on account of its own qualities and as a substitute for the baritone oboe.

The body of the heckelphone is turned from hard Austrian maple wood and is for convenience made in three sections. At the top is a short metal crook to carry the reed, and at the lower end an almost spherical bell. As built in modern 'flat pitch' the total sounding length is 138·5 cms. The main bore is truly conical and double the mean *diameter* of the German style oboe. The conicity is therefore more marked than that of the baritone oboe in the same pitch. Two varieties of bell have appeared at different times, the original with a plain open end and a large vent hole in the side, and a more modern one with three smaller vents and a perforated wooden stopper which is designed to mute the lower register a little. All through the instrument the note-holes are large in relation to the bore, and are controlled by key mechanisms which the makers build to correspond with the principal accepted systems of oboe fingering. As might be expected, so large an air column requires a fairly strong reed and one similar to that of the bassoon and nearly as large is usual. Some players, however, prefer an enlarged version of the cor anglais reed. When well controlled the tone of the heckelphone is rich and satisfying, with great body and considerable prominence in the orchestral ensemble.

At the present day there exists a group of three heckelphones of different sizes. The largest of these pitched in C stands exactly one octave below the oboe, but has an extended lower register. Its full compass is from *A* below four-foot *C* to *g''* with exceptionally three higher semitones. This is the accepted range of the instrument today, though a fingering chart issued by the makers indicates that when first brought out the compass was less. A choice of *B* or *B♭* as the lowest note was then offered. The Terz-Heckelphone, pitched in E♭, and the piccolo-heckelphone in high F complete the series. For these the written compass is *b* to *e'''*, sounding respectively a minor third and a fourth higher. It is customary to write for the heckelphone in the treble clef, placing it in full score between the cor anglais and the bassoons.

# CHAPTER 9

# *Acoustics*

IT is now getting on for a century since the first really scientific approach was made to the problems of acoustics as found in wind instruments. Certainly the general behaviour of musical pipes in its simpler aspects has been known and more or less understood for hundreds of years, but the first real insight into the structure of complex tones (which include practically every sound known to Music) came with the work of Helmholtz in the early 1860s. It was he who by beautifully conceived experiments proved the truth of Ohm's earlier statement that the ear senses, as pure tones, only simple harmonic vibrations in the air, and that the quality of a complex musical sound depends only on the order, number, and intensity of simple tones which are its components.[1]

Much early tonal investigation could only be qualitative, as, for instance, Helmholtz's classical analyses by means of selectively tuned resonators, and syntheses with tuning-forks. It was not till the advent of the telephone receiver and the phonograph in the '70s that the first quantitative work came in sight. At this stage the extreme complexity of the whole matter began to be evident, and it remained for Dayton Miller with his 'Phonodeik' and later workers with electrical methods[2] to begin to get things formulated. At the present time a great deal of research is going on, though the work is still far from complete. All the standard orchestral voices have been subjected to tonal analysis and their characteristics plotted. We can now compare them both qualitatively and quantitatively. What we still do not know is exactly how the tonal qualities of instruments are affected by certain traditional features of their construction. Conversely, we find that in trying to make wind instruments to a given tonal specification, an empirical method is still almost universal. In this respect the organ-builder is nowadays probably in advance of, say, the bassoon-maker, though his problem is simpler in that he only requires each pipe to sound one note.

It is evident that the field of orchestral acoustics is far too large even to be outlined in these pages, and we must confine ourselves to a few important general statements which will clear the way for a more specialised study of the oboe.

From the point of view of physics all wind instruments appear as highly complex vibratory systems and present very considerable problems. All have, however, certain easily recognised common features. First, there is always some form of *generator* or *exciter* which initiates and maintains the sound. In the oboe this is the reed, as already described. Next comes the *resonator*, commonly taken to be the tube or body of the instrument, though more properly it is the column of air contained within the body. Taken together, the generator and the resonator form a coupled dynamic system, and the vibrations of the two are associated in a very complex and intimate way. The resonator is, however, the dominant partner which determines and stabilises the pitch of the sound produced and, that this may be so, the mass of the air column is made large and its coupling with the generator fairly tight. If the coupling should momentarily fail, as sometimes happens if a mouthpiece fits its socket badly, the generator will take charge and emit its own unfettered note. Hence the appalling squeaks and quacks which sometimes embarrass even the best of reed players. An inadvertent slackening of the lip will also have the same result, which is one reason why beginners on reed instruments are almost as unpopular with their neighbours as novice violinists.

The third common factor among wind instruments is that all are provided with means of altering the length of the resonating air column, and so varying the note sounded. In the oboe this is done by making holes in the side of the tube which can be opened and closed by the fingers. The effect of opening a side-hole is nearly, but not exactly, equivalent to cutting off a portion of the body, and of course the note concerned is then propagated mainly from the hole rather than from the end of the tube. The exact behaviour of the air in the tube below an open side-hole was for a long time a puzzle, though its influence on tone and tuning was well understood by practical musicians from the earliest days. Today the question has been reduced to a matter of fairly simple mathematics.[3] More will be said about this later in connection with special fingering.

Finally, we must consider a common feature which comes into being only during the act of playing. Then the generator is coupled both to the resonator and to the air cavities of the head, throat, and chest, and the air in them is also set in vibration. This is clearly to be discerned with the aid of a stethoscope. It follows that during performance the oboe player and his instrument together form a coupled system of *three* elements, all of which he can in some degree control. He can vary the length of the resonator with his fingers; he can 'humour' the reed with his lips, pinching or relaxing it as required, and he can modify the shape and volume of his air cavities by the use of chest and especially throat muscles. Here, then, is the source of that flexible intonation so much valued by musicians, and here, too, some physical basis for the advice so often given by teachers 'Imagine yourself singing the note you are trying to play'. It has already been indicated that under the varying conditions of musical performance the vibrations of the generator, the resonator, and the air cavities are connected in a complicated manner. Research into these relations goes on today in a number of institutions, and from time to time the results of experiments are published in technical papers. Much of this material is, however, not readily accessible, nor is it at all easy for the layman to understand. For him, therefore, Richardson's book already cited in a footnote is recommended. Although this volume was issued as long ago as 1929, it remains most valuable for its almost non-technical account of the phenomena.

Let us now turn to some acoustical matters which affect the oboe family in particular. First, what are the factors which make its tone so characteristic, especially in the lower register? Advanced text-books quote both demonstrations and mathematical proofs that a conical tube closed at its vertex resonates to the entire series of harmonic overtones having frequencies twice, three times, four times etc. that of the fundamental—i.e. to the musical octave, twelfth, fifteenth, etc. The oboe, being in the main such a tube, we might expect to find all these overtones (which are also those of a cylindrical tube open at *both* ends) present in the notes of its basic scale. This is the reason for the common generalisation that 'the oboe behaves acoustically like an open organ pipe'. Unfortunately musical instruments rarely satisfy in full the simple first assumptions of the text-books. These take no account of the way in which the sound-waves have been generated; of the changes in magnitude, range, or pitch of overtones due to the coupling of generator and resonator; of altered resonances due to the need for side-holes and many other features which practical use imposes on an instrument. The orchestral oboe is in fact far from the ideal postulated by simple theory.

If we listen to a steady upward scale played throughout the compass of an oboe, it does not take a very sensitive ear to distinguish changes in quality between successive notes and a progressive thinning of tone, even though the total impression is one of general homogeneity. It is common experience that the more interesting tones to the ear—the bright and brilliant ones—are those of complex structure containing many powerful overtones. These are more prominent in loud than in soft sounds. The tonal structure of an instrument also generally gets less complex as we progress into the higher registers. Modern research confirms all these points in the case of the oboe.

It is customary nowadays to refer to the products of tonal analysis as 'tonal spectra' by analogy with the line spectra we obtain when examining light with a spectrograph. A very useful type of comparative diagram can be made from tonal spectra by plotting the intensity of each component found in a complex tone at its appropriate frequency along a base line. In these diagrams a uniform or linear scale of frequency is adopted, as this makes it easy to recognise whether the components (partials) are harmonic or not. It is, however, convenient to use a logarithmically divided scale of intensities, since the microphone used in modern methods of investigation measures the pressure of sound-waves falling upon it, and this convention allows weaker partials to be more readily displayed.[4] Such a diagram for three notes on the oboe is shown below and it reveals three remarkable facts about the instrument.

1. That there are no important overtones of a greater frequency than 7,000 cycles per second in any part of the compass.
2. The low and middle registers are rich in overtones up to about the sixteenth harmonic, but the upper is comparatively poor.
3. In the low register the first five overtones are nearly equal in strength to the fundamental. The fundamental becomes relatively more prominent in the harmonic array as we ascend.

In general the larger members of the oboe family show similar characteristics.

So far we have not made much progress towards a general answer to our question. Our information is, indeed, little more than Ohm or Helmholtz give us, supplemented by the slightly disquieting fact that there is inconsistency between adjacent notes on the oboe, at least as regards the intensity of partials. Each successive note does *not* reproduce exactly the same harmonic pattern with merely a shift of fundamental. It is evident that basic theory

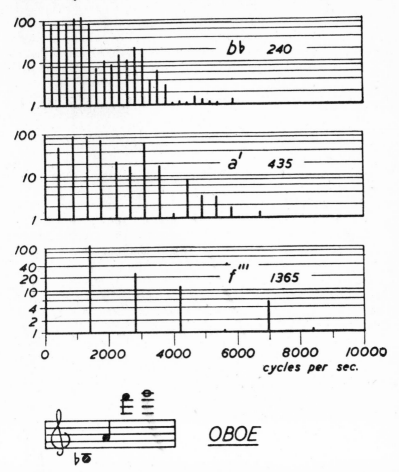

Fig. 14. Tonal spectrum of typical oboe. (By permission of Prof. Bernard Hague.)

cannot take us further, and we must enquire in some other direction.

I have already pointed out that, in spite of the audible differences between adjacent notes, a scale played on the oboe leaves the ear with an impression of homogeneity—a sense of 'oboeness', as it were, throughout the entire range. This may be purely subjective, and perhaps it is due to the listener becoming conditioned to accept any quality of sound within certain previously experienced limits as characteristic of the instrument. It seems, however, to go much deeper. We suspect, in fact, that there really is some common factor running through the entire compass of the oboe and that so far we have failed to identify it. The theory of *Formants* appears to supply the clue.

The idea of formants is a fairly recent and very advanced one, with far-reaching implications throughout the whole field of practical music. No more than a simplified outline can be included in such a book as this, but further references will be found in the bibliography.

As long ago as 1837, while investigating speech sounds, Sir Charles Wheatstone proposed a 'fixed-pitch' theory of vowels which later on was established by Helmholtz. Briefly, the Wheatstone–Helmholtz conception was that every vowel, no matter on what note it is uttered, is identified by certain vibration frequencies which are invariably present. Experiment has confirmed the theory to a very great extent, and, indeed, the sensitive methods of Dayton Miller have revealed the characteristic frequencies even in whispered vowels. For example, if I, a baritone, sing the vowel *ah* on every note in the range of my voice, measurements show that there is always present a dominant vibration of around 824 cycles a second. Now let somebody else, say a soprano, sing the same vowel on her complete range of notes. We shall find again the outstanding 824 cycles. This is because when we sing *ah* the lips, tongue, and soft palate take up a definite position and the mouth becomes a resonating chamber which responds chiefly to 824. Conversely, every time we adjust our mouths to that particular shape and sing a vowel it will come out as *ah*. For the sake of simplicity I have referred to the mouth only, but it has been proved that the other cavities, the sinuses, also play a considerable part.[5] It should be noted, too, that some vowels show more than one outstanding permanent frequency. We can conveniently describe this situation by saying that the air-cavities of the head possess qualities of *selective resonance*. The distinctive frequencies found in all vowels were named in 1897 by the physicist Hermann-Goldap, who invented for them the word *Formant*.

Now, considering again the body of a wind instrument, we know that such a tube, whatever its material, cannot be absolutely rigid and unyielding. In fact the stiffer we try to make it the more likely it is to develop mechanical resonances of its own. In many instruments quite a lot of the energy put into the generator is used up in making the walls of the body vibrate at their own natural frequencies and these vibrations may be passed on to the air column inside. Moreover, a tube with fairly thick walls pierced by side-holes will behave as an 'acoustic filter' reinforcing some frequencies and perhaps completely suppressing others. Thus the body of an instrument has properties of selective resonance not unlike those of the vocal cavities. Bearing this in mind, it is not unreasonable to expect some analogy between the behaviour of a wind instrument and that of the human voice machine. Assuming this analogy, Hermann-Goldap analysed the tones of a number of orchestral instruments and satisfied himself that each showed a characteristic array of frequencies present throughout the compass. He therefore announced that orchestral instruments, like the voice, possessed *formants*, and in them he claimed to have identified the source of instrumental *timbre*.

To the acousticians of his time Hermann-Goldap's theory was revolutionary, and it has been slow of acceptance in spite of the early corroboration of Dayton Miller and that of Stumpf in 1926. Today the theory is gaining ground, though a few authorities are still sceptical. We shall be wise, I think, to recognise that it still requires further extension, and in fact some of the originator's own observations show this clearly. For example, two instruments of very different character which he investigated, an oboe and a clarinet, both showed the same formant range, but in the oboe it proved to be more powerful than the fundamental tone, while in the clarinet the fundamental was predominant. The conclusion is that the mere presence of a formant is not the *sole* determinant of timbre.

Beyond its application to single instruments the idea of formants can be extended to an infinite degree and opens up vast fields for speculation. Just as simple tones will 'beat' together to produce a 'difference tone', so, we may conceive, will the components of a formant range. Perhaps we may find that the formants of two different instruments playing together will unite to give a new formant characteristic of the combination. Consider, too, that instruments playing in unison with each other may yet perhaps have formants whose components are dissonant. Multiply these simple cases by the number of individual instruments which now appear

I

together in the symphony orchestra, and the complexity of the
resultant sound almost baffles the imagination. Yet it is probably
in this very complexity—in what Bonavia-Hunt has called 'the
clash of myriads of formants'—that we find the brilliance of the full
orchestra or the grandeur of the organ chorus; brilliance and
grandeur that no single instrument possesses.[6]

## THE INFLUENCE OF THE BELL

The acoustical experiments so far mentioned have in the main,
and for obvious reasons, been carried out with modern oboes. In
this book, however, we are equally concerned with the older types,
and since some of them show features now abandoned, we must
consider, as far as we can, the effect of these. Let us take first the
bell. In modern instruments this is often a not very impressive
feature, and indeed it is on occasion omitted altogether. Bell-less
oboes are, nevertheless, not common and their tone is not typical.
It has usually a 'snarling' quality which most players dislike. In
most well-made modern instruments[7] the bell takes the form of a
gently curved expansion, taking up the last sixth of the bore and
increasing in diameter from about 17 mm. to 38 mm. at the open
end. Recently some makers have shown a tendency, possibly for
manufacturing reasons, to replace the curved section with a perfectly straight-sided cone, while yet others combine a series of
cones to form an approximate curve. The difference between these
is negligible in playing.

The actual function of the bell in woodwind instruments still
requires adequate investigation, but theory suggests that a small
and simple one, as on the modern oboe, will have little effect beyond reducing to some extent the power of the higher partial tones.
The influence of the bell will also presumably become less as more
holes above it are opened.

The bell of the early oboe is obviously quite a different matter.
Here we have a comparatively large structure with rather thin walls
and a complicated internal form which does not develop smoothly
out of the main bore of the instrument.

If we compare the inner shape of average bells, old and modern,
we notice at once that the narrowest diameter of the former is considerably greater than the widest part of the main bore. The two
meet in fact in an abrupt 'step'. It is therefore probably better to
regard the older type of bell, not as an extension of the main tube,
but as a sort of supplementary resonance chamber whose charac-

teristic responses will colour the tone of the instrument. Some of
these responses will, no doubt, fall within the formant range, and
so influence all notes, while others will affect individual notes in
particular. Before we can speak positively on this matter we shall
require a large number of tonal spectra for old instruments, and so

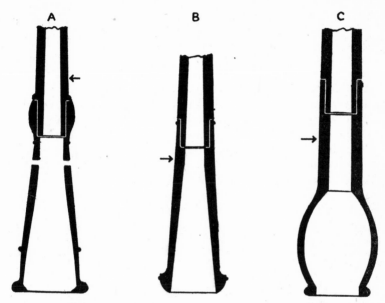

Fig. 15. Three characteristic oboe bells in section

A. Late 18th-century type with 'tuning holes'
B. Modern French type
C. Cor anglais; Triébert model *c.* 1880
   The arrows indicate the position of the lowest note-hole in
   each case

far these are not available. We can, however, make some attempt
to assess bell characteristics in the light of general knowledge. The
upper part of the old bell is conical, and so may be expected somewhat to reduce the higher partial tones. In the middle there often
comes an almost cylindrical section. This is small in relation to the
whole length of the instrument, but it may still serve to em-
phasise the odd-numbered harmonics a little. The lowest section
is again a conical or curved flare ending in a heavy rim. In the

great majority of examples this rim is slightly in-curved, and so reduces the mouth diameter of the bell by about 4 mm. This very distinctive feature has aroused the interest of many scholars, most of whom, in the past, have assumed that it was designed to mitigate the harshness of the lower notes. In fact this supposed harshness is open to doubt, and recent research has done much to disprove it.[8] The modern idea is that the heavy rim was intended merely to strengthen a rather vulnerable part of the instrument, though why it should require an internal ridge remains unexplained. It has been suggested that the undercutting of the rim may have been intended to relieve stresses in the wood as it matured and to prevent incipient splits from 'running'. Certainly the favourite woods of the 18th-century instrument-maker, box and pear, are notably liable to warping. Even after two hundred years specimens twist and bend under changing atmospheric conditions, as almost every collector has discovered. The peculiar thing is, however, that the inner ridge to the bell persisted long after these variable materials had been superseded by more permanent hardwoods and, in any case, strengthening rings of ivory or metal were in use from very early times. Why also is the inner ridge peculiar to the oboe alone? Whatever its initial purpose may have been, it can be shown experimentally that it contributes to the tone nothing that can be detected by the unaided ear.

A last remarkable feature of the older type of bell joint is its elongation, which gave the assembled instrument considerable more length than was required to make the lowest nominal note. The effective length was, however, adjusted by the presence of two permanently open holes placed about 7 cm. below the $c^\sharp$ hole and the 'great key'. This construction is evidently a link between the three-jointed and the one-piece reed instruments—the shawms— and it is interesting to find it so fully retained, since in nearly all other respects even the earliest true oboes were much in advance. In the shawms the body was often as much as one-third longer than the chosen scale required and the extra length beyond the lowest note-hole was vented by two, four, or even six so-called 'tuning holes'. The full function of these holes has not always been clearly understood, and even reliable writers have sometimes been unintentionally misleading. Writing of the 18th-century oboe one recent worker has said, 'No note is sounded from the part of the bell below the $C$ holes'. Such expressions are unfortunate, as they seem to imply that the active part of the air-column stops short at these holes. Certainly their position (and size) determines the pitch of the fundamental note sounded, but the remaining part of the column has a definite effect on its timbre. Were it not for the great expansion of the bell we should expect pitch effects also. We have here in fact a special case of 'open pipe, one hole uncovered' where the impedance of the part below the hole approaches zero.[9]

Pressure waves travelling down the tube from the reed, when they reach an open side-hole find alternative paths offered, and some at least of the frequencies which make up the complex tone are undoubtedly propagated from the open end. This is clearly shown when we plug the bell of an 18th-century oboe as far as the 'tuning holes'. The lowest note then remains the same as regards pitch but its quality is much altered. (See also 'Muting' in the Chapter 'Technique'.)

The lower members of the oboe family are nowadays regularly furnished with a different sort of bell which has in general been in vestigated even less than the normal soprano type. This is the so-called 'd'amore' bell—in German *liebesfuss*—pear-shaped outside, spheroidal within, and with a constricted opening. Though often regarded as a product of the early 1700s, the bulb-bell has in fact been associated with double-reed instruments at least since the 13th century, thereby antedating the true oboes by some five hundred years. The earliest information we have about it is provided by two beautiful illustrations in the 'Cantigas de Santa Maria'—a most important manuscript prepared for Alphonso the Wise of Spain (1221–84) and now preserved in the Escorial. Despite its ancient origin, the bulb-bell seems to have had a curiously disjointed life. For long periods at a time it disappeared altogether, only to be re-introduced—perhaps even re-invented— later on by some thoughtful specialist. Concerning its reappearance on the tenor oboe in the 18th century I have already offered some speculations in a previous chapter.

During the period of the true oboes the bulb-bell has shown a curious inconsistency both of form and dimension, even in the hands of makers working at the same time; and instruments of identical pitch with both bulb and plain bells are known to have existed side by side. It is also occasionally found associated with the larger clarinets up to about 1850. All this suggests some degree of uncertainty as to the true worth of the d'amore bell, and there is no doubt that at various times it has been credited with more virtues than it really possesses. Older writers have often tended to regard it as something of a mystery and to talk rather extravagantly of the 'melancholy' quality it imparts. Probably the chief explanation of the difference in tone-colour between larger and smaller oboes is found in the 'scaling' of their tubes—a relationship between mean diameter and length well understood by the organ-pipe maker. It is to be noted, however, that many excellent oboe makers declare that in the cases of the oboe d'amore and the cor anglais, if the instrument is reasonably well designed in the first place, all necessary fine tuning can be done by adjusting the inner curves of the bell alone. We note also that in the late 18th and early 19th centuries the neck of the bulb was frequently made very long and compensated by 'tuning-holes'.

Quite recently an investigation of the bulb-bell has been started by Professor Bernard Hague of the University of Glasgow, and I am privileged to quote here some of his results. Dr. Hague, besides being an excellent oboist, is a skilled mechanic who has actually made instruments for his own use, and his findings, which embody the viewpoints of both musician and physicist, are therefore particularly valuable. Working with an oboe d'amore to which he has fitted alternative plain and bulb bells, he concludes that the latter has little effect that the unaided ear can detect beyond the first few notes of the lowest register. A typical cor anglais bell examined by Dr. Hague showed as its chief characteristic a pronounced cavity resonance in the region of 680 cycles per second. We may assume therefore that this bell would affect the tone colour of its associated instrument by reinforcing the 680-cycle frequency and its multiples wherever they occur. This fact connects rather remarkably with some purely qualitative observations of my own. A number of inexperienced listeners at different times had a cor anglais solo played to them and were asked to describe the sound. The usual adjectives, 'nasal', 'melancholy', etc., were forthcoming, but the interesting point was that several descriptions confirmed the impression that I myself formed many years ago when first I heard the cor anglais, namely that in the lowest octave it sings 'aw'. Now in his investigation of the vowels Dayton Miller found 730 cycles to be characteristic of the sound 'aw'. Fletcher, pursuing the matter rather further, concluded that each vowel shows two ranges of characteristic frequencies, a higher and a lower, and from his published table[10] it appears that the nearest frequency in a recognised speech sound to 680 cycles is the lower one (704) typical of the shortened ŏ as in the word 'hot'. My observations cannot be regarded as scientific, since conditions were not in any way controlled, but they are still interesting as suggesting the presence of the same formant in a natural voice sound as in that of an artificial musical instrument.

To sum up, we may say that the type of bell associated with the earliest oboes of which specimens survive was a good deal more specialised than that of even the contemporary shawms. It behaved chiefly as a selective resonator and influenced notes throughout the entire range of the instrument in varying degree. The acoustic properties were due to various details of construction which makers clearly recognised as desirable though they employed them in the light of empirical knowledge only. This type of bell survived until nearly the middle of the 19th century, after which, as the entire oboe underwent general refinement, it became simplified and reduced till it assumed its present form. The pear-shaped d'amore bell, though somewhat variable in its relative dimensions, shows comparatively little change from the earliest form in which we know it. It too has properties of selective resonance, but its influence on tone, except in a limited part of the scale, appears to be less than commonly supposed.

## THE OCTAVE OR 'SPEAKER' KEY

In all modern oboes the octave key is so important that, in addition to the historical and descriptive references in foregoing chapters we must also examine briefly its acoustical functions and its defects. The simplest way to do this will be to consider first certain general points about the behaviour of air columns of the appropriate shape.

We know that when the oboe player breathes into his reed, the chink between the blades opens and closes extremely rapidly, and thus transmits tiny bursts of energy to the air inside the instrument. If at the instant that one of these impulses is generated the chink is closed we can regard the tapering body of the oboe as a cone closed at its vertex. When energised, the air column in such a pipe will vibrate with maximum motion, but no change of pressure at the open end, while at the closed end there will be minimum motion but violent alternations of pressure. This is the simplest mode of vibration in a closed conical air column and explanations and demonstrations can be found in most elementary text-books.[11] By a loose analogy with the behaviour of vibrating strings the points of greatest motion in air columns are termed *antinodes* or *loops*, and those of no motion *nodes*. Modern methods of investigating the conditions inside the tubes of sounding wind instruments and organ pipes have been described by W. Steinhaus in 1915, and by R. W. Young and D. H. Loughridge in 1936.[12]

Now the air column in any tube can in suitable circumstances be made to break up into parts which, because of their lesser length, will vibrate faster than the whole column, and so we shall hear an *harmonic* of the fundamental note. (The fact that in nearly all wind instruments fundamental and segmental vibration go on at the same time without any special effort on the part of the player and give rise to the overtones mentioned earlier can here be disregarded.) The vibration speeds of these parts are related to that of the whole column in inverse ratio to their respective lengths. This fact enabled the early oboists to sound the second register of their simple instrument. They worked with their lips on one member of their coupled system, the reed, till they established a condition where the air column divided itself in two, and so sounded the octave. The process is not unduly difficult, and the degree of lip adjustment needed soon becomes a matter of instinct. There is, however, one very tiresome thing about reeds—they are very inconsistent, varying remarkably from one to the other, and even changing their characteristics during use. Even the best player on an 18th-century oboe could never be confident that his 'overblowing' would come off every time, and something to reduce the uncertainty was much needed.

The desired improvement, the 'speaker' key, seems to have arrived early in the 19th century—perhaps a little earlier—though exactly when and by whom it was added we do not know. It was an extremely simple affair: just a plain key convenient to the left thumb and covering a very small hole towards the top of the instrument. Though it was a complete innovation in regard to the oboe, the idea was probably not entirely new, for something of the sort was certainly involved in Denner's experiments of *c.* 1700, which are generally regarded as having led to the primitive clarinet.

To understand how the speaker works, let us turn again to our closed conical air column. When sounding its fundamental note this vibrates as a whole with a node at the vertex and an antinode at the open end. (Fig. 16A.) To sound the octave the column divides in two and a new antinode appears at the middle. If we open a tiny vent at this point the pressure there cannot rise above or fall below that of the surrounding air, and so a node, which is a point of maximum pressure variation, cannot form. Conversely, an anti-node is encouraged to form, and thus the process of overblowing becomes much more positive. (Fig. 16B.)

Although the octave key was the greatest boon to oboe players, it still has one great defect. Looking again at B in the diagram, we see clearly that we cannot have two antinodes next to one another with-

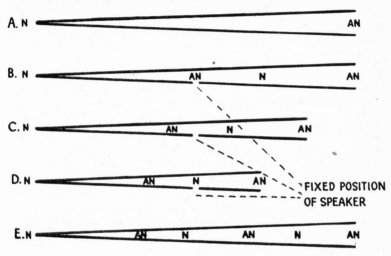

Fig. 16. Vibration of closed conical air column

A. Sounding its fundamental
B. Sounding the octave (vent open)
C. As B, the tube shortened. A node approaches the vent
D. As B, the tube further shortened. A node has reached the vent and the system ceases to function
E. Sounding the 3rd harmonic (the musical 12th)

out an intervening node. The combined length of the segments equals that of the whole column, and the individual length of each bears a fixed mathematical ratio to that whole. Now, opening successive holes as we do in running up a scale on any wind instrument is roughly equivalent to shortening the tube in stages. Although the tube, and so the air column, becomes shorter, the ratio of its length to those of the segments must remain the same, and so the nodes and antinodes get progressively closer together. From this it is evident that for every step by which we shorten the tube there must be a fresh position where theoretically the speaker vent should be. If we cannot move the speaker, we shall finally arrive at a state of affairs where a node is required exactly where the presence of the vent forbids it. We are then worse off than with no vent at all.

Fortunately, in practice, circumstances are not quite so rigid, and it has been found that until the limit condition (Fig. 16D) has almost been reached a well-designed speaker will function even when quite considerably removed from its theoretical position. This has enabled instrument makers to work out certain compromise placings in which a single speaker can be used to 'octave' several notes. Some time after the middle of the 19th century the situation was further improved by the provision of two speakers, each placed at an average position designed to assist a group of notes, and in modern times a third has been added. This is of particular value with the long tubes of the cor anglais and baritone oboe. We should note also that, when operated, the 'half-hole' mechanism on modern oboes provides what is really a further speaker in a situation which is at other times occupied by a normal note-hole.

None of the vents is, however, quite theoretically placed, and the positions on the tube used by different manufacturers seem to have been selected by trial-and-error methods and to vary considerably. For this reason casual comparison of different oboes gives little useful information, and may indeed be very deceptive. The positioning of vent-holes is another aspect of instrumental acoustics which deserves more truly scientific investigation than it has yet had, though the necessary experiments would probably be difficult to plan in view of the many factors involved, some of which are by no means obvious at first sight. For instance, it is now known that in a conical tube sounding an harmonic the nodes do not occur symmetrically between the antinodes, but tend to be shifted towards the apex, and this is only one of many such points which have to be allowed for in making calculations.

Finally we should put on record that, in spite of the practical efficiency of modern instruments with two or three speakers and the half-hole mechanism certain experimenters have never quite abandoned the idealist's dream of an individual speaker corresponding to every note of the fundamental scale. Alfred Morton is reputed to have devoted much time to making such an oboe, but to have given it up in the end as mechanically impracticable.

### THE SIZE AND POSITION OF NOTE-HOLES

In any wind instrument whose notes depend on the opening of side-holes, the size and position of these are plainly matters of the greatest importance. That these two factors are related was clearly understood by woodwind makers from very early times, and they used this knowledge extensively, though in a purely empirical manner. They knew that, within limits, a small hole drilled higher up on an instrument will sound the same note as a larger one placed lower down, and this fact enabled them to keep the holes (on small instruments at least) tolerably in tune and still within the reach of the fingers. On large instruments, unfortunately, the latitude available was often insufficient, and then intonation was bound to suffer, since the holes had of necessity to be kept within the stretch of the normal hand.

During the last thirty-five years a great deal of research has been done in this connection, with the result that today we possess formulæ which relate all the different factors that govern the note sounded by any given hole—i.e. the diameter of the hole; its position on the body of the instrument; the length, diameter, and wall thickness of the main tube; and whether or not other holes are open at the same time.[13] To follow out these formulæ in any detail would, however, involve us in a much deeper dive into mathematics than is desirable in a small book. A few general statements must therefore serve.

First, we can express our formulæ in the shape of equations which we can solve by graphs for all sorts of different conditions. It is therefore no longer beyond the bounds of possibility to design a wind instrument from first principles to a given specification as far as compass and tuning go, though the scientific control of tone quality still eludes us, as I have already said when discussing formants. Whether instrument makers will find any great advantage in mathematical methods is, however, another matter, for their rule-of-thumb procedure, guided by the experience of centuries, has by now become almost a fine art and seems to serve all practical needs very adequately. Moreover, in the modern oboe with a compass of almost three octaves there are serious additional complications. Certain holes, besides sounding simple notes in the first and second registers, serve also as vents to aid the production of higher harmonics, and so call for some compromise. Secondly, most modern work has been based on a conception introduced by the late Professor Webster in 1919—that of 'acoustic impedance'. We can perhaps most usefully think of impedance as a sort of reluctance to permit the free oscillation to and fro of the air particles, and it is a property which all tubes and holes have in some degree. The word has been borrowed from the behaviour of electrical conductors carrying alternating currents, and indeed our knowledge of electricity has provided many analogies which have been of service to modern acoustics. Many years ago Lord Rayleigh defined what he called the 'conductivity' of a side-hole as the ratio of its area to its depth, but added that in measuring the depth a little more—actually nearly one-third of the diameter—must be allowed because the interference with air-motion extends a little beyond the limits of the hole. Rayleigh's definition can be simply written down as

$$c = \frac{\text{area}}{\text{depth} + \frac{1}{3}\text{ diameter}}$$

The same thing occurs at the open end of pipes, and in dealing with them we make a similar allowance, which we call 'end correction'. After all, a side-hole is only a rather special sort of pipe, very short but very wide in proportion. Now the impedance of a hole is not the exact converse of its conductivity; there are other things involved, in particular the inertia of the air, and all these make our formulæ extremely complicated. We shall therefore skip a number of stages and accept that in the end we can define the impedance, denoted by $I$, as $\frac{fda}{c}$, where $d$ = the density of the air, $a$ = the velocity of sound, $f$ = the frequency, and $c$ = conductivity as defined by Rayleigh. For practical purposes it is often useful to think of the converse of impedance for which we use the rather obvious name 'admittance', denoted by $A$. Therefore $I = \frac{fda}{c}$ or $A = \frac{c}{fda}$, which here we may call the 'admittance equation'.

Let us now think of an open pipe with a hole bored in the side. Call the conductivity of the hole $c$. The air 'admitted' to the surrounding atmosphere from inside the pipe comes partly from the section above the hole and partly from that below it, so we can say that the admittance of the hole equals the sum of the admittances of the two sections. We apply our admittance equation and, since we know the value of $c$ from measurements and can assume $d$ and $a$ to be constants for all practical purposes, we can calculate $k$. This gives us the pitch of the note sounded. Conversely, if we know the pitch of the note we want, our equation will tell us how big to make the necessary hole and where to put it. Our third point to consider is that we can extend the above principle as far as we wish. If we regard the tube of our instrument as being made up of a series of sections each cut off by a note-hole at either end,[14] we can apply the admittance equation as often as necessary, and so determine the note sounded by a hole when other holes below it are also open. We can go still further, and evolve a theory of fingering for our instrument which will cover not only the progressive opening of holes, as in running up as scale, but will also explain quantitatively the effect of opening intermediate holes. This is of importance as, even with modern keywork, wind players still use 'fork fingerings' a great deal.[15] In the days of primitive keywork many necessary semitones could be obtained only by sounding the next note above and by some means flattening it. Two ways were open to the player: he could either partly close the hole in question, or he could leave it fully open and completely stop one or two immediately below. On the oboe, with its very small holes, the former was very difficult to do with the needed accuracy, and was in fact confined to half closing the bottom or 'great' key in an effort to make a $d\flat$ as the second lowest note on the instrument. The latter was more useful, though the note obtained usually required some work with the lips on the reed to pull it into tune. On modern instruments special provision is often made, so that notes which are frequently forked as a matter of convenience in playing are as well in tune as any others. The principle behind both methods of flattening a note is simply that of reducing the admittance of the hole sounding it, and this will be easily understood if we look again at the formula. In the first case partial stopping reduces the area, and so the conductivity of the hole, and, in turn the quantity $c$. In the second, closing the lower holes increases the effective length of the section of pipe below the operative hole, or in other words makes *that* deeper. This also, according to Rayleigh's definition, will reduce the quantity $c$. The reader who may wish to follow up in detail the calculations outlined in the foregoing paragraphs is referred once again to Richardson's excellent book, in the appendix to which he will find a number of typical cases fully worked out with graphical solutions.

Before ending this sketch, however inadequate, of the mathematics of instrumental tubes it will be well to notice just two more things. The writers of some text-books have likened the motion of the mass of air contained in a note-hole to that of a piston in a cylinder. The illustration is, however, only partly valid, for it is now known that such an air-body does not oscillate as a whole, but is much more active near the walls of the hole than in the centre. In this matter again our knowledge of electricity furnishes an analogy, for the behaviour of the air particles is almost exactly like that of alternating currents which tend to crowd into the outer layers of large conductors. This is called the 'annular' or 'skin' effect, and in both the electrical and the acoustic sense, it tends to increase the resistance. Unfortunately, we are at present unable to measure the extent to which this occurs in the acoustic case, but we do know that the effect increases with the speed of vibration. Now, we know also that the sounds of most woodwinds are highly complex and are made up of a number of frequencies. Is it not possible, then, that the annular effect may influence different components of a note to different degrees, and so give to the note-hole a filtering property? Here perhaps is the explanation of the difference in quality of the same note when sounded from a larger or a smaller hole suitably placed. On the oboe the holes are traditionally small in relation to the bore, and players have always attributed the particular tone quality they admire to this fact. Possibly also the unpopular tone of the bell-less oboes is due to the fact that they have usually been designed on the lines laid down by Boehm for his improved flute, and have, in consequence, exceptionally large holes.

Finally, I have mentioned before in connection with bells the abrupt 'step' which often occurs in the bore of old oboes (and in modern Austrian ones) at the lowest joint. The student of antique instruments will have noticed that the same thing is to be found in some 18th- and early 19th-century examples at the middle joint as well. As far as I am aware, the acoustic result of this has not yet been investigated fully, but the feature occurs so frequently that we must suppose that the older oboe makers introduced it deliberately. Since (as Webster worked out) resonating pipes themselves have the property of impedance, no doubt the application of a suitable form of the impedance formula would tell us what effect the abrupt expansion has.[16] We do know that, in the case of a cylindrical pipe, a widening of the bore near an antinode of the note it is sounding will raise the pitch of that note, and, conversely, will lower it if near to a node. It seems likely, therefore, that the 'step' was connected with the system of tuning used by early makers.[17] We must consider also that an irregularity in the bore which is near an antinode when the fundamental is sounding may be approached by a node when the air-column breaks up to give a harmonic. Thus it is possible for harmonics to be out of tune with their prime tones, a state of affairs not uncommon in old oboes. Here is another defect which the early player had to rectify as best he could with his lip or by variations of fingering. The matter was not, however, left entirely to the player; instrument makers were well aware of the difficulty, and they did much to adjust the relative intonation of the fundamental and over-blown registers by under-cutting or coning out the holes where they met the bore. The process is still employed, for, though oboe making has today reached a high degree of accuracy, the registers still have to be adjusted to each other, and fine tuning is invariably necessary.

[1] In 1701 Sauveur of Paris had demonstrated that the peculiarities of *string* tone could be attributed to vibrations both complete and segmental occurring simultaneously in the same string.

[2] Wegel and Moore, 'An Electrical Frequency Analyser', *Trans. Amer. Inst. of Electrical Engineers*, Vol. 42 (1924), pp. 457–65.
E. Meyer and G. Buchmann, 'Die Klangspectren der Musik Instrumente', *Sitzungsberichte der Preuss. Akad. der Wissenschaft*, 1931, pp. 735–778.

[3] E. G. Richardson, *Acoustics of Orchestral Instruments*, London, E. Arnold and Co., 1929, pp. 145 *et seq*.

[4] Bernard Hague, 'The Tonal Spectra of Wind Instruments', *Proc. Roy. Mus. Ass. London*, Session 1946–47, p. 72. The article includes also a valuable specialised bibliography of the subject.

[5] G. Mackworth-Young, *What Happens in Singing*, London, Newman Neame, 1953, pp. 20, 25, and 98–9.

[6] N. A. Bonavia-Hunt, 'What is the Formant?' *Musical Opinion and the Organ World*, Dec. 1948, p. 151, and Jan. 1949, p. 209.

[7] We must except certain oboes made under Austrian influences which by design retain 18th-century features. These, however, are so rarely seen, except in Austria, that they can be disregarded in any generalisation.

[8] Josef Marx, 'The Tone of the Baroque Oboe', *Galpin Society Journal*, No. 4, London, 1951, pp. 3 *et seq*.

[9] E. G. Richardson, *op. cit.*, Appendix, p. 148.

[10] H. Fletcher, *Human Speech*, Keegan Paul, London, 1930.

[11] E. G. Richardson, *op. cit.*, pp. 22–3; also Alexander Wood, *The Physics of Music*, Methuen, London, 1944, pp. 110–12.

[12] W. Steinhaus, 'Untersuchung stehender Luftschwingungen (insbesondere in Flöte und Orgelpfeife)', *Annalen der Physik*, Vol. 48, p. 695 (1915).
R. W. Young and D. H. Loughridge, 'Standing Sound Waves in the Boehm Flute measured by the Hot Wire Probe', *Journal of the Acoustical Society of America*, Vol. 7, No. 3 (1936), p. 178.

[13] E. G. Richardson, *op. cit.*, Appendix, p. 129.
E. J. Irons, 'On the Fingering of Conical Wind Instruments', *Phil. Mag.*, Vol. 11 (1931), pp. 535 *et seq*.

[14] V. C. Mahillon, *Elements d'acoustique musicale et instrumentale* (1874). Also vide Irons and Richardson.

[15] As long ago as 1775 Lambert published a theory of fingering for the conical flute in the Memoirs of the Academy of Berlin; again vide Irons.

[16] Readers familiar with the more advanced aspects of alternating current electricity will find an excellent analogy in the matching or otherwise of wave guides.

This year F. C. Karal has published an investigation of the effects of abrupt changes in the cross section of circular tubes. He sums up as follows: 'The constriction inductance can . . . be interpreted physically as an increase in the equivalent length of the tube.' The converse appears to hold good also. Since, as Richardson has pointed out, the formulae pertaining to cylindrical tubes, such as the flute, apply with but little modification to gently tapering tubes, we may expect similar effects from abrupt changes in the cross-section of the oboe. We shall probably not be far wrong if we say that the general effect of the 'steps' in some antique instruments was equivalent to some over-all shortening of the tube quite apart from any selective 'filtering' effect on certain partial tones. This may to some extent account for the surprising length of some antique instruments in relation to their actual pitch.

F. C. Karal, 'The Analogous Acoustical Impedance for Discontinuities and Constrictions of Circular Cross Section', *Journal of the Acoustical Society of America*, Vol. 25, No. 2 (1953), p. 327 *et seq.*

[17] Hugh W. Loney, American patent 2,602,364, April 10th, 1950. In his specification the claimant writes: 'The different registers produced by the register key in woodwinds have different intonations, owing to the change in the effective diameter-to-length ratio.' He quotes specifically the case of the clarinet and finds that an alternating smooth expansion and contraction of the bore, the proportions of which he has plotted, greatly improves the intonation.

# CHAPTER 10

# Materials and Manufacture

THE various materials which have been used for the body of the oboe make an interesting study, and one which has at times given rise to a deal of controversy. While nowadays African Blackwood, called also Grenadilla and 'Ebène de Mozambique', is almost universally employed, there remain some older players who affirm that the tone of a rosewood oboe is the sweetest, and a few ultra-conservatives still give the palm to the now rarely obtainable Box. African Blackwood—*Dalbergia melanoxylon*—was, according to Holtzapffel,[1] first imported into Europe over a century ago as 'Black Botany Bay Wood', though whether it really came from that part of the world seems uncertain. Today its sources are Tanganyika, Uganda, and Portuguese East Africa. It is nearly the hardest and most dense of all timbers and, owing to its irregular growth, one of the most wasteful in use. In favourable conditions it turns and bores very well indeed, and takes a high polish from the tools, which is, of course, of great advantage in making such finely adjusted works as the tube of a modern oboe. Blackwood has occasionally been confused with ebony (at one time used a good deal in flute making), but the properties of the two woods are by no means alike. Furthermore, not all specimens of African Blackwood show quite the same characteristics, and the examination of a large number of instruments suggests that several botanical varieties may be included in the general trade name. *Dalbergia latifolia*, for instance, is definitely known to have been used, though experts usually regard it as inferior. Of *D. melanoxylon* some examples are so compact as to show no sign of any grain on the finished surface, while others appear to be finely porous and, curiously enough, many of the best clarinets seem to be those made of this more 'grainy' wood. Some pieces on cutting yield a soft brown sawdust, while the waste of others is greyish and gritty in texture. On cutting into the rough logs, blackwood often displays purplish-black streaks, which by degrees turn deepest black. There appears to be no objection to this uneven colouring, and indeed some of the finest wood shows it, but players do not seem to

K         129

like it, and modern makers who cannot wait for them to darken naturally often anoint the finished joints of their instruments with printer's ink.

Box—*Buxus sempervirens*—which is excellent for all sorts of turned work, was at one time the favourite wood for all the smaller musical instruments, and the so-called Turkish variety could be found with a beautiful curly grain which yielded a very handsome finish when polished. English box, which is perhaps a little softer and tougher than other growths, was formerly held in high esteem, and the older turners tended to attribute its virtues to the method of its preparation. This is said to have included burial underground to season for periods of up to twenty years. At a time when crafts were handed down from father to son this sort of thing was of course possible, but material seasoned like this is quite unobtainable today and, in an ever-hastening world, it is unlikely that it ever will be again.

It seems rather strange that Cocus—*Brya ebene* D.C.—so much esteemed for flutes and clarinets, appears never to have gained great popularity among oboists. A. M.-R. Barret, whose opinion carried great weight in the mid-19th century, does not consider it in his writings at all. In the preface to the first edition of his famous Tutor, published *c.* 1850, he mentions only box and rosewood, claiming all-round superiority for the latter but by 1862, when his second edition appeared, he had found both surpassed by violet wood. Nowadays violet-wood oboes are exceedingly rare, though a few old ones may still be in use.

Oboe tubes of metal, either silver or plated alloy, have been introduced at various times, but on the whole have never become very popular. They are naturally useful in extreme climates, where wood splits easily and even ebonite tends to warp, but their tone is frequently unsympathetic. As long ago as 1855 Von Gontershausen wrote of the sound of the metal oboe as 'hard and pointed' and lacking in tenderness. Coming from one who was presumably accustomed to the strong tone of the German oboes of the time, this remark is especially significant. Compare this with the case of the metal Boehm flute, which is, if anything, increasing in popularity at the present time.

Of the modern materials, only ebonite is as yet important. This substance has many advantages in instrument making, and is fairly widely used. It is easily worked to a high finish, is more stable than wood in a bad climate, and is not subject to the great fluctutions of temperature that affect metal instruments in playing. In spite, however, of all this, many musicians object to ebonite and appear to distrust it on tonal grounds. At the time of writing, synthetic plastics, which have already invaded the fields of flute, clarinet, and bassoon, appear to have made little progress in the territory of the oboe, though at least one Continental firm has exhibited a most elegant instrument with a tube of transparent perspex.

The connection between the tone of a wind instrument and the material of its tube has deeply interested conscientious musicians for many years, and from time to time comparative trials have been made. Until fairly recently the consensus of scientific opinion has been that, provided it be dense enough, the substance of resonating tube has no effect on tone quality. On this point, however, practical players have continued to outface the scientists,[2] and recently their attitude has found some justification. Experiments with sets of organ-pipes of like dimensions and pitch have shown quite definitely that different materials tend to reinforce different groups of partials.[3] (See 'Formants' in Chapter 'Acoustics'.) The same may reasonably be expected to apply to orchestral instruments. We have here, then, a third factor affecting the tone of woodwinds (the other two being the type of generator and the size and shape of the resonator), but in the present state of our knowledge it seems to be the least important.

Although certain special woods have been preferred for instrument making,[4] the older oboes preserved in musical collections show a surprising variety of material. That the woods favoured by early makers gave satisfactory musical results can hardly be doubted, but it seems, nevertheless, that these may often have been selected in the first place for their good turning and boring qualities. Mersenne, in reference to the flute, writes of 'plum tree, cherry tree, and other woods that may be easily bored', and goes on to say, 'It is customary to choose wood of a beautiful colour, that will bear a high polish, to the end that the excellence of the instrument may be combined with beauty of appearance'. This conjecture is supported, in the case of English makers at least, by the fact that between 1694 and 1849 the Register Book of the Company of Turners of London contains the names of many celebrated wind instrument makers, and shows that in youth they were all bound apprentice as turners pure and simple.

A survey of antique oboes listed in the principal European and American collections is extremely revealing. Between 1690 and

1830 they were regularly made of the 'fruit' woods, pear and
cherry; maple and allied trees; very rarely of cedar; most frequently
of box. Solid ivory was used only for specially rich examples.
After the first quarter of the 19th century we encounter ebony,
cocus wood, rosewood, and violet-wood; maple and box are still
there, though the latter less frequently than before; finally metal,
African blackwood and ebonite make their appearance. For the
mounts that strengthened the bell-rim and sockets, ivory was much
the commonest material till nearly the middle of the 19th century,
with horn as a poor second on Continental instruments. It is to be
noted, however, that these embellishments were much less common
on the oboe than on other early woodwinds, and in very many
cases the sockets were strengthened merely by making the surrounding wood thicker. As regards the keys, brass, and silver for
high-class work, were the usual thing till supplanted about 1830
by the hard white bronzes known as German silver, maillechort,
etc. These alloys were of course also used for rims and strengthening rings for sockets. Today they are universally employed, either
plain or plated, and their only rival is sterling silver. In view of the
amount of wear to which delicate keywork is subject, and because
some perspiration is very corrosive to copper-based alloys, it has
been suggested that stainless steel might be substituted, but so far
the difficulty (and hence the cost) of working this material has
proved prohibitive. Chromium plating, though a good protection,
makes the keys too slippery for comfort in playing. Occasionally
in the finest keywork hard steel inserts are used at the points of
maximum wear, and these have proved valuable.

## TURNING AND BORING

In the early days the making of oboe bodies involved no operations that were not then the common currency of the master-
turner's art. The joints were shaped externally on the recipro-
cating pole lathe, and the boring was done with long 'shell' bits and
reamers or D-bits of suitable shape, while the free end of the work
was supported by a perforated steady or 'spectacle plate' attached
to the lathe bed. After the advent of the fully rotary lathe these
methods continued, and they still remain the essential basis of the
much more complex modern technique. The special tools formerly
used in instrument making are illustrated in some of the classic
works on turnery, notably those of Plumier,[5] a contemporary of Dr.
Talbot, and of L. E. Bergeron.[6] These clearly show that in their

day the work was regarded as within the province of the general turner, though probably only the most skilled undertook it. There are also four plates in the 'Luthérie' section of Diderot's *Encyclopédie* of 1747 which, for the details they give, are well worth study.

The piercing of side-holes is always a matter of some anxiety to instrument makers, on account of the risk of splitting a joint, and before the days of power tools this must have been even more acute. Some early makers are believed to have avoided the danger

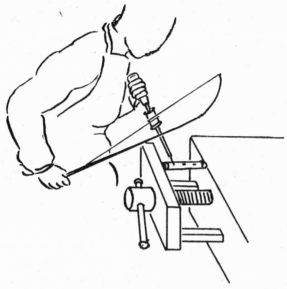

Fig. 17. The Bow-drill in use

by burning out finger-holes with hot irons, but simple openings were usually made with a spear-point bit driven by the drill-bow. This, in skilled hands, gave fast, clean cutting and a sensitive control of direction (Fig. 17). In Vol. 2 of his great treatise on turning, Holtzapffel illustrates two special tools, one for boring simple holes, the other designed to form the seatings for key-pads. Both are modifications of the common centre-bit, and they appear to have been used with the much slower hand brace. In this connection Holtzapffel says that the holes in flutes and clarinets were undercut when necessary by means of a stout knife.[7] In this, however, he seems to be behind his time, for thirty years earlier Bergeron had depicted a much more elegant tool which is used today

with but little improvement. This implement, sometimes called a
'fraise', will be easily understood from Bergeron's engraving reproduced here (Fig. 18). It consists of two parts, a fluted conical
cutter, and a stem with a wooden handle like that of an awl. The
stem has a screw thread at its end, and the cutter is pierced down
the centre and tapped to correspond. In use the cutter is slid into
the bore of the instrument and the stem passed through the hole to
be treated. A turn or two serves to pick up the cutter, which can
then be drawn up till its apex enters the hole. Since the stem has a
*right-handed* thread and the teeth of the cutter slope to the *right*,
the resistance encountered in cutting tends only to screw the two
parts more firmly together. A gentle pull on the handle puts the
necessary feed on the fraise. Modern versions of the tool have
certain refinements which make it easier to control, and the stem
has even been adapted for use in the lathe chuck, but the operative
principle remains exactly the same as it was in Bergeron's day.

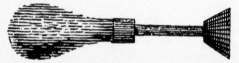 

Fig. 18. The 'Fraise', from Bergeron's
'Manuel du Tourneur' 1816

Let us now consider a little the processes involved in making a
modern blackwood oboe in an up-to-date factory. The rough
timber, already seasoned in the open air for some three years, is
first cross-cut into billets slightly longer than finally required for
the joints. These are up-ended on a chopping-block and *cleft* into
pieces of suitable size. This procedure, though much less economi-
cal than sawing, is essential in all the best-quality work, since it
brings to light any incipient cracks and flaws which might open up
later in the finished joints. The final cost of an oboe so begun is, of
course, high, on account of the quantity of wood discarded, but the
difference in price between first- and second-class instruments
(whose joints are usually sawn from the log) is well spent, since it
buys the nearest approach possible to a guarantee against splitting
in use. After cleaving out, the joints are roughly chopped to shape
by hand, then rough turned, and bored with a small hole from end
to end. There follows another period of seasoning, the longer the
better, though it is to be noted that with air circulating through the

central hole, the wood now comes into condition much more quickly. When judged ready, the joints are turned to their final shape and the conical bore is developed with suitable taper bits and reamers. Formerly this part of the work took up a good deal of time and, if the bore were at all complex, required quite a number of tools. The advent of modern superhard tool steels has, however, shortened the process considerably, and indeed I have recently seen an impeccable bore produced by one pass only of a single reamer. At this stage there follows yet another prolonged seasoning, this time in an oil-bath.

To the onlooker, the 'setting out', which comes next, is probably the most interesting part of the whole business. For this are employed 'setting-out machines', which differ in detail according to the ideas of different makers, though all embody the same essentials. In general such a machine consists of a short lathe bed carrying two poppet heads between which the turned and bored joints can be mounted. One head carries a plain cone centre, while the other has a spindle fitted with a self-centring chuck to grip the work. The spindle can rotate freely or be rigidly locked, and its position is shown by an indexed dividing plate. The small bed slides longways upon a second rather larger bed, and this, too, carries an index-scale and a lock. The third component is a sensitive drill-press mounted exactly over the axis of the two poppet heads. By means of the two motions, rotary between the heads, and longitudinal along the main bed, any point on the surface of the blank joint can be brought accurately beneath the drill and retained there by the locks. The combined readings of the two indices provide a formula which gives the precise position of every hole drilled, and enables the most perfect repetition work to be done. In cases where large numbers of identical joints are required, as in the clarinet trade, some makers replace the longitudinal index with a sort of 'master bar'. This is a metal cylinder full of holes so placed that when one of them engages with a small bolt attached to the travelling bed that member is held rigid, and in consequence the workpiece is automatically positioned as well. Near each hole in the master is stamped the corresponding reading for the dividing plate on the chuck spindle and the size number of the drill required. This arrangement speeds the work up greatly and each bar represents in fact the maker's own specification for a particular joint. A further refinement, used mostly by bassoon makers, consists in having the column of the drill-press movable through an arc so that holes can be drilled not only perpendicular to the axis of the work, but at any other angle to it as well. The actual drills used nowadays for this work are double-edged fly-cutters, which at high speed cut extremely freely and leave virtually no 'burr'. As these cutters are made from flat steel—they are in fact only a development of the primitive spear-point drill—there is little difficulty in shaping them for special purposes. It is, for instance, the regular thing to bore a note-hole and cut out the surrounding seating for a key-pad with the same tool, and so get them absolutely concentric. Certain of the cutters, too, are made with a stop which prevents them from penetrating the full thickness of the wood. These are used to make the blind holes, which are subsequently tapped with a coarse thread to take the key pillars. Others, again, are designed to mill out any surface recesses which the keywork may require. When the joint leaves the setting-out machine it is ready to receive its pillars and keys.

The last stages—pillar and key fitting, springing, and padding—are ones in which machinery cannot help, except perhaps in making the actual key components. Formerly these were shaped by hand from sheet or bar metal and finally assembled by soldering. In France, where by the end of last century the cheap woodwind trade was most highly organised, this work was often farmed out. Workers turned out enormous numbers of keys in their own homes, and in certain districts the business became almost a domestic industry, as did chain-making in the Midlands of Victorian England. With such a system the French were able, before the First World War, to make keys more cheaply than any other nation, and they exported many thousands of sets made to foreign specifications. The French key maker, in fact, seldom, if ever, saw the instrument to which his labours contributed. At the present day keys are often cast in comparatively soft metal in an effort to approach the cheapness of the former French product. Recently, too, in high-class key making, hand forging has largely given place to power pressing or hammering. The metal so treated becomes 'work-hardened', and the makers claim this to be advantageous. Somehow, however, machine-formed keys never seem to be quite so elegant as the old hand-made type.

We have digressed, and must return to our half-finished oboe. From the setting-out machine the joints pass to the pillar setter. The holes for the pillars have been tapped, and these are now screwed firmly home. Here occurs an interesting point of manufacturing technique which appears to be quite a modern invention. In order that the pivot holes in corresponding pairs of pillars shall be perfectly aligned, these are fitted in the form of blanks with solid globular heads. A jig is then applied which supports both pillars rigidly, and a drill is passed through both heads together. The jig removed, the heads are then faced off flat where the tube of the key will bear against them. All work on the actual wood of the tube being now finished, the bore is again checked and gauged for the last time. The keys, which have in the meantime been assembled, are mounted and padded. The actual fabrication is over, and the instrument passes to the tuner for the most subtle operation of all. A touch with a small hand reamer here, or the fraise there, a hair's-breadth of adjustment to the rise of this key or that, and under his skilled hands a beautiful mechanism becomes a work of art.

From the foregoing it is clear that the methods used by the modern woodwind maker are almost exactly those of his predecessor of two hundred or more years ago. Certainly the mechanism he provides is more reliable in some respects, and machinery has reduced the physical labour and time spent on some operations. Machinery has made some processes more exact, but it has done nothing to replace the skill of individual craftsmen, nor does it seem likely to do so at least as long as natural wood remains the principal raw material. It is true that where large output justifies the initial cost—as in providing the enormous number of clarinets absorbed by military and school bands in America—some factories have introduced a certain amount of automatic machinery. Finished clarinet bodies of great accuracy are turned out in quantity by automatic copying lathes, but even these cannot eliminate the personal skills called for in assembling, fitting, and above all in tuning. The oboe is not at present required in vast numbers, and though in consequence its price may remain high, traditional methods of building seem to meet its case. It is only when one considers the possibility of moulded plastics replacing wood that the picture begins to change. These substances already play a large part in our life, and if ever one should be developed that is cheap and has all the necessary characteristics for a good woodwind body, then indeed may the old methods go by the board.

[1] C. Holtzapffel, *Turning and Mechanical Manipulation*, London, 1843, Vol. I, p. 74.
[2] See letters from Theobald Boehm to W. S. Broadwood, 1865, 1866, and 1867. Published in *Boehm on the Flute*, London, Rudall Carte and Co., 1882, pp. 47–51.

[3] Dayton C. Miller in *Science*, 1909, Vol. 29.
Boner and Newman, *Journal of the Acoustical Society of America*, Vol. 12 (1940), p. 83.

[4] Box is mentioned in the *Oeuvres* of J. P. Coutant, published in Poitiers in 1628. Constant Pierre points out that the reference concerns an industry that was then at least a century older.

[5] Charles Plumier, Religieux Minime, *L'Art de Tourner en Perfection*, Lyons, 1701.

[6] L. E. Bergeron, *Manuel du Tourneur*, Paris, 1792 and 1816.

[7] C. Holtzapffel, *op. cit.*, Vol. 2, p. 541 (London, 1846).

# CHAPTER XI

# Obsolete Constructions

THE CURVED COR ANGLAIS

In the previous chapter we examined briefly the methods of the oboe maker of *c.* 1700 and saw that, except in the one matter of key mounting, the modern techniques follow directly in the same tradition and represent no more than a development of the old principles with perhaps the assistance of power-driven lathes and drills. In the group of oboes which we know today each likewise had its counterpart in the late 17th or 18th century. During that period, however, one member of the family progressed in a manner different from that of the others. This was the tenor, which, after beginning as a straight instrument like the treble, soon began (in Continental Europe, at least) to acquire a curved form. As the oboe da caccia and cor anglais this at last became the dominant type, and remained so for many years. Though rivalled by a very efficient new straight instrument as long ago as 1839, the curved cor retained some devotees until the present century.

The strange metamorphoses of the tenor oboe have puzzled scholars for a long time, and some of their opinions are discussed in the Chapter 'The Larger Oboes'. The subject is reintroduced here only because the curved instrument presented special problems of construction and, as far as I am aware, dependable evidence regarding the techniques employed has come to light only during the past year.[1] These techniques rather set the instrument apart from the others, and I have therefore thought it best to deal with them separately.

The student of obsolete wind instruments is bound to become familiar sooner or later with bent wooden tubes. He encounters them in the crumhorns and curved cornetti (instruments which belonged really to the Medieval period and which were in their last decline by the time that the oboe appeared), and most commonly in the serpent. In use, the latter alone overlapped the oboe by some two hundred years and survived long enough to benefit by comparatively modern keywork. The construction of surviving examples of all these instruments is fairly obvious. They were produced by hollowing out two shells of plank-wood and glueing and pinning these together, subsequently binding the tube so formed with strips of cloth and covering the whole with a skin of leather.

Concerning the larger oboes writers have repeatedly insisted that the curved tenor of the 18th century was made by the same method. There is, in fact, almost no justification at all for this statement. Very few specimens show any sign of a join along the length of the tube, and indeed I am personally acquainted with but a single example. This was formerly in the Galpin collection, and is now No. 142 of the Leslie Lindsey Mason collection in the Museum of Fine Arts, Boston, Mass. The instrument is a two-keyed one of the flared bell type with rather wide bore, for which Bessaraboff has reserved the designation 'oboe da caccia'. It is very doubtful if the narrow-bored cor anglais was ever constructed by the 'plank' method and there is a very good practical reason against it. If we look at any contemporary picture of a cornett-player we see that the instrument was held with the curve in a more or less horizontal plane and that the finger-holes were bored perpendicular to this; i.e. through one of the component shells. The playing position of the bent cor anglais, on the other hand, required the holes to be bored along the outer curvature in the same plane as the supposed junction between the two halves. This is obviously a most unsatisfactory arrangement with a glued join and where undercutting might be required. There is also the objection that, in playing, the glued join on the inner curve would lie just where all the condensed moisture tends to collect. It appears that, on grounds of practical efficiency as well as on the evidence of all but the most exceptional specimens, the idea of a long-ways join in the curved tenor must be rejected.

If this is so, what alternative can we offer? Towards the end of the 19th century certain French cors anglais were made with the upper joint alone quite gently curved. In such cases the top section was built up of five or six separate pieces united by tenons and, as there was no outer covering, the seams were clearly visible. Most curved tenors were, however, leather-covered like the serpents, and both joints were quite strongly bent. That was the commonest form of the instrument and, if the evidence of musical literature is to be trusted, it seems, quite unaccountably, to have escaped adequate examination or description. Some very strange theories have, nevertheless, been advanced and have till quite recently been left unchallenged. For instance, it has been suggested that the joints were turned and bored in the usual manner and afterwards forcibly bent with the aid of heat and perhaps moisture.[2] This theory will not stand up in the light of practical experiment. Also, among other things, it offers no explanation of how the curve was to be prevented from changing under the varying conditions of use, a very serious matter with those instruments fitted with much key-work. Certainly such wooden objects as the ribs of violins and the frames of tennis racquets are formed in this way, but these are invariably subject to some permanent restraint which prevents subsequent shifting. The idea of simply boring and bending will not do and we must conclude that some method of building up, other than in longitudinal halves, was employed.

It is here that the late French instruments give us a lead. If such a construction as theirs was used the outer seams would of course be hidden by the leather; but what about the inside of the tube? Surely the joins, if any, would show there? The fact is that they do, and it is surprising that so many students seem for so long to have missed this point. Recently a considerable number of specimens of different dates have been viewed internally with the aid of a modified surgical inspection lamp and, so far, every one examined has shown distinct transverse joins. The final evidence appeared less than a year ago. A two-keyed cor anglais, probably of early 18th-century Italian origin, came to hand. This had suffered badly by damp, and from both joints the leather had partly peeled away. Inside it showed the usual transverse joins, but *outside* the corresponding seams did not pass right round the tube. The various sections comprising each joint were not entirely separate, as in the French examples, but had been produced by cutting out a series of wedges across a normally turned tube (Fig. 19). The apex of each wedge removed penetrated quite half the thickness of the tube wall, leaving only a strip of wood thin enough to bend without undue strain and allowing the gaps to be closed and glued. The process was in fact the same as used by a joiner who will notch the back of a moulding before applying it to a curved surface. Before sawing out the wedges a flat had evidently been planed on the tube, and when the bending was complete this formed a bed on the inner curvature to which a thin wooden 'splint' was glued and pinned. The resultant structure was completely firm and solid and showed no sign of ever having moved.

Here was positive evidence of a very interesting and completely practical method of building; but it was afforded by a single example only. It was felt necessary to have some confirmation. As no collector could be expected to allow cherished specimens to be 'skinned' even in the interests of research, it was decided to try

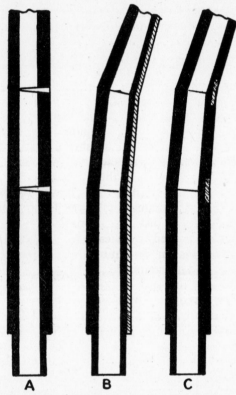

Fig. 19. Construction of the bent Cor Anglais

A. The tube turned and bored; wedges cut out
B. The tube bent. Retaining 'splint' shaded
C. Alternative method. Retaining 'keys' shaded

X-ray examination. This was a fortunate decision, for further and unsuspected details came to light. A series of bent cors anglais were screened and photographed and no less than four structural varieties were revealed. The oldest type was exactly as already described. A ten-keyed German instrument of the early 19th century showed the same structure, but with a *metal* splint along the inner curvature, this being screwed to each section between the notches. The third variety was exemplified by a Triébert instrument of *c.* 1850 with ten German silver keys. Externally this appeared to have no remarkable features, but by X-ray each joint proved to be built up of several detached sections butted together without any tenons. Instead, each section was attached to the next by three or four wooden 'keys' which bridged the join. Each key was let into a deep groove in the wall and pinned into place with wooden pegs.

A second 18th-century example, this time by the Florentine maker G. Bimboni, showed an interesting variation, combining features of both the above types. In this case the body had been notched and bent but, instead of by a splint, the curve was maintained by a series of inset keys each shaped like two keystones joined at their narrow ends. These prevented the seams from opening by virtually 'dovetailing' them together. Finally, one of the late Triébert upper joints without leather was X-rayed for comparison and another surprising thing was found. It had been recognised from the outset that here tenons were indeed employed, but the photograph revealed that these had not been turned down from the actual sections but were quite independent small wooden tubes. Again they had been pinned in place with wooden pegs, and altogether there were five such unions in one very gently curved joint. The X-ray has confirmed that in general the bore of the bent tenor oboe passed through a series of very obtuse angles and was not a true curve, although in the later examples a very fair approximation was achieved. In all cases, however, the smoothness and finish were those of the original boring and could be as good as in any straight instrument of the same period.

---

[1] The evidence may in fact have been available for nearly sixty years and lain unrecognised for lack of an adequate description. There is a rather obscure entry in the catalogue of the César Snoeck collection, published in Ghent in 1894, which reads as follows: '962—*Vielle taille de hautbois.* En arc du cercle, à deux clefs. Instrument de transition entre la taille de hautbois et le cor Anglais. Deux de ses parties sont recouvertes de cuir: la troisème l'a été également; cette partie dénudée, met sous les yeux le moyen qu'employaient les facteurs au 17$^{me}$ siècle pour produire des tubes courbés.'

Unfortunately this instrument does not figure in Sach's list of 1,145 specimens from the Snoeck collection transferred in 1902 to the Berlin Hochschule nor among the 436 Flemish examples presented to the Brussels Conservatoire in 1908, and its fate is unknown. We are therefore without information as to the method of construction Snoeck mentions; neither have we his reasons for assigning the instrument to the 17th century.

My own researches in the matter only began late in 1952, but first results were happily available and were communicated to the late F. G. Rendall in time to be used in Chapter X of his book on the clarinet in this series.

² E. Halfpenny, 'The Tenner Hoboy', *Galpin Society Journal*, No. 5, p. 25.

P. A. T. Bate, *op. cit.*, No. 6, p. 100.

CHAPTER 12

# Technique and Capabilities

THE technique of the oboe is today a highly developed and complex matter which can only be discussed authoritatively by an experienced player. The subject therefore is in general outside the scope and intention of this book, which is certainly not to teach the art of oboe playing. The viewpoint of the professional oboist, however, is as a rule sternly practical. He seldom has time to philosophise or to concern himself with the past history of the instrument which he finds at once both a good servant and an exacting master. He will have decided which solution to certain difficulties suits his own case best, and he may even be unaware of certain facilities of which he himself has never felt the need. Thus professional opinion may sometimes become biased. It is because of this that I have here attempted to present a few points of technique which may be of general interest as seen by a non-professional onlooker.

The dictionary definitions of technique as concerned with instrumental playing may be summed up as 'the mechanical skill and dexterity necessary for performance'. The reference books in general give us a description of technique from a purely physical standpoint—mastery over the physical problems of an instrument, in fact—but they make little attempt to explain its deeper purpose or to relate it with the vital matter of æsthetics. In the recent past this outlook has obtained in many music schools and academies. The purely technical part of a musician's training has often been more or less walled off from the interpretative or the creative. There have been times when executive brilliance has been admired above all else, and many players have cultivated it as an end in itself. At the present day, however, a more just and balanced view is growing up and it is usually held that, while the individual performer may, according to his natural gifts, excel on the one side or the other, his technique should contribute to and be disciplined by good musicianship in the widest sense.

To the musicologist technique in its 'gymnastic' sense is of no particular concern but it does interest him deeply where it involves

L     145

those procedures unavoidably imposed on the player by the acoustics of his instrument or the limits of his natural equipment of fingers and thumbs. One such is the device of 'fork-fingering' on woodwinds, which is still the most convenient way of producing certain notes in certain combinations in spite of the abundance and efficiency of modern keywork. In the 18th century these notes could be obtained in no other way, and there is little doubt that the lay-out of note-holes on many old instruments, which today appears rather curious, was conditioned by this fact. Forked notes had, if possible, to be as good as the natural ones, and if an over-all consistency could be obtained by some slight sacrifice of the latter the compromise was often worth making. (See p. 49, *ante*.) With the rational placing of holes now possible a curious anomaly has sometimes appeared. For the sake of convenience the player may wish to 'fork' a note and then be chagrined to find that the hole involved, though now ideally placed for its primary function, is out of tune for anything else. The solution has been provided by yet more mechanism, this time operating automatically whenever the fork fingering is employed. (Cf. M. Bonnet's invention, p. 70.)

There is another matter which has greatly complicated the technique of the oboe in modern times, and this too is the result of the growth of mechanism. We have already noticed in Chapter 4 that even the simple two-keyed instrument afforded a choice of fingerings for certain notes; with the numerous additional holes introduced by a key system such as Barret's or the full Conservatoire many more alternative fingerings have become available. Some of these are useful for passing notes or shakes only, while others are of general service, and the choice of the best fingering in any given circumstances can be quite an embarrassment to an inexperienced player. For example, Barret in his 1862 *Méthode* shows no less than four versions of both the $c'''$ and the $d'''$, though not all are equally servicable. Some of them, he points out, cannot be attacked with the tongue but may only be slurred to from the preceding note.

Again, it must be observed that the advent of a new facility has sometimes taken away a former one. For instance, the fully automatic octave action invalidates several alternative fingerings for extreme high notes, as does the very useful coupling between the low $b^{\natural}$, $b^{\flat}$ and $c^{\natural}$ keys. In these cases the choice between facilities must be a matter for the individual player, and for the inexperienced it may be a most difficult one.

Yet another point which falls under the heading of 'technique' is the production of a good tone. A generally agreeable tone is essential to any instrumentalist, for without it, though he may be the most brilliant executant, his audience will be unsympathetic. Occasionally oboists whose tone is recorded as harsh have become celebrated because of surpassing execution (the Bessozis and A. J. Lavigne are notable examples) but such are indeed rare. Good tone is, however, a difficult thing to define and, as I have pointed out earlier, different countries have different ideas. Bad tone by whatever standards is easily recognised, though its causes are sometimes obscure. Given a reasonably good reed, bad tone is often due either to faulty breathing or a wrong embouchure but perhaps most frequently to the player not being clear in his mind as to what kind of sound he is trying to produce. It is well known that a violinist whose habits are formed tends to produce his own personal tone on any instrument, be it a Stradivarius or a modern fiddle, and the same is true of wind players. The oboist should always try to imagine the sound he wants to make and listen to himself critically for both tone and intonation. It is not enough just to blow and expect the instrument to do all the rest. By the same token, it is a great mistake for the beginner to imagine that he can make a good start without professional aid. One can do a great deal by oneself after the initiation is over, and very sound and helpful books[1] are obtainable for use at this stage, but it is at the beginning that bad habits are formed or avoided, and this is the time when an ounce of experienced guidance is worth many pounds of text-book.

Since the beginning of the 18th century many alleged 'masters' have written instruction books for the oboe and today these are much sought after by collectors. Often the texts were quite shamelessly 'pirated' from earlier publications, and we even find pulls from identical plates appearing with different title-pages—an interesting side-light on music publishing before the laws of copyright were properly established. Every so often, however, a good 'Tutor' by a real master made its appearance. Such were usually designed in the first place as study material for the author's own pupils, and, if he held a professorship in some leading school of music, he could sometimes insist on their exclusive use in his classes. As the means of making known the newest technical inventions and improvements those books were, however, valuable to wider public, and today they are of much service to the musical historian, since they indicate what was expected of the oboe at various stages of its development. For a condensed survey of the progress of oboe technique the following short list is suggested:—

1. *The Sprightly Companion*, 1695.
2. *La Véritable Manière d'apprendred à jouer en perfection du Hautbois* ——, Freillon Poncein, 1700.
3. *Principes de la Flute Traversière—et du Haut-bois—*, Hotteterre-le-Romain, 1707.
4. *The Modern Musick Master*, 1731.
5. *New and Compleat Instructions for the Oboe or Hoboy*, *c.* 1790.
6. *Méthode*, Garnier, *c.* 1800.
7. *Méthode*, Vogt, MSS. post 1813. } Covering the rise of the modern French oboe.
8. *Méthode*, Brod, 1835.
9. *Complete Method*, Barret (2nd edn.), 1862.
10. *Oboeschule*, Sellner, 1825. } These two devoted to the
11. *Oboeschule*, Niemann, 1899. } Vienna type oboe.

If we compare the descriptive paragraphs in such a selection of tutors as the above, it soon becomes clear that modern oboe playing embodies the sum of almost all the procedures that have been worked out during more than two hundred and fifty years of laborious development. Indeed, throughout the long life of the instrument only three technical devices of any significance have been discarded, namely the half closing of the low *c* key to obtain *c♯*, the use of the 'twin' holes, and the practice of muting. The first of these was rendered needless by the advent of a proper *c♯* key early in the 19th century, though it had in fact fallen out of use many years earlier, leaving a gap in the scale which was generally accepted, as most 18th-century fingering charts show. The second was obsolescent though still possible in respect of the *g♯'* on some instruments as late as the 1860s. The third, though unknown to the majority of modern players, is still very occasionally demanded by composers.

BREATHING

It surely goes without saying that a first essential in playing the oboe, as in singing, is controlled and unlaboured breathing, and in view of its manifest importance it is surprising how little space the great teachers such as A. M.-R. Barret have given to it in their writings. It is evidently a matter which even the experienced player finds difficult to describe and would much prefer to demonstrate. Recently, however, at least one detailed study has appeared from the pen of a distinguished English oboist[1] and this can be heartily recommended for its clarity and good sense. There, perhaps, in a book such as this, the matter might be allowed to rest but for the fact that even among leading professionals there are differences of opinion that deserve to be put on record.

It is evident that in playing any wind instrument the natural and unconscious rhythm of breathing must be more or less disturbed by the demands of musical phrasing. The instrumentalist must therefore get used to a method of respiration which will at the same time supply his bodily needs, serve his instrument, and meet the requirements of the music. Ideally this should be as unselfconscious during playing as is normal breathing at other times. With practice it becomes so, though the novice without experienced help may at first find himself at a loss.

In the case of the oboe the chief difficulty is due to the fact that the reed with its narrow opening will pass only a very small volume of air in a given time but requires that little at a fairly high pressure. This, incidentally, has no bearing on whether the actual embouchure or muscular control of the reed is 'tight', 'loose', 'flexible', or whatever else the player may choose to call it. Widely divergent opinions are held on this matter of embouchure, and what is best for one player may not necessarily be so for another, but the breathing difficulty affects them all alike. In everyday life few of us breathe to the full capacity of our lungs. An average man standing at rest in normal circumstances breathes about sixteen times a minute and in that time passes in and out some ten litres of air, or when walking easily at two miles per hour between eighteen an nineteen litres.[2]

Such conditions are clearly very different from those often imposed by musical phrasing and, moreover, the steady stream required to operate an oboe reed satisfactorily calls for quite a considerable volume of air in reserve, even though comparatively little of this will actually pass between the blades. The problem, then, is to adjust the respiration so as to clear the lungs of stale air from which the body has used up the oxygen long before so great a volume can pass through the instrument. If this is not done the player will very soon become distressed and be unable to carry on. Most oboists are agreed that their needs are best met by deep and unhurried breathing both in and out through the mouth, taking advantage of every opportunity the music offers, and using the abdominal muscles to the full. There will, of course, be times when a full breath is not possible but even then the player should try to avoid gasping and hunching the shoulders, which is both unmusical and physiologically bad. Though apparently far removed from the normal, such breathing, if consistently practised, very soon becomes a matter of unconscious habit and the muscular development acquired is generally beneficial. This was recognised as long ago as the 16th century, for in 1533 in *The Castel of Helthe* Thomas Elyot recommended the playing of shawms as a healthful exercise. 'The entrayles which be undernethe the middreffe', he writes, 'be exercised by blowing . . . or playing on shalmes . . . which do requyr moche wynde.' If by 'moche wynde' Elyot implied 'much wind control', as I think we may assume he did, his advice is today as good as ever it was. The above, I have indicated, seems to be the opinion of a majority of players but it is only fair to observe that there is also a school of thought which advises inhaling only as much air at a time as will serve for each phrase of music, so that there will always be a minimum to get rid of when the need arises.

Before leaving the subject of breathing there are one or two matters which are worthy of note rather as curiosities than as regular features of oboe technique. In the eleven-line paragraph which is all that he devotes to breathing, Barret writes, 'If in playing a phrase, the pupil should find he has retained too much air he must let a portion escape, taking care to have sufficient remaining to finish the passage'. This would seem to suggest that Barret favoured the 'minimum air' method, and his advice to the pupil touches on what appears to be one of its great difficulties for the inexperienced, i.e. that of gauging accurately the amount of air necessary for any given passage. Barret does not say how the excess air is to be allowed to escape, but I have known players to use either the corner of the mouth or the nose as a sort of 'safety valve'. In spite of Barret this seems to be an undesirable practice, for it sometimes gives rise to the most uncouth wheezings and snorts. Occasionally skilled oboists find it advantageous to leave the embouchure undisturbed and to breathe momentarily by the nose, but this is, of course, a different matter.

There is another form of nose-breathing which is sometimes practised but which is nowadays generally deprecated. The method is to allow the cheeks to relax somewhat without altering the set of the lips, thus forming a sort of elastic reservoir which maintains an air-stream while the lungs are emptied and re-filled via the nose. The technique is just that employed by jewellers and others who use the simple mouth blowpipe. The device can be learned by anyone, but some people have a particular gift for it, and certain oboists have used it to produce a quite phenomenal sostenuto. Though at times this ability has undoubtedly been abused we should not dismiss it as a mere vulgar trick. The late Charles Reynolds, for instance, was a much-respected player who used it, and an occasion is still remembered when, at a rehearsal of 'Tristan' at Covent Garden, Richter with admiration called the orchestra's attention to Reynolds' feat in playing the famous cor anglais solo in the third act without any apparent pause for breath. In point of musical taste the achievement may not have been above criticism, but the fault surely lies with the composer who wrote forty-one slow bars full of ties and without a single rest, rather than with the musician who was so gifted as to be able to play them exactly as written. All too often composers are inconsiderate to their instrumentalists, or even ignorant of their physical needs. As another member of the orchestra on this occasion observed, 'Even shepherd boys have to breathe'.

The cor anglais solo just mentioned is only one example of the excruciating demands composers sometimes make. As a rule these can only be met by a compromise, and a wise conductor, unless he has very decided views of his own, will leave the matter to the judgment of his solo player. No one else can know as well as the instrumentalist the practical difficulties which may lie hidden in an apparently simple passage of music and, for this reason, nearly all the most valuable improvements in keywork have been invented by players. In the case of the oboe this inventiveness has at least once been directed to the problem of sustained blowing also. Some years ago the late Albert Coates told me that once in his young days in Russia he had encountered an oboist who played the longest sustained passages without giving any sign of breathing at all. At the distance at which this man sat from the conductor his appearance showed nothing unusual, but, on questioning, he admitted that he was able, while keeping a normal control of his reed, to retain in one corner of his mouth a tiny indiarubber tube. This passed beneath his clothing to a small bellows which he worked with his foot, thus providing his seemingly inexhaustible wind supply. The story seemed to me at the time somewhat apocryphal,

but later it was strangely corroborated. One day I repeated it to
the well-known London expert Mr. B. Manton-Myatt, who immediately recalled that an invention of the sort had some years ago
been offered to the firm with whom he was then employed. The
inventor demonstrated his apparatus successfully and then offered
it for trial by some of the witnesses. One or two did use it, but
judgment on its commercial possibilities was deferred. Unfortunately, in the course of the next few days all the gentlemen who
had tested the device developed an unpleasant and painful mouth
infection. The inventor and his apparatus forthwith disappeared
and nothing more has, to my knowledge, been heard of it.

## VIBRATO

The question of *vibrato* or no *vibrato* in the playing of woodwinds is one which seems to arouse the most violent feelings among
instrumentalists. Although by no means universally accepted (few
German or Italian players use it), vibrato is nowadays regarded in
English-speaking countries as a legitimate and useful part of the
oboist's technique, while in America it has become the subject of
considerable study. Once again the matter is evidently one of taste
and musical purpose. A good vibrato used with judgment is not,
I think, detrimental to the natural tone of the instrument, but it
must be said that in excess it can soon become vulgar and cloying
and may even upset intonation. Poor intonation which ought to be
corrected may also be masked by excessive vibrato. One would not
wish the violinist to abandon an effect which adds much richness to
his performance; on the other hand, it is unthinkable that all our
music should be blurted out as though by the tremulant of the
cinema organ, and the same considerations of good taste should
surely govern wind playing.

Vibrato is engendered by pulsating the wind stream more or less
rapidly, and is a faculty which some oboists develop naturally as
their powers increase. Others require to cultivate it specially. The
effect can be produced by the lips and jaw; by the throat muscles;
or by the abdominal muscles. Obviously the first method is apt to
disturb the embouchure, and most fine players use the third, since
they have already developed good abdominal control.

## MUTING

The practice of muting has no regular place in the accepted
technique of any present-day reed instrument, except perhaps, in

special circumstances, that of the saxophone. In the 18th and 19th centuries, however, some players seem regularly to have muted the oboe, and in the tutor published c. 1772 by Longman and Lukey of London the celebrated J. C. Fischer is credited with introducing the idea in England. Fischer was held in high esteem in this country and no doubt his methods were widely copied. In his instructions he recommends the insertion of a plug of cotton or lamb's wool in the bell of the instrument, but warns the player that this must not be pushed up beyond the 'air holes'. Recent experiments with a series of old oboes have shown that when the bell is plugged the lowest note can as a rule be sounded well in tune through these holes. The effect is not so much to reduce the volume of the note as to alter its quality and bring it more into line with those sounded by the very small holes higher up on the instrument. This is, of course, what we should expect from acoustic considerations. A more permanent and probably rather later device than the wool plug was a pear-shaped mute of turned hardwood, and the survival of examples in company with certain old oboes affords more evidence of the usage. The final disappearance of the 'air holes' in the bell occurred at a time when the whole instrument was undergoing a process of refinement and its scale was becoming more even throughout.

In the modern oboe, where the bell appears to be of less acoustic significance than formerly, some degree of muting is still possible as long as one or two of the lowest holes are left open. This is called for by Stravinsky in the last few bars of the score of 'Petroushka', but one cannot help feeling that here the effect desired is not any change of tone quality but only the most extreme pianissimo possible by any means. In most performances the results are of doubtful value, and the great majority of oboists will simply play the passage as softly as they can by normal methods of lip and breath control. On the other hand, I am informed by Mr. Alfred Livesley of Manchester that the late Stephen Whittaker was a firm believer in the value of a cotton-wool mute which he used consistently for all playing except, of course, in passages involving the two lowest notes of the instrument.

EXTRA HARMONICS

In addition to the thirty-six notes which make up the chromatic compass of the oboe today, users of modern instruments have at their disposal some eight more (sometimes fewer if there is fully automatic octave mechanism) which professional players term the *harmonics*. Properly speaking, of course, all notes from $c\sharp''$ upwards, where the fingering of the primary scale repeats itself with the addition of the 'half-hole' or a speaker key, are harmonics, but the player makes no distinction about them in his mind and regards them as normal. The extra harmonics, however, are not obtained by simply octaving regular first register fingerings. Since two octave keys became universal on the oboe and the tube of the instrument was lengthened to give the low $b\flat$ it has been found that the first four notes of the scale, together with the first speaker key and the second four plus the second speaker, all provide excellent twelfths with a peculiar character of their own.

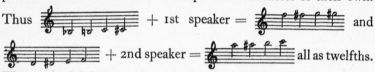

Thus ___ + 1st speaker = ___ and ___ + 2nd speaker = ___ all as twelfths.

These special harmonics are a useful addition to the oboist's resources, particularly in solo work, but they require care in production and cannot be played *forte*. Used with discretion their very individual tone colour can be most telling.

While on the subject of harmonics generally it may be well to mention again the different fingerings for the extreme high notes of the normal scale which are sounded either as twelfths or as super-octaves. When the player has mastered the accepted ones he will soon notice minute differences between them both in quality and intonation. He may even find out additional or modified fingerings which suit his own instrument particularly well. The oboist should try to take advantage of such alternatives as his ability and musicianship dictate, for this is all part of technique. Such things transform a competent performance into an artistic one and greatly increase the pleasure of both the player and his audience.

## CAPABILITIES

To conclude this chapter here is a short summary of the capabilities of the modern oboe. In the first place, the instrument is undoubtedly at its best in a medium compass, say $f'$ to $b''$, and in this range its tone is at its sweetest, neither too reedy as it sometimes tends to be lower down, nor thin as in the acute register. Within these rather narrow limits of an octave and a fourth the widest dynamics from a full singing *forte* to the faintest *pianissimo* are readily obtained, and within them too most composers from the time of Gluck onward have written their most satisfying orchestral solos. The symphonies of Beethoven and Schubert are full of perfect examples. In more modern works oboe solos are at times carried up to the extreme notes with great effect, but in these the *vocal* quality of the middle register is replaced by an unique incisiveness which has a particular value of its own.

Scale and arpeggio passages, diatonic and chromatic, are readily played both *staccato* and *legato*, as well as wide skips, grace notes, and shakes. If the mechanism is kept in good order (as it always should be by regular overhauls) the oboe has very considerable agility, little, if any, inferior to that of the flute and in this connection it seems that its full capacity in the way of articulation is not always realised. Although, because of the character of the reed, only single tonguing is really satisfactory on the oboe, a good player can produce a charming and most effective quick *staccato*, as, for example, in the solo in Act I of Rossini's 'William Tell'. Occasionally modern composers will write passages that demand double or even triple tonguing but these are seldom effective. 'Flutter' tonguing as sometimes used by flute and clarinet players (although it has sometimes been asked for), is not practicable on the oboe.

In the matter of shakes the oboe is well enough equipped, although there are some notable difficulties. With his instrument of 1860–62 Barret claimed to have achieved perfect shakes on every note but few players today would regard them all as practical in all circumstances. The reader who is particularly concerned will find in any up-to-date work on orchestration lists of shakes and other conjunctions of notes which are best avoided. Present-day requirements in all departments are well illustrated by such books as the *Orchester Studien*, edited by Heinze (Breitkopf and Hartel), or Louis Bas' *Etudes d'Ochestre* (Costellat), both of which contain selected difficult passages extracted from standard orchestral works.

Since the four principal types of oboe have become standardised a number of modern instruction books have appeared in various languages. Most of these are excellent, though all contain much the same material. The chief difference among them lies in the authors' personal approach to the problems of teaching. It is interesting to note that although Barret's own oboe has passed entirely out of use, his *Méthode*, now over ninety years old, is still regarded as one of the very best on account of the excellence of the studies he wrote for it. This work, I believe, is still part of the prescribed material in the leading oboe schools in France.

We may sum up, then, by saying that though both the technique and the physical capacity of the oboe are more advanced today than at any previous time, they still have certain limitations, a fact which some composers seem to find more difficult to appreciate than players to admit.

[1] Evelyn Rothwell, *Oboe Technique*, London, O.U.P., 1953.

[2] The various factors concerned with human respiration vary a great deal between different individuals, and for this reason it is difficult to define the normal save in terms of quite broad averages. Thus the breathing rate at rest, though usually much nearer to sixteen, may be as high as twenty-four breaths per minute without indicating any abnormality.

A concise description of the mechanism of human breathing will be found in Vol. 19 of the *Encyclopaedia Britannica* (14th Edn.), from which it will be sufficient to quote here that the *vital capacity* (i.e. the quantity of air which can be expelled from the lungs by the deepest possible expiration following the deepest possible inspiration) as tabulated by Colonel Flack in the cases of seventy-three British Air Force pilots varied from 2,800 to 5,500 ccs.

# CHAPTER 13

# Celebrated Oboe Players—some Biographical Notes

THE progress of any musical instrument over the ages has always been influenced by two main groups of men: the players or player-teachers on one hand, and the purely technical instrument makers on the other. From time to time the two activities have been combined in one individual and when this has happened the greatest advances have been made. In the case of the oboe, its very origin, as well as its fullest flowering in mid-19th century Paris, lay in the hands of such *artistes-ouvriers*. Those who are definitely known to have made physical modifications to the instrument are easily accounted for, but there may have been many improvers whose names are now lost and to whom no tribute can be paid. There are also many whose contribution to the art of the oboe was not physical at all, but who were important in their time as exemplars of taste or virtuosity. Their legacy also has come down to the modern player, for music teaching is a continuous process. Each successive teacher adds something to the sum-total of knowledge.

I feel, therefore, that any history of the oboe, however limited, must include some account of its great players. The difficulty, on the evidence we possess today, is to choose among them those of the greatest importance in one field or the other, and to avoid giving a mere catalogue of names. Such a selection is bound to be, to a great extent, a personal one. There are some players, about whom we have a great deal of information, who will inevitably figure in any list. Others, less well known, must depend for inclusion on the compiler's own assessment. The English writer will almost certainly show some preference for French or French-trained players, since their school rather than the German has had most influence in English-speaking countries. The reader, then, is asked to bear these points in mind if he feels that some deserving names have not been included among the following short biographies. For obvious reasons living or quite recent players have not been discussed.

PHILIDOR. The *Philidors* were a large and celebrated family of musicians who flourished in the service of the French Court from the mid-17th century onwards. The fullest account of them is given in 'Les Philidor', a set of excellent studies by Ernest Thoinan published in *La France Musicale* in 1867–8.[1] The family name was originally Danican, and tradition (unfortunately not documented) has it that the 'Philidor' was bestowed on the first recorded musician among them by Louis XIII after one Filidori, an 'oboist' of Siena who had some time before made a great impression in Court circles. Concerning this first Philidor, however, there appears to be some disagreement among scholars. Grove's *Dictionary of Music* (4th edn.) takes him to be one of two presumed brothers Michel and Jean. On the other hand, Josef Marx[2] believes him to have been an earlier Michel, father of the above two, whom he accepts as undoubted brothers. Regarding Filidori little or nothing is known except his name, but it is clear on datal evidence that his instrument cannot have been the true oboe as we now understand it.

The Philidors are of particular interest as an example of family tradition in music. Like all the men in the Royal service they were versatile, most of them playing the trumpet-marine and crumhorn in addition to the double-reeds of their time. The most important in oboe history are the following:—

*Michel* (?–*c.* 1659). He is recorded as a member of the band of the Grande Ecurie in 1651, playing the trumpet-marine, crumhorn, and 'hautbois'. It is he who has been tentatively suggested by Josef Marx as the co-inventor of the true oboe.[3] He died without issue.

*Jean* (*c.* 1620–79), from whom all the rest of the family were descended. He also served in the Grande Ecurie, beginning as a fifer and going on later to the trumpet-marine, crumhorn, and oboe (perhaps this time the true three-jointed instrument).

*André*, eldest son of Jean, known as 'Philidor l'aîné' (*c.* 1647–1730). He played the bassoon (*bass de hautbois*) at the Court of Louis XIV in addition to the other family instruments, and composed music for Court entertainments. His chief fame, however, comes from his appointment in 1684 as musical librarian to the King. Between that date and his death he compiled the famous 'Collection Philidor' comprising Court music of all sorts from the reign of Henri III to the end of the 17th century. A portion of this collection still survives, and is of the greatest value to musical scholars. André was the most prolific of the family, having sixteen children by his first wife, Marguérite Mougiant, and five by his second, Elizabeth Le Roy. Several of these became musicians in their turn.

*Jacques* (1651–1708), known as 'Philidor le cadet', was the younger brother of André. In addition to playing the family instruments he composed marches, dance tunes, etc. He was an especial favourite of Louis XIV, who marked his approbation by the gift of landed property at Versailles.

*Anne* (1681–1728), eldest son of André, became in 1704 an oboist attached to the Chapel Royal. We may reasonably assume that his instrument was the true oboe, since he was born exactly ten years after the production of Cambert's 'Pomone', though he may possibly have known also the shawm in his earlier days. The familiarity and condescension shown by the French Royalty to their favourite musicians are well illustrated by the life of Anne Philidor He was the godson of the Duc de Noailles, who exerted much influence on his behalf, and he was often invited to play the oboe privately for the King and to sing duets with him. On one occasion, at the *appartement* of Mme. de Maintenon, the then aged King did him the singular honour of singing for him an aria which had not been heard since 1655, nearly sixty years earlier. In 1725 he founded the 'Concert Spirituel'.

From the above we see that the Philidors form a link between the old and the newer reed instruments, the first of them having been brought up on the shawms, while the later generations played only the true oboe. It is interesting to note that in the younger members of the family professional music was not the only concern. François André (1726–95), André's first son by his second marriage, became the leading chess player and theoretician of his time. As a chess virtuoso he travelled triumphantly on the Continent and in England, till, in 1754, he was summoned back to France and devoted himself seriously to musical composition. His successful production in 1759 of a light opera, 'Blaise le Savetier', led to a number of others before his death in London in 1795.

PAISIBLE, *James* (?–1721), also spelt 'Paisable' and 'Peasible', may well have been the first to use the true jointed oboe in England. The circumstances surrounding his arrival in this country and the evidence leading to the above surmise are discussed in Chapter 3, p. 35. Unfortunately our information about him is by no means as full as we could wish, though a good deal of relevant material has been collected by W. J. Lawrence.[4] This includes his will. During his service at the English Court he was notable not only as an oboist, but also as a composer of entertainment music, overtures, 'act tunes', etc.

GALLIARD (*Gaillard*), *Johann* (1687–1749), was born of French parents at Zell in Hanover, where his father was a hairdresser. As a young man he became a virtuoso on the oboe, being appointed Court musician to Prince George of Denmark at the age of nineteen. Later he travelled to London and became leader of the orchestra to Queen Anne. Galliard died in London, having been noted in this country principally as a composer of theatre music. A full account of his activities in this field will be found in Grove's *Dictionary*.

HOTTETERRE. Between the mid-17th and late 18th centuries a dozen or more members of the Norman family of Hotteterre served in the Royal Music of France. Besides being most able musicians, a number of them were particularly distinguished as instrument makers and turners. Instrument making was indeed traditional in this family, and was practised also by several members of a collateral branch who did not enter the Royal service. A very full study of them all has been made by Ernest Thoinan.[5]

From the point of view of oboe history the most important Hotteterres are Jean I (?–*c.* 1678), first of the main branch of the family, his second son, Nicolas I (?–*c.* 1694), and his grandson, Jacques (?–*c.* 1761). Jean I was a most outstanding maker, as is proved by a number of his instruments still to be seen in different Continental collections, and both he and his son are highly praised in Borjon's *Traité de la Musette* of 1672. 'The father', says that writer, 'is a man of unique talent for the making of all kinds of instruments of wood, ivory and ebony: bagpipes (musettes), recorders, flageolets, oboes, crumhorns . . .' This is the man whom Josef Marx has singled out as possibly the father (with Philidor) of the true three-jointed oboe.[6] Jean's third son Martin gained particular fame as a player on this form of bagpipe and he improved the instrument greatly in a number of ways. The family indeed, as a whole, seem to have had a special gift for bagpipe playing which was exceedingly fashionable in Court circles in their time, and in this aptitude some musicologists claim to recognise a legacy from their French provincial origin.

Jacques, who was Martin's son, assumed that name also on his father's death. In his youth he spent a long period in Rome, whence he was later distinguished by the sobriquet 'Le Romain'. From 1705 to 1707 he served in the band of the Grande Ecurie, playing the basse de hautbois. He was, however, particularly remarkable as a performer on the transverse flute, and many authorities hold that his skill on that instrument hastened the demise of the flute-à-bec. Be that as it may, his *Principes*, published in 1707, treated in great detail of both instruments. The same work includes a short article on the hautbois, and the writer points out many affinities with the transverse flute, deriving all the natural fingerings save one from his tablature for that instrument. He postulates a compass of *c'* to *d'''*, a whole tone more than admitted by several later teachers, though he omits the low *c♯*. In addition to the instruction book Hotteterre-le-Romain wrote a considerable quantity of music with important parts for oboe, as well as sonatas and suites for flutes with *continuo*. He has sometimes been credited with the invention of a double chanter with six keys applied to the musette, but most leading authorities, including Constant Pierre, believe this to have been the work of his father Martin I.

CHEDEVILLE. The three brothers *Chédeville* (another typically Norman name) were also musette and oboe players in the French royal service. The eldest was born in 1694 and died in 1725, while the youngest lived until 1782-3. Besides being contemporaries of the younger Hotteterres, they were connected with them by marriage. Again Ernest Thoinan is our best authority.

HOFFMANN. According to tradition, one of the most important contributors to the advancement of the oboe in the 18th century was *Gerhard Hoffmann* (1690-1757). Born at Rastenburg, Thuringia, Hoffmann was one of those remarkable products of the late Baroque period, a man of outstanding accomplishment in both the arts and sciences, with gifts also as a leader of men. At Jena he studied mathematics and architecture, and in 1719, as architect or surveyor, he entered the service of the Duke of Weimar. Under the *Capellemeister*, J. W. Drese,[7] he studied musical theory, later turning to the composition of cantatas and other church music. Hoffmann also turned his attention to the defects of the instruments of his time and is reputed to have made improvements to both the flute and the oboe. It has often been said, mainly on the evidence of Walther's manuscript (Chapter 4, p. 40), that in 1717 he added keys for *g♯* and *b♭* to the oboe. Unfortunately no oboes so equipped are known earlier than the end of the 18th century, while Walther's notes are so ambiguous that modern musicologists frankly admit that they cannot interpret them

M

adequately. This may well be doing an injustice to Hoffmann, but the most that we may safely say is that he seems to have devised some method of improving the intonation of the enharmonics $g\sharp$ and $a\flat$. In 1736 Hoffmann was elected burgomaster of his native town, where, at the age of sixty-seven, he died.

SAMMARTINI (*San Martini*), *Giuseppe* (*c.* 1693–*c.* 1750) was a composer and oboist of Milan whose works, together with those of his brother, were much esteemed in England in the first half of the 18th century. His chief interest to us here lies in the quality of his playing. According to Dr. Burney, who is our chief source of information, his performance was superior to anything that had been heard previously in this country, being marked by a refinement of tone which was evidently unusual at the time. Some of Sammartini's contemporaries believed that his fine effect was due to a secret method of manipulating the reed before inserting it in the instrument. It seems more likely, however, that he was an unusually skilful reed maker who appreciated more than most the tonal effect of subtle adjustments to the size and scrape of the blades. There are some disagreements among historians as to Sammartini's dates, Hawkins placing his first arrival in England as 1729, while Burney makes it six years earlier.[8] According to Quantz he was to be heard in Milan in 1726, while he published twelve sonatas in London towards the end of 1727. He was well received by leading musicians in this country, and through the influence of Bononcini obtained a place as oboist at the opera. Having relinquished this post, Sammartini was fortunate in gaining the patronage of Frederick, Prince of Wales, and entered his household as musical director of the Chamber concerts.

VINCENT, *Thomas* (*c.* 1720–83), another oboist and composer, became the pupil of Sammartini. According to Dr. Burney, again our chief informant, the Sammartini method which Vincent had learnt raised the oboe to a position of eminence as a solo instrument. On the other hand, W. T. Parke (*q.v.*) clearly had a poor opinion of Vincent's tone in spite of his prominent position in London music before the arrival of J. C. Fischer. Together with Festing the violinist, and Weideman the flautist, Vincent was one of the founders of the charitable fund which in April 1738 became the Royal Society of Musicians. It is said that these three were moved to inaugurate their fund by the desperate straits of the orphan children of KYTCH, another oboist of great repute in his day.

QUANTZ. Although famous above all as a flautist, *Johann Joachim Quantz* deserves to be noted also as a player on the oboe. Full details of his life will be found in article 838 of Rockstro's monumental volume on the flute, together with many references. It is sufficient to mention here that, having studied the violin, violoncello, viola da gamba, trumpet, and oboe from the age of ten, he obtained an engagement to play the latter instrument in the Royal Chapel at Warsaw in 1718. The following year he returned to Dresden, a city which had attracted him from his earliest independent days. In 1719 also he adopted the flute as his chief instrument. By March 1728 he had completely abandoned the oboe, since he found that it interfered with the perfection of the flute playing to which he was now devoted. Quantz was born at Oberscheden in Hanover in 1697 of quite humble parents and died at Potsdam in 1773 having achieved fame, fortune, and honour.

BESOZZI. A notable Italian family of reed and flute players whose activities in Turin, Parma, Dresden, and Paris extended from the early 18th century till nearly the end of the 19th. The first two generations of the family, to which the most outstanding players belonged, could have known only the two-keyed oboe. Their performances and compositions are better documented than most, and are therefore valuable as evidence of what this instrument could do in the hands of experts. The earlier Besozzis were renowned for the technical brilliance of their playing, though some critics condemned it as flashy and noisy. (See Braun below.) In Great Britain the style and virtuosity of the Besozzis were much admired, and Gaetano, the youngest of four brothers of the first generation, ended his career in London, where he died in 1798. Carlo (son of Antonio, the second brother), who was born during his father's tenure of a post in the Dresden Court band, was especially noted for his phenomenal dynamic range and endurance. In *The Present State of Music* (France and Italy), Burney writes with admiration of three of the Besozzis whom he had heard and in particular, in 1770, of an oboe concerto played by 'Besozzi, nephew of the celebrated bassoon and oboist of Turin'. No doubt Burney's enthusiasm together with Gaetano's example influenced English taste for some considerable period. Probably the last Besozzi to call for particular notice here is Louis-Désiré. He was born at Versailles in 1814 and, after winning a Grand Prix de Rome, devoted a long life almost exclusively to teaching. He died in Paris in 1879.

M 2

FISCHER, *Johann Christian* (1733–1800), though born a German at Freiburg-im-Breisgau, established his home and spent the latter part of his life in England. Here he was greatly admired, and became probably the most influential oboist of the 18th century. In spite of almost Johnsonian eccentricities, he was accepted in quite distinguished social and intellectual circles and (rather against her father's will) married Mary Gainsborough, daughter of the celebrated painter.[9]

Authorities differ strongly in their opinions of Fischer's style and tone, and contemporary reports should be read with due regard to the circumstances and manners of the time. In his youth Mozart expressed great admiration for Fischer but later in life criticised him strongly in a letter to his father, Leopold.[10] Some recent critics have tried to interpret Burney's verbose comparison of Fischer and Carlo Besozzi to the disadvantage of the former, but in his favour we have the direct testimony of the younger Parke, who, as a prominent London oboist in Fischer's day, would appear to have no reason to accord undue praise. Parke was at times an acid commentator yet he wrote, 'the tone of Fischer was soft and sweet, his style expressive, and his execution was at once neat and brilliant'. It is known that in his last years Fischer's powers failed rapidly, though he continued, as many other artists have done, to make public appearances. This was probably against his own best interests and he may indeed have already been declining when Mozart penned his bitter comments. He died, it is said, on April 29th 1800, following on an apoplexy which occurred while he was playing a difficult solo at a concert in the presence of the King and Queen.

BARTH, *Christian Samuel* (1735–1809), was born at Glauchau in Saxony, and became a scholar under J. S. Bach at the St. Thomas School, Leipzig. He soon became an oboist of distinction and began also to compose for the instrument. As a player he was successively employed in the Court bands at Rudolstadt, Weimar, Hanover, Cassel, and finally Copenhagen. His son *Philipp* was born at Cassel and also became a notable oboist. He later succeeded his father in the Copenhagen appointment.

RAMM, *Friedrich* (1744?–1811), was born at Mannheim. At the age of fourteen he was appointed to the celebrated electoral orchestra there, a very remarkable distinction for one so young, and he remained a member throughout its finest period. In 1760 Ramm, then sixteen years old, made his first concert tour, visiting

Frankfurt-on-Main and later The Hague, where he played before the hereditary Governor, the Prince of Orange. In 1722 he visited the Court of Joseph II at Vienna and appeared also in Paris and Bologna.

The removal of the Electoral Court from Mannheim to Munich caused Ramm to transfer his activities to that city in 1779. Throughout his career he repeatedly obtained leave of absence to tour in Europe, no inconsiderable favour in those days of musical patronage. In 1784 he was able to accept an invitation to go to London as a soloist and the following year he accompanied his friend the eminent violinist Carl Cannabich to Rome and Naples.

In the mid-1770s Ramm was a regular visitor in the household of Christian Cannabich, father of the violinist and at that period director of music to the Elector. There he made the acquaintance of the young Mozart, who presented him with a concerto for the oboe which became a favourite item in his repertoire.[10]

PARKE, *John* (1745–1829) and *William Thomas* (1762–1847), were two brothers prominent as oboists in London in the late 18th and early 19th centuries. Of the elder Parke's manner of playing we have little evidence save some complimentary notices in news-sheets, etc. It is recorded, however, that he was a pupil of *Redmond* SIMPSON, whose tone was considerably disparaged by the younger brother. In his *Musical Memoirs* (London, 1830), writing of Fischer, William Parke says: 'He arrived in this country in very favourable circumstances, the oboe not being in a high state of cultivation, the two principal players, Vincent and Simpson, using the old English oboe, an instrument which in shape and tone bore some resemblance to that *yclept* a post-horn'. Unfortunately we have no accurate contemporary description of this 'old English oboe' nor any idea of how, if at all, it differed from the instruments of visiting foreign artists. In the latter part of the 18th century it can hardly have been the same instrument to which Dr. Talbot applied the name in 1700.

*W. T.* PARKE studied the oboe under the guidance of his elder brother, and obtained his first regular engagement as a principal oboe player at the age of twenty. According to his own account he excited great admiration by his abilities in the extreme register of the instrument, extending its compass to $g'''$, which he claimed had not been done before. An oboe with an unusual $c^\sharp$ key, bearing his name, is noticed in Chapter V. Parke's other claim to fame rests on his *Musical Memoirs* mentioned above. Though much that he wrote is no more than racy and slightly malicious gossip, the memoirs of one who was for forty years principal oboe at the Theatre Royal, Covent Garden, are valuable to the historian as a supplement and corrective to the more ponderous and sometimes irritating contemporary writers.

LEBRUN, *Ludwig August* (1759–1824), like a number of other 18th-century instrumental virtuosi, was also a composer. In addition to playing officially in the Court orchestras of his native Mannheim and of Munich, he toured frequently as a soloist in Germany and other European countries. He died in Berlin.

In 1790 Lebrun was succeeded in the Munich orchestra by *Anton* FLADT, born in Mannheim in 1775 and a pupil of Ramm in Munich. He appeared also in Paris and London with the greatest success.

At this point strict chronology would require the introduction of Antoine Sallantin, professor of the oboe at the foundation of the Paris Conservatoire, and the first of a line of distinguished teachers who have maintained unbroken the tradition of the French school until the present day. Because of this very continuity, however, it seems best to treat all the Conservatoire men as a group, and I have therefore placed them together at the end of this chapter.

BRAUN, *Johann Friedrich* (1759–1824), born at Cassel, held during his lifetime posts in various German court orchestras. Braun is another player concerning whom historians differ. He was, according to Bechler and Rahm, at first a pupil of Philipp Barth, but comparison of dates sheds some doubt on this. The reference in *die Oboe*[11] is not clearly worded, and it seems unlikely that in normal circumstances a budding instrumentalist should become the pupil of a man fourteen years his junior. It is possible that his instructor was in fact C. S. Barth.

Later on Braun went to Dresden at the expense of the Landgrave of Hesse-Cassel to study under Carlo Besozzi, but their association did not last long. Braun regarded the bravura of the Besozzis as trivial and foreign to the true nature of the oboe, and his influence, which later in life was considerable, tended to foster a quiet and pastoral style of playing. Braun's two sons, *Carl Anton Philipp* (1788) and *Wilhelm* (1791), both born at Ludwigsluft, became in their turn notable oboists, the elder at Copenhagen and the younger in his native town, Berlin and Stockholm. Both adhered closely to their father's style and opinions.

GARNIER, *Joseph François* (1759–1825), a pupil of Sallantin, was noted both as a teacher and a performer. His *Méthode*, through its publication in Berlin in German translation, makes an interesting link between the French and German schools of playing and seems to suggest that in his day at least the two ideals of tone were not so divergent as they were later to become.

GRIESBACH. An instrumentalist of evident importance in England, but one concerning whom we have no very satisfactory data, is *Johann Friedrich Alexander Griesbach* (?–1824). He is on record as a member of the Royal Society of Musicians in 1794, as first oboe in the Opera before 1808, and with the Philharmonic Society from 1813 to 1821. Griesbach appears to have been a man of generous disposition and possibly of some humour, for Parke relates that in 1808, when the great Catalani was at the height of her power and popularity, she exerted her influence to place her brother, a quite inferior oboist, in the first desk at the Opera House. Griesbach not only accepted the second position gracefully but helped the usurper out in passages beyond his ability, a point which could not fail to be remarked in orchestral circles.

It is generally held that Griesbach was the last outstanding player in this country to use the old-fashioned broad reed, a conclusion supported by an article published in *The Harmonicon* for 1830. The writer recalls Griesbach's clear and powerful tone, which he attributes to 'a large and strong reed' and then goes on to speak of his successor, *H. A.* GRATTAN-COOKE (1808–89), whose reed, he says, was smaller and finer. This smaller reed was, however, almost certainly used with a heavy English instrument with eight or nine keys—the type which was so soon to be replaced in this country by the first Triébert models, and which has been likened to 'a kitchen chair-leg adorned with salt spoons'. (See Plate IV, No. 2.) The late E. W. Davies gave it as his opinion that Grattan-Cooke, and possibly his contemporary, CROZIER, were the last prominent English players to stand out against the invasion of French instruments in the mid-19th century.

Although Grattan-Cooke's name appears frequently in programmes, etc., he seems to have been a much less distinguished man than Griesbach, and little is remembered now of his musical career except his friction with Mendelssohn. He died after a very long period of retirement. It has to be admitted that, with the brilliant exceptions of Barret and Lavigne, professional oboe playing in England soon after Griesbach passed into a phase of mediocrity and did not really recover until about the last twenty years of the century.

THURNER. A Continental player much esteemed at the beginning of the 19th century was *Friedrich Eugen Thurner* (1785–1827). Born in Mumpelgard, Württemberg, he studied under Ramm during his Munich period and no doubt acquired from him that quality which made the Mannheim wind players in general so much appreciated. Thurner held orchestral appointments in Vienna, where he made a great impression on Beethoven, in Brunswick, Cassel, and Frankfurt-on-Main. In this latter city he played under the direction of Spohr. In 1818 he removed to Amsterdam, where he died aged only forty-two. In spite of the shortness of his working life, Thurner gained considerable fame as a pianist and a composer in addition to his accomplishment on the oboe.

SELLNER, *Josef* (1787–1843), who may well be regarded as the father of the modern German oboe, was born at Landau in the Bavarian Palatinate. In the years 1811–17 he was principal oboe in the theatre orchestra at Prague, latterly under the direction of Weber. By 1821 Sellner was established in Vienna, the city with which he is chiefly associated in the mind of the oboe student, and there he was attached to the Court orchestra as well as being professor of the oboe and director of the students' concerts at the Conservatoire. The thirteen-keyed oboe which he perfected about this time is discussed in Chapter 5, pp. 56 and 74. Sellner's tutor for this instrument first published in 1825 became subsequently the basis of a number of standard 'methods', being translated into both French and Italian.

BROD, *Henri* (1799–1839), was a pupil of Vogt, second in the line of Professors at the Paris Conservatoire, with whom he later shared the oboe desk at the Opéra and Conservatoire concerts. In spite of the respect in which he held his master he became dissatisfied with the four-keyed oboe favoured by Vogt, and soon made valuable improvements. Although Brod died young he made a great mark as player and teacher and his *Méthode* is still valued for the excellent studies he wrote for it. (See also Chapter 5, pp. 58–61.)

SOLER. In the prize lists of the Paris Conservatoire foreign names are comparatively rare, and we notice therefore especially that of *Pierre-Joachim-Raymond (Pedro) Soler* (1810–50). Though born at Vidra in Spain, Soler's musical education was completed in Paris, where he won the first oboe prize in 1836, and thereafter joined the orchestra of the Opéra-Comique. Soler was an enthusiast for the Boehm system oboe (see Chapter 5, p. 72), and his proficiency on this instrument was much praised by *Enrique* MARZO of Madrid. Marzo was himself a distinguished oboist and teacher who in 1870 issued a tutor with a fingering chart for the oboe 'sistema Bohem segun el último modelo modificado por Triébert'. The instrument illustrated differs in some details from the Buffet-Boehm, which was apparently the type used by Soler.

LAVIGNE, *Antoine Joseph* (1816–86), was born at Besançon and received his early musical instruction from his father, a musician in an infantry regiment. He entered the Conservatoire in Paris in 1830 but his studies were interrupted in 1835 when his father's regiment was ordered from the city. In 1836 he was able to resume, however, and the next year he won the first oboe prize. Thereafter he was for several years principal oboe at the Théâtre-Italien.

It was in England, where he settled during the last forty-five years of his life, that Lavigne gained his greatest fame. In 1841 he first appeared as soloist at the Drury Lane Promenade Concerts, and from 1861 he was for many years a member of the Hallé Orchestra in Manchester. In spite of great professional ability, Lavigne in later life fell into poverty and distress, and in 1885 he was admitted to the Infirmary of St. Saviour's, Southwark. He was then transferred to the Royal Infirmary, Manchester, where he died.

About the time of Lavigne's removal to England he became much interested in the ring-key experiments which Louis Auguste Buffet was then making. Besides perfecting a ring-keyed clarinet according to the ideas of Klosé, Buffet had been in consultation with Boehm with regard to applying the latter's mechanism to the oboe. The instrument which resulted attracted Lavigne at once, and he became a complete convert, remaining faithful to this type of oboe for the rest of his life, and indeed continuing to experiment and modify till the end. (See Chapter 5, pp. 71–73.)

During his professional life Lavigne did not escape a good deal of criticism, mainly on the score of his tone, which many regarded as too loud and unyielding. Some critics laid the blame for this entirely on the instrument he favoured, though his almost fabulous lung power and endurance (he was a nose-breather) may have contributed. All are agreed, however, that he was an admirable musician with quite remarkable gifts of execution and phrasing.

LALANDE. Through his tenure of leading orchestral appointments both in the north and south of England, as well as for a time in Scotland, *Desiré Alfred Lalande* (1866–1904) had undoubtedly a profound influence on musical taste in Great Britain in the last decade of the 19th century. Born in Paris, son of a former bassoonist of the Hallé Orchestra, Lalande became a pupil of Georges Gillet. In this country his example did much to foster a preference for the French school of oboe playing at a time when in other branches of music German instrumentalists were in the ascendant. The late Edward Buttar, a man of wide practical experience and in the fullest sense an amateur of the oboe, gave it as his considered opinion that throughout his career Lalande was unquestionably the finest oboist to be heard in the United Kingdom.

DE BUESCHER. Another London player of the early 1900s who should undoubtedly be mentioned here is *Henri de Buescher*. The late Sir Henry Wood, for whom he played for some years in the old Queen's Hall orchestra, spoke of him as 'incomparable'. He was, however, possessed of a very small tone, which, for some people, detracted from an impeccable style and musicianship. Shortly before the First World War de Buescher went to America, where he became extremely influential, although he still did not escape criticism on the score of limited volume.

### English Teachers in the 19th Century

A survey of the records of the last seventy years, such as they are, suggests that the revival of a superior style of oboe playing in England followed very soon after the establishment of three important academies: the Royal and Trinity Colleges, and the Guildhall School of Music. The Royal Academy of Music had, of course, been active since 1822, and for many years after 1829 its oboe professor was A. M.-R. Barret, who has already been mentioned as one of the two exceptional men during a poor period. The three new foundations were as follows: 1872, Trinity College of Music; 1873, the National Training School of Music, reorganised as the Royal College in 1882; 1880, the Guildhall School of Music, and the opening of three such bodies in London in a single decade indicates clearly a growing recognition of the importance of proper academic instruction in all branches of the art. In 1893 the North followed with the creation of the Royal Manchester College of Music. The evident importance of the oboe in professional circles made the instrument an essential subject in the curriculum of all these institutions.

BARRET, *Apollon Marie-Rose* (1804–79), was born at Saint-Brieuc, Côtes-du-Nord, France. Like Brod and Lavigne he became a pupil of Vogt at the Paris Conservatoire, where he was first prize-man in 1824. At the conclusion of his formal studies he obtained engagements as solo oboe at the Odéon Theatre and the Opéra-Comique, but remained in Paris only a few years. London music, as it then was, offered opportunities to a young oboist of ability and, in 1829 Barret secured the first oboe desk at the Italian Opera, a position which he retained until 1874. He thus over-lapped Grattan-Cooke, and according to reports of the Royal Musical Festival, played eighth oboe to him at Westminster Abbey in 1834. At the same time he held the R.A.M. professorship already mentioned. Although quickly established as an influential London professional, Barret kept up his Paris connections, in par-ticular with the firm of Triébert, whose instruments he pushed assiduously in this country. In 1850 he published the first edition of his celebrated instruction book, and with the second (1862) he introduced his own special key system which is fully discussed in Chapter 5.

At the time of writing Barret's playing is, of course, beyond living memory, but about 1910 E. W. Davies, who heard him in his later years, described his tone as rather large but more reedy than was popular at that time when the smoothness of Gillet and La-lande was most admired. Till the very last Barret is reputed to have preserved his magnificent technique. Davies recalled that on one occasion when he met Barret in Morton's workshop the latter complimented the old man on this. Barret's reply was wryly humorous: 'Ah!' he said, 'if I play badly now people say "Poor old Barret!" and if I play well they still say "Poor old Barret!" ' Honoured by musicians the world over, Barret died, not in London as is often stated, but in Paris where he had spent the last few years of his retirement.

In 1880 the oboe teaching at the Royal Academy was placed under the care of *George* HORTON (1820–92), who had been a member of Queen Victoria's private band in the days of the Prince Consort. He is reported to have had a very reedy tone and to have been a player of no great refinement. In 1883 Horton was also given the professorship at the Royal College, thus instituting a plurality of appointment at the two schools which continued until 1931.

After the death of Horton the oboe chairs at both the Royal Academy and the Royal College passed to *William* MALSCH (1855–1924), a man who was much loved both for his personal qualities of kindness and integrity and as a great teacher. A performer of supreme technical ability and great endurance, Malsch is regarded by many as the best London player of his day, although there were some who did not altogether admire his tone. In his earlier days he used a German style oboe but about 1897 relinquished it in favour of one by a Paris maker, probably in deference to the growing popularity of French tone in this country. It is reported that the French firm were for commercial reasons most anxious to have one of their instruments in the hands of a leading English player and that Malsch rejected several examples before finding one that satisfied him and that he felt he could recommend to other players.

In 1924 both the Royal Academy and the Royal College appointed *Leon* GOOSSENS, happily still with us as the teacher of a group of players whose characteristics have brought them recognition as virtually a 'school' on their own. Goossens continued teaching at the Royal College until 1939, and was then succeeded by *William* SHEPLEY (1875–1947), who has already been mentioned in connection with the Sharpe oboe. (Chapter 5, p. 79.) Goossens had relinquished his Royal Academy appointment in 1935, being followed by *Alec* WHITTAKER.

As regards oboe teaching in the other two London schools, Trinity College and the Guildhall, it was again Malsch who guided matters in their early days. He was appointed professor at Trinity in 1880, having as his assistant after a few years *A. J. B.* DUBRUCQ and being followed in 1924 by *J. A.* McDONAGH. By the 1890s Dubrucq had removed to Manchester and was no longer to be heard in London, save at the Opera. There, however, he was supreme, and it is recorded that more than once eminent visiting singers interrupted rehearsals to come down to the footlights and applaud the oboist. A contemporary has described his tone as 'simply heavenly' and his technique as equally beyond reproach.

At the Guildhall School Malsch was named professor at the foundation but was joined in 1889 by *George* FORMAN. The latter was a devotee of automatic octave mechanism and designed a particularly ingenious system which both he and his son used. Malsch and Forman retired together from the Guildhall in 1910 and were replaced by *Arthur* FORMAN.

From the foregoing we can conclude that without doubt William

Malsch was the most influential oboe teacher of his time in this country.  For seventeen years he had the unique distinction of directing the oboe studies simultaneously in all four of London's leading academies as well as playing in the most important concerts.  In consequence he started on their careers a large number of pupils, many of whom attained distinction in later life.

The first professor of the oboe to be named in the records of the Royal Manchester College of Music is *Charles* REYNOLDS (1843–1916), who was already a well-known player of many years standing when the College was founded.  A member of the Hallé Orchestra from the season of 1871–2 till his death, Reynolds played beside Lavigne for six years, and it is not impossible that he was a good deal influenced by this partnership.  Edward Buttar, who frequently heard him play in the early 1900s, stated that Reynolds then had a very large and broad tone (which would, of course, have been necessary to balance with Lavigne) as well as quite remarkable technical ability.  It has already been observed that Hans Richter was particularly impressed by Reynolds' performance at Covent Garden where he appeared season after season for many years, and it may well be that his somewhat Germanic tone appealed especially to the great conductor.  It seems unlikely that the actual oboe used had much influence on Reynolds' tone, for, although he employed a key-system modified according to his own ideas, he did not favour the large bore and note-holes of Lavigne.  Reynolds' professorship in Manchester dated from 1898, and during his tenure he taught a considerable number of young players who later became important, among them Leon Goossens. His successors were, in 1917 *Arthur* NICHOLLS, and in 1926 *Stephen* WHITTAKER, whose own key-system has also been noticed in a previous chapter.

## Professors at the Paris Conservatoire

Since its foundation in 1793 the fountain-head of French oboe playing has always been the Paris Conservatoire.  Its teachers have each in turn been eminent men whose influence has been felt far beyond the frontiers of their own country, and their names cannot be omitted from any commentary on the instrument.  The present account is necessarily much condensed but detailed information is readily available in musical dictionaries etc.[12]

As might be expected, the Paris Professors have had much influence on the physical growth of the French oboe.  Doubtless the

conservatism of the earlier ones held up its mechanical development for some years but, on the other hand, later men, such as
Charles Triébert, were associated with the most revolutionary
innovations. These matters have been discussed in Chapter 5
under 'The Rise of the French Oboe'.

The sequence of teachers at the Conservatoire began with
*Antoine* SALLANTIN (1754–*post* 1816) already a noted Paris instru-
mentalist when he was appointed to the Chair at its foundation.
He occupied a leading place in the Opéra orchestra from 1773 till
1813, and is known to have used an oboe with only four keys.
Sallantin studied with Fischer in London from 1790 to 1792.

Concurrently with that of Sallantin two other names appear in
the records of the Conservatoire as professors of the oboe. They
are *P.* DELCAMBRE, from 1795 to 1802, and — SCHNEITZHOFFER,
1800 to 1802. These men appear to have held a sort of parallel
appointment with the first professor as did VOGT for several years
before he succeeded to the Chair.

The life of the second professor, *Auguste-Gustave* VOGT (1781–
1870), is particularly interesting as showing the vicissitudes
through which a musician might pass in those days of political
upheaval in Europe. Born in Strasbourg, Vogt gained the first
oboe prize in 1799 and then became principal oboe in the imperial
chapel and private band, retaining this position until 1814 and
during the Hundred Days. 'Musician 1st class' in the Foot
Grenadiers of the Imperial Guard, Vogt found himself in Milan
for Napoleon's coronation and then received his discharge in 1808.
In 1814 he occupied the first oboe desk in the royal chapel but was
'purged' for suspected Bonapartist opinions and for having, as an
Imperial Guard, fought against the invading armies supporting
Louis XVIII. The post was restored to him in 1819 and he retained it until 1830. From 1839 till 1848 he was again a member of
a royal private band, this time of Louis-Philippe.

In addition to the various military appointments listed above,
Vogt occupied a number of distinguished civilian posts. He
belonged to the orchestra of the Opéra-Comique from 1803; transferred to the Opéra from 1812 to 1834; was solo oboe to the Société
des Concerts in 1828; and made a first appearance in London with
the Philharmonic Society in 1825. His association with the faculty
of the Conservatoire began in 1802, when he was appointed joint
Professor, and from 1816 to 1853 he held the position absolutely.
He also was a confirmed devotee of the four-keyed oboe.

VERROUST, *Stanislas* (1814–63), was born and died at Haze-brouck. He studied under Vogt, becoming first prize-man in 1834, and thereafter, like his master, held both civil and military appointments. He became Professor at the Conservatoire in 1853 and held the position for ten years.

TRIÉBERT, *Charles-Louis* (1810–67), was the elder son of Guillaume Triébert, founder of the celebrated Paris firm of wind instrument makers. He too was a pupil of Vogt and won the first prize at the Conservatoire in 1829, five years ahead of Verroust, whom he was afterwards to succeed. Although born into the instrument-making business, and later a partner in the family concern, he preferred the life of a virtuoso performer. Between 1830 and 1850 Triébert appeared in the orchestras of the Opéra-Comique, the Opéra, and the Théâtre-Italien, and then with the Société des Concerts in 1853. He was appointed to the Conservatoire chair in 1863 and held it till his death four years later.

BERTHELEMY, *Felix Charles* (1829–68), another Conservatoire first prize-man, was born at Saint-Omer. He completed his academic studies in 1849, and from 1855 till 1868 had a distinguished career in the Opéra and with the Société des Concerts. Berthélemy was appointed to the Conservatoire in 1867, on the death of Triébert, but survived less than a year.

Probably the most remarkable academic career of any of the Paris professors was that of *Charles Joseph* COLIN (1832–81), sixth holder of the oboe chair at the Conservatoire. Born at Cherbourg, his musical studies took him to Paris, where at the age of twenty he won the first oboe prize, the next year those for harmony and accompaniment, and at twenty-two that for the organ. In 1857 he crowned his successes by winning the second Grand Prix de Rome. Colin directed the teaching of the oboe at his former academy from 1868 till his death in 1881.

On the death of Colin the Conservatoire appointment passed to *Georges* GILLET (1854–1934), another most remarkable oboist. Gillet was born at Louviers in the département de l'Eure, but his precocity in music soon brought him to Paris. He entered the Conservatoire at an unusually early age, gaining the first oboe prize when only fifteen. At twenty he was solo oboe at the Théâtre-Italien. His further career was equally brilliant. He was in 1872 a founder of the Colonne concerts, where he remained as solo oboe for four years, and then held the same position with the Société des

Concerts until 1899. In addition he was soloist at the Opéra-Comique and later, between 1878 and 1904, at the Opéra.

The delicacy of Gillet's tone has often been praised, indeed it was sometimes described as almost 'fluty', while his technical mastery is witnessed by the series of supremely difficult studies he published in 1909.

In 1881 Gillet was appointed professor at the Conservatoire, and at this time he introduced the 'Système 6' oboe of Triébert as the standard instrument for all his pupils. He retired from the professorship in January 1929, being followed by L. F. A. BLEUZET (1874–    ). Gillet died five years later, after an unusually long and distinguished professional career.

[1] See also A. Pougin, 'André Philidor' in *La Chronique Musicale* for 1871 and G. E. Bonnet, 'Philidor et l'évolution de la musique française au XVIIIᵉ Siècle', Paris, 1921.
*N.B.* Eitner has erroneously attributed the 'France Musicale' articles mentioned in the text (p. 158) to Pougin.

[2] *Galpin Society Journal*, Vol. IV, 1951, p. 13.

[3] *Ibid.*

[4] W. J. Lawrence in *Mus. Ant.*, Vol. II, pp. 57 and 241; Vol. III, p. 177; and Vol. LV, p. 191.

[5] E. Thoinan, *Les Hotteterre et les Chédeville*. E. Sagot, Paris, 1894, (limited edition). N. Mauger, supplement to above. Fischbacher, Paris, 1912.

[6] *Galpin Society Journal*, Vol. LV, 1951, pp. 11 *et seq.*
It should be noted that in 17th- and 18th-century France the term *musette* was applied to a most elegant and refined form of bagpipe blown by bellows held under the arm and not, as today, to the small pastoral oboe. As late as 1769, and possibly after, a musette player was listed among the staff musicians attached to the Paris Opéra.

[7] Until his death in December 1716 Johann Samuel Drese was Capellmeister to the Duke of Weimar, with his son, Johann Wilhelm, as his deputy. In 1714 J. S. Bach, who had formerly been simply a member of the Duke's select string orchestra, was appointed Concertmeister, a post which carried additional duties as a composer. On Drese's death Bach had hoped to succeed to the directorate but was passed over in favour of the less gifted Johann Wilhelm.
See C. Sandford Terry's *Bach's Orchestra*, O.U.P., London, 1932, p. 4.

[8] Sir John Hawkins, *A General History of the Science and Practice of Music*, London, 1776.
Dr. Charles Burney, *A General History of Music*, London, 1776.

[9] See *Memoire of Dr. Burney*, by Mme. D'Arblay. Also *Parke's Musical Memoirs*, London, 1830, Vol. I, pp. 334 *et seq.*

[10] See Mozart's letters to his father February 14th and April 4th, 1778. *The Letters of Mozart*, ed. Hans Mersmann, translated into English by M. M. Bozman, J. M. Dent, London, 1928.

[11] Bechler and Rahm, *Die Oboe*, Merseburger, Leipzig, 1914, p. 28.

[12] In particular the *Encyclopedie* of Lavignac and de la Laurencie, Delagrave, Paris, 1927. (Article contributed by L. F. A. Bleuzet.)
Constant Pierre, *Le Conservatoire National—Documents Historiques et Administratifs*, Imprimerie Nationale, Paris, 1900.

# The Musical Instrument Trade in 19th-Century France and Germany

ALTHOUGH the different circumstances affecting wind-instrument making in France and German-speaking Europe between 1800 and 1880 are clearly to be discerned in the general music literature of the period, it has been felt necessary to make some comparative analysis of properly authenticated data.

As an experiment, therefore, twenty-four pages were taken at random from the most complete list of wind-instrument makers at present available (Lyndesay G. Langwill, Edinburgh; first issued privately, cyclo-styled, in 1941 and revised and supplemented at intervals up to date). From these all the names of makers definitely known to have been working in France and Germany between 1800 and 1850 were extracted and tabulated. As a result the names of fifty-one French domiciled manufacturers appear as against fifty-three German. Of the French list forty-four show Paris addresses and seven provincial ones. The German makers are distributed over no less than ten different States, taking Prussia collectively.

Taken a stage farther, the analysis showed that, of the German towns concerned, Dresden and Munich had by far the largest number of instrument makers. This would seem to be in keeping with the leading position taken by these centres in the orchestral music of the time. The pre-eminence of Munich, it will be recalled, began with the transfer thither from Mannheim of the Electoral Court in 1778. As the musical fame of Munich increased, so that of Mannheim declined, showing very clearly the effects of princely patronage on the Arts in Germany even as late as the Classical period.

Such an experiment as the above can, of course, be only rough and ready, but the resultant figures are none the less interesting as indicating a reason for the inconsistency between different makes of German oboe in the years after Sellner. (See pp. 74–76 *ante.*)

# A Selective Bibliography of the Oboe
# (Short Title)

THE following list is divided for convenience into four sections: A. Instruction Books and Tutors, but excluding technical exercises pure and simple; B. Works valuable mainly for their historical or descriptive matter; C. Technical works; D. Catalogues of Collections and Exhibitions, and Commentaries thereon. No claim is made as regards completeness, but all works which I have found of most general value or interest under each heading are included. In a number of cases secondary or specialist references will be found in the chapter notes. With one or two important exceptions printed articles in foreign languages other than French, German, or Italian are not included. Wherever known, dates and the names of publishers are indicated.

As regards *music* for the oboe it has been thought best to attempt no new list. As recently as 1953 an excellent detailed table of nearly five hundred items compiled by Evelyn Rothwell has been published as an appendix to her *Oboe Technique* (O.U.P.) and readers will find additional material in Philipp Losch's supplement to *Die Oboe* by Bechler and Rahm (Merseburger, Leipzig, 1914) and in W. Altmann's *Kammermusik Katalog* (Merseburger, 1931) and Supplement (Hofmeister, Leipzig, 1936).

The comparatively few tablatures and instruction books for the oboe which appeared in the 17th and 18th centuries refer, of course, to the two and three-keyed instrument only. It is thought that the similarity between some of them, as well as their minor variations, may best be appreciated by considering them in order of publication and they are therefore listed here in that way. In the remainder of the bibliography the customary alphabetical arrangement is used.

## A. Tutors and Fingering Charts (18th Century)

Anon. *Plain and Easie Directions—to learn the French Hautboy.* (Known only from the Term Catalogue for May 1695 and possibly never issued.) *Henry Playford, London.*

Banister, John? *The Sprightly Companion——.*
*Henry Playford, London, 169⁵*

*Military Music or the Art of playing on the Haut-bois explained——.* (Known only from the Term Catalogue.)
*Thomas Crosse, London, 1697.*

*The Second Book of Theatre Music—proper to play on ye HAUTBOY—a scale is added—.* (This scale forms the basis of all English instructions as late as 1757 and may be derived from the Crosse publication above.)
*John Walsh, London, 1699.*

*The James Talbot Manuscript* (Christ Church MS 1187). Tablature provided by Mr. la Riche, *c.* 1695–1700.

Freillon Poncein, Jean-Pierre. *La Véritable Manière d'apprendre à jouer en perfection du Hautbois.* *Colombat, Paris, 1700.*

Hotteterre-le-Romain. *Principes de la Flute Traversière—et du Haut-bois.*
*Christophe Ballard, Paris,* 1707, 1713, 1722.
*Estienne Roger, Amsterdam,* 1708.
New edition with added tablature for Clarinet and Bassoon.
*Bailleux, Paris, c.* 1765.
Reprinted in facsimile from the Amsterdam version and German translation by H. J. Hellwig.                                    *Cassel,* 1941.
Anon. *Complete Tutor to the Hautboy.* (Possibly derived from the Crosse publication above, reprinted several times since 1750.)
*Walsh and Hare, London, c.* 1715.
Prelleur. *The Modern Music Master.* (Oboe section derived verbatim from the *Compleat Tutor.* According to Dayton C. Miller the Flute matter is taken from Hotteterre-le-Romain via an English translation of *Les Principes* issued by Walsh and Hare in 1729.) *London, c.* 1731.
Eisel. *Musicus Autodidaktos.*                              *Erfurt,* 1738.
Minguet Y Yrol. *Reglas, y Advertencias Generales que ensenan el modo de taner todos los instrumentos mejores——etc.*      *Madrid,* 1754, 1774.
? Charles, *Apollo's Cabinet or the Muses Delight.* (Doublets of *The Modern Music Master.*)          *Mr. Charles, Liverpool,* 1754, 1757.
Anon. *New and Complete Instructions.* London, various imprints. (Attributed to J. C. Fischer, or at least supervised by him for the original publishers.)                           *Longman and Lukey, c.* 1772.
*Longman and Broderip, c.* 1780.
*T. Cahusac, c.* 1790.
*Muzio Clementi,* 1802.


*19th Century and after—alphabetical order*

Anon. *Gamme pour le Hautbois.*                          *Andre, Paris.*
*Schott, Mainz.*
*Gamme pour le Hautbois à 14 Clefs.*                     *Schott, Mainz.*
*Gamme f.d. Hoboe.*                                 *Gombart, Augsburg.*
*Tabelle aller Griffe.*                                 *Diabelli, Vienna.*
*Tabelle aller ausfuhrbaren Triller.*                     *Diabelli, Vienna.*
*Tabelle fur die Hoboe.*                               *Cranz, Hamburg.*
*Heckel, Biebrich-am-Rhein.*
*Zimmermann, Leipzig,* 1891.
*Tablature de Hautbois (Système Conservatoire et Système G. Gillet.)*
*Leduc-Bertrand, Paris,* 1910.
*Tonleiter für die Oboe*                               *Bachmann, Hanover.*
*Witzendorf, Vienna.*


Asioli, B. *Tavola—dell' Oboe moderno.*                    *Ricordi, Milan.*
*Breve Metodo.*                                        *Ricordi, Milan.*
Barret, A. M.-R. *A Complete Method for the Oboe.* 2nd edn. (enlarged).
*Jullien and Co., London,* 1852.
*Lafleur and Son,* 1860.
Barth, L. *Theoret-prakt. Schule fur Oboe.*         *Koster, Pankow,* 1907.
Bas, L. *Méthode nouvelle de Hautbois.*            *Enoch et Cie., Paris.*
Brod, H. *Grande Méthode.*                  *Schonenberger, Paris,* 1835.
Capelli, G. *Metodo teorico-practico.*                     *Ricordi, Milan.*
Garimond, H. *Méthode elémentaire.*                      *Leduc, Paris.*
Garnier, F. J. *Méthode de Hautbois.*            *Andre, Paris, c.* 1800.
*Extrait de la Méthode.*                               *Andre, Paris.*
Gillet, F. *Méthode pour le debut du Hautbois.*      *Leduc, Paris,* 1940.
Hinke, G. *Praktische Elementarschule.*            *Peters, Leipzig,* 1888.

Hofmann, R.  *Kurtzgefasste Schule für Oboe.*    *Domkowsky,* 1902.
Kastner, G.  *Metodo elementare p. Oboe.*    *Ricordi, Milan.*
Kling, H.  *Grifftabelle für Oboe.*    *Oertel, Berlin,* 1894.
Kuffner, J.  *Principes—et Gamme de Hautbois.*    *Schotts Sohne, Mainz.*
    *Oboeschule.*    *Schotts Sohne, Mainz,* 1894.
Langey, O.  *Tutor for the Oboe.*    *Riviere and Hawkes, London,* 1885.
    *Tutor for the Oboe.*  (Revised edition.)  *Hawkes and Son, London,* 1911.
Mariani, G.  *Método poplare p. Oboe.*    *Ricordi, Milan, c.* 1900.
Marzo, E.  *Método de Oboé.*    *Romero, Madrid,* 1870.
Mazarov, N.  *Shkola dlia Goboya.*  Vol. 1.    *Muzgiz, Moscow,* 1939.
    *Shkola dlia Goboya.*  Vol. 2.    1941.
Nemetz, A.  *Allgem. Musikschule f. Militarmusik.*
    *Diabelli, Vienna,* 1844.
Niemann, T.  *Oboeschule.*    *Zimmermann, Leipzig,* 1899.
Parès, G.  *Cours d'ensemble instrumental. Hautbois.*
    *Lemoine, Paris,* 1899.
Petrow, J.  *Tonleiterschule.*    *Zimmermann, Leipzig,* 1912.
Pietzsch, G.  *Schule fur Oboe.*    *Hofmeister, Leipzig,* 1911.
Reinhardt, A.  *Theor.-prakt. Oboeschule.*    *Benjamin, Hamburg,* 1912.
Rosenthal, R.  *Grosse praktikalische Oboeschule.*
    *Schmidt, Heilbronn,* 1908.
Salviani, C.  *Metodo completo p. Oboe.*    *Ricordi, Milan.*
Schubert, F.  *Praktikalische Oboeschule.*    *Merseburger, Leipzig.*
Sellner, J.  *Theor.-prakt. Oboeschule.*    *Diabelli, Vienna,* 1825.
    *Theor.-prakt. Oboeschule.*  (New edn. revised Rosenthal.)
    *Schotts Sohne, Mainz,* 1901–3.
    *Theor.-prakt. Oboeschule.*  (Original edn. in Italian translation.)
    *Ricordi, Milan, c.* 1827.
Singer, S.  *Méthode pour Hautbois.*    *Gebethner, Warsaw,* 1913.
Veny, L.  *Méthode complète pour le Hautbois.*    *Cotelle, Paris.*
Vogt, A.-G.  *Méthode*  (MSS. according to Bleuzet.)    *c.* 1813.

### B.  Historical and Descriptive

Agricola, M.  *Musica Instrumentalis deudsch.*
    *Wittemberg,* 1528, 1532, 1542, 1545.
    *Musica Instrumentalis deudsch.*  (Reprint in facsimile.)
    *Breitkipf and Hartel, Leipzig,* 1896.
Apel, W.  *The Harvard Dictionary of Music.*    *Cambridge, Mass.,* 1945.
Bonanni, F.  *Gabinetto armonico.*    *Rome,* 1722.
Brancour.  *Histoire des Instruments de Musique.*  *H. Laurens, Paris,* 1921.
Burney, Dr. C.  *A General History of Music.*    *London,* 1776.
    *The Present State of Music in France and Italy.*    *London,* 1771.
    *The Present State of Music in Germany and the Netherlands.*
    *London,* 1773.
Carse, A.  *The History of Orchestration.*    *Macmillan, London,* 1925.
    *Musical Wind Instruments.*    *Macmillan, London,* 1939.
    *The Orchestra in the 18th Century.*    *Heffer, Cambridge,* 1940.
    *The Orchestra from Beethoven to Berlioz.*    *Heffer, Cambridge,* 1948.
Catrufo, J.  *Traité des Voix et des Instruments.*    *Paris,* 1832.
Chatwin, R. B.  *Some Notes on the History of the Oboe.*  (Ex 'Musical
    Progress and Mail'.)  *Boosey and Hawkes, London, Feb.–April,* 1939.
Cobbett, W. W.  *Cyclopedic Survey of Chamber Music.*    *Oxford,* 1929.
Comettant, O.  *Histoire d'un Inventeur (Ad. Sax).*    *Paris,* 1860.
Cucuel, G.  *Etudes sur un orchestre au 18ᵐᵉ siècle.*
    *Fischbacher, Paris,* 1913.

Dalyell, J. G. *Musical Memoirs of Scotland.*    *Pickering, London, 1849.*
Diderot and d'Alembert. *Encyclopédie.*    *Paris, 1767, 1776.*
Donnington, R. *The Instruments of Music.*    *London, 1949.*
Doppelmayr, J. *Historische Nachricht von den Nürnbergischen Mathe-
    maticis und Kunstlern.*    *Nürnberg, 1730.*
Euting, E. *Zur Geschichte der Blasinstrumente in 16 und 17 Jahrhundert.*
    *Berlin, 1899.*
Farmer, H. *Rise and Development of Military Music.*
    *W. Reeves, London, 1912.*
Fetis, F. J. *Biographie Universelle des Musiciens.*
    *Firmin-Didot, Paris, 1868.*
Francoeur, L. J. *Diapason général—des instruments à vent.*    *Paris, 1772.*
    *Traite général—des instruments d'orchestre.* (Revised by A. Choron.)
    *Paris, 1813.*
Galpin, F. W. *European Musical Instruments.*
    *Williams and Norgate, London, 1937.*
    *Old English Instruments of Music.* (3rd edn.)
    *Methuen, London, 1932.*
Gerber, E. L. *Historisch—biographisches Lexikon.*
    *E. Breitkopf, Leipzig, 1792.*
Gevaert, F. A. *Nouveau traite d'instrumentation.*    *Lemoine, Paris, 1885.*
Grove, G. *Dictionary of Music and Musicians.* (3rd edn.)
    *Macmillan & Co., London, 1927.*
Halfpenny, E. *The English Debut of the French Hautboy.* (Ex. *Monthly
    Musical Record.*)    *Augener, London, July 1949.*
    *The Tonality of Woodwind Instruments.* (Ex. *Proceedings, Royal Musical
    Association,* Vol. LXXV.)    *R.M.A., London, 1949.*
Hawkins, C. *A General History of Music.*    *London, 1876.*
Heckel, W. *Der Fagott.*    *Merseburger, Leipzig, 1899.*
    English translation by L. G. Langwill.    1931.
    Ex. *Journal of Musicology,* Vol. 11.    *Ohio, U.S.A., 1940.*
Hipkins and Gibb. *Musical Instruments, Etc.*
    *A. and C. Black, Edinburgh, 1888, 1921.*
Junker. *Musikalischer Almanach.*    1782.
Kappey, J. A. *Short History of Military Music.*
    *Boosey and Company, London, c. 1890.*
Kastner, G. *Manuel Général de Musique Militaire.*
    *Firmin-Didot, Paris, 1848.*
Kinsky, G. *A History of Music in Pictures.*    *Dent, London, 1930–37.*
Kircher, A. *Musurgia Universalis.*    *Corbeletti, Rome, 1650.*
Koch, H. *Musikalisches Lexikon.*    *Offenbach, 1802.*
Koch-Dommer. *Musikalisches Lexikon.*    *Heidelberg, 1865.*
Laborde, J. B. de. *Essai sur la Musique.*    *Paris, 1780, 1781.*
Langwill, L. J. *The Waits.* (Ex. *Music Book,* Vol. VII. Contains an im-
    portant list of local references.)    *Hinrichsen, London, 1952.*
    *Town Musicians.* (Ex. the *Scotsman.*)
    *The Waits of Exeter.* (Ex. the *Express and Echo,* December 10th, 1938.)
    *The Alto-Fagotto etc.* (Ex. *Musical Progress and Mail.*)
    *Boosey and Hawkes, London, April 1934.*
    *Two Rare Eighteenth-century London Directories.* (Ex. *Music and
    Letters.*)    *London, Jan. 1949.*
    *London Wind-instrument Makers—17th and 18th Centuries.* (Ex. *The
    Music Review,* Vol. VII.)    *Heffer, Cambridge.*
Lavoix, H. *Histoire de l'instrumentation.*    *Firmin-Didot, Paris, 1878.*
Lucinius, O. *Musurgia.*    *Joan Schött, Strassburg, 1536.*
N

Macdermott, K. H.  *Sussex Church Music in the Past.*  2nd edition.
*Moore and Wingham, Chichester,* 1923.
Majer, J.  *Neueröffneter Musik Saal.*  (2nd edition.)
*Kremer, Nürnberg,* 1741.
Marx, J.  *The Tone of the Baroque Oboe.*  (Ex. *Galpin Society Journal,* Vol. IV.)
*London,* 1951.
Mattheson, J.  *Das neueröffnete Orchestre.*  *Hamburg,* 1713.
Mersenne, M.  *Harmonie universelle.*  *Baudry, Paris,* 1636.
Miller, G.  *The Military Band.*  *Boosey and Co., London,* 1912.
Norlind, T.  *Musikinstrumentenhistoria i ord och bild.*
*Dordish Rotogravyr, Stockholm,* 1941.
Parke, W.  *Musical Memoirs.*  *Colburn and Bentley, London,* 1830.
Pierre, C.  *Les facteurs d'instruments de musique.*  *Sagot, Paris,* 1893.
Pontecoulant, L. G. le D.  *Organographie.*  *Castel, Paris,* 1861.
Praetorius, M.  *Syntagma musicum.*  *E. Holwein, Wolfenbüttel,* 1619.
Reprint.  *Trautwein, Berlin,* 1884.
Prestini, G.  *Notizie intorno alla storia degli strumenti etc.*
*Bongiovanni, Bologna,* 1925.
Profeta, R.  *Storia—degli strumenti musicali.*  *Florence,* 1952.
Redfield, J.  *Music, a science and an art.*  *Knopf, New York,* 1928.
Riemann, H.  *Musik—Lexikon.* (Various editions.)
*Mainz, Leipzig, Berlin,* 1882–1922.
Rockstro, R. S.  *A Treatise—on the Flute.*
*Rudall Carte, London,* 1890, 1928.
Sachs, C.  *Handbuch der Musikinstrumentenkunde.*
*Breitkopf, Leipzig,* 1930.
*Real-Lexikon der Musikinstrumente.*  *Berlin,* 1913.
Schlesinger, K.  *Oboe: Cor Anglais.* (Ex. *Encyclopaedia Brit.,* 11th edn.)
1910.
*Modern Orchestral Instruments.*  *W. Reeves, London,* 1910.
Schmidl, C.  *Dizionario universale dei musicisti.*  *Milan,* 1928–38.
Schneider, W.  *Historisch-Technische Beschreibung, etc.*
*Hennings, Leipzig,* 1834.
Speer, D.  *Grund-rightiger Unterricht der Musikalischen Kunst.*
*Ulm,* 1687, 1697.
Stephen, G.  *The Waits of the City of Norwich.*
*Goose and Son, Norwich,* 1933.
Sundelin.  *Die Instrumentirung—Militär Musik-Chöre.*
*Wagenfüht, Berlin,* 1828.
*Die Instrumentirung fur das Orchester.*  *Berlin,* 1828.
Terry, C. S.  *Bach's Orchestra.*  *O.U.P., London,* 1932.
Teuchert, E., and Haupt, E.  *Musik-Instrumentenkunde in Wort und Bild.*
(Vol. II.)  *Breitkopf, Leipzig,* 1911.
Virdung, S.  *Musica Getutscht.*  *Basle,* 1511.
Reprint in facsimile.  *Trautwein, Berlin,* 1882.
*Kassel,* 1931.
Wickerlin, J. B.  *Nouveau Musiciana.*  *Paris,* 1890.
Wright, R.  *Dictionaire des instruments de musique.*
*Battley Bros., London,* 1941.
Zacconi, L.  *Prattica di Musica.*  *Venice,* 1596.
Zedler.  *Universal Lexikon.*  1735.

## C. Technical

Andries.  *Apercu théorique de tous les instruments de musique.*
*Ghent,* 1856.

Berlioz, H.  *Traite de l'instrumentation.*       *Schonenberger, Paris,* 1844.
 *Instrumentationslehre. Erganstz u. revidiert von Richard Strauss.*
                                                          *Leipzig,* 1905.
Buck, Percy.  *Acoustics for Musicians.*       *O.U.P., London,* 1918.
Bonavia-Hunt, N. A.  *What is the Formant?*  (Ex. *Musical Opinion.*)
                                            *London, Dec.* 1948, *Jan.* 1949.
Forsyth, Cecil.  *Orchestration.*            *Macmillan, London,* 1922.
Hague, B.  *The Tonal Spectra of Wind Instruments.*  (Ex. *Proc. Roy. Mus.
 Ass. Session LXXIII.*)                                          1947.
Helmholtz, H. L. F. von.  *The Sensations of Tone,* trans. A. J. Ellis. (2nd
 edn.)                          *Longmans, Green and Co., London,* 1885.
Hopkins and Rimbault.  *The Organ.* (3rd edn.)
                                        *Robert Cocks, London,* 1877.
Lloyd, Ll.  *The Musical Ear.*            *O.U.P., London,* 1940.
Mackworth-Young, G.  *What Happens in Singing.*
                                        *Newman Neame, London,* 1953.
Mahillon, V.  *Elements d'acoustique.*       *Mahillon, Brussels,* 1874.
Miller, D. C.  *The Science of Musical Sounds.*
                                        *The Macmillan Co., New York,* 1922.
 *Sound Waves.*                         *The Macmillan Co., New York,* 1937.
Richardson, E. G.  *The Acoustics of Orchestral Instruments.*
                                        *Arnold, London,* 1929.
Rothwell, Evelyn.  *Oboe Technique.*         *O.U.P., London,* 1953.
Smith, Robert.  *Harmonics.*      *T. and J. Merrill, Cambridge,* 1757.
Wood, Alexander.  *The Physics of Music.*       *Methuen, London,* 1944.


                                  *Periodicals*

*Acoustical Society of America. Journal.*           *Menasha,* 1929.
*Allgemeine Musikalische Zeitung.*       *Leipzig,* 1798–1849, 1863–1882.
*Cäcilia.*                                       *Mainz,* 1824–48.
*Galpin Society Journal.*                           *London,* 1948.
*Musical Opinion.*                                   *London,* 1877.
*Royal Musical Association, Proceedings, London.*       *London,* 1875.
*Sitzungberichte der Preuss, Akad. der Wissenschaft.*       *Berlin,* 1882.
*Woodwind Magazine.*                           *New York,* 1948.
*Zeitscrift fur Instrumentenbau.*                   *Leipzig,* 1880.


D.  *Catalogues of Collections and Exhibitions (including Commentaries)*

AMSTERDAM.  Rijksmuseum—Musiekinstrumenten uit het Rijksmuseum
 te Amsterdam, 1952. (Exhibition in The Hague.)
BASLE.  Historisches Museum, Basel. *Katalog* No. IV, KARL NEF, 1906.
BERLIN.  Sammlung der Staatlichen Hochschule. *Beschreibender Katalog.*
 CURT SACHS, 1922.
BOLOGNA.  Esposizione internazionale di Musica in Bologna, nel 1888.
 *Catalogo ufficiale.* (Parma 1888.)
BOSTON, MASS.  Boston Museum of Fine Arts, Boston, Massachusetts.
 *Ancient European Musical Instruments, An organological study of the
 Musical Instruments in the Leslie Lindsey Mason Collection at the
 Museum of Fine Arts, Boston.* N. BESSARABOFF, Harvard University
 Press, 1941.
BRESLAU.  Schwebisches Museum. *Catalogue.* EPSTEIN–SCHEYER, 1932.
BRUSSELS.  Musée instrumental du Conservatoire Royal. *Catalogue des-
 criptif et analytique.* V. C. MAHILLON, 5 vols., 1893–1922.

BIRMINGHAM. Birmingham and Midland Institute. *Catalogue*, 1953 (*stencil*).

COLOGNE. Musikhistorisches Museum von Wilhelm Heyer in Cöln. *Kleiner Katalog*. GEORGE KINSKY, 1913.

COPENHAGEN. Music History Museum. *Das Musikhistorische Museum, Kopenhagen*. ANGUL HAMMERICH, 1911. German translation of Danish text, ERNA BOBE, pub. Breitkopf and Härtel, Leipzig. (179 illustrations.)

Claudius Collection. *Catalogue* 1900 and enlarged edition Danish and German texts, 1921.

FLORENCE. *Catalogo de Instrumentos antigos de Leopold Francolini*. R. Instituto L. Cherubini. *Gli strumenti raccolti nell Museo* etc. LETO BARGAGNA, 1911.

Collezione Etnografico-Musicale Kraus. *Catalogo Sezione Instrumenti Musicali*. A. KRAUS FIGLIO, 1901.

GHENT. Collection d'Instruments de Musique Anciens ou Curiex formée par C. C. Snoeck. *Catalogue* 1894. (This collection was subsequently divided between the Berlin Hochschule and the Brussels Conservatoire Museums but certain specimens mentioned in the Catalogue are no longer to be found in either of these.)

GLASGOW. Kelvingrove Art Gallery and Museum. *The Glen Collection of Musical Instruments*. HENRY GEORGE FARMER, 1943, (ex *The Art Review of the Glasgow Gallery and Museums Association*.) The collection, which was formerly to be seen in Edinburgh, was not yet on exhibition in Glasgow in 1953.

HAGUE, The. D. F. Scheurleer Collection. *De Muziek-Historische Afdeling*. Gemeente-Museum, 's-Gravenhage, door DIRK J. BALFOORT, 1935.

HAMBURG. Museum für Hamburgische Geschichte. *Verzeichnis der Sammlung alter Musikinstrumente*. HANS SCHRODER, 1930.

INNSBRUCK. Museum Ferdinandeum. *Catalogue*.

LEIPZIG. Instrumenten-Sammlung von Paul de Wit. *Perlen aus der I–S* etc. German, French and English texts in parallel columns and 16 plates in colour. 1892.

LISBON. Museu Instrumental em Lisboa. *Catalogo summario*. MICHEL'ANGELO LAMBERTINI, 1914.

Collecções Keil. *Breve noticia dos instrumentos de musica antigos e modernos*. ALFREDO KEIL, 1904.

LIVERPOOL. Rushworth and Dreaper Collection. *General Catalogue*, 1923.

LONDON. Exhibition 1852. *Exhibition Lecture on the Musical Department*. W. W. CAZALET.

*Douze jours à Londres. Voyage d'un mélomane à travers l'Exposition Universelle*. COMTE AD. DE PONTÉCOULANT, 1862 (Paris).

South Kensington Museum. *Descriptive catalogue of the Musical Instruments*. CARL ENGEL, 1870.

South Kensington Museum. *Catalogue of the Special Exhibition of Ancient Musical Instruments* (1872), published 1873.

International Inventions Exhibition, 1885. *Guide to the Loan Collection and List of Musical Instruments* etc.

Royal Military Exhibition, 1890. *Descriptive Catalogue of the Musical Instruments*. C. R. DAY, 1891.

Crystal Palace Exhibition. *Catalogue*, 1900.

Loan Exhibition, Fishmongers' Hall, 1904. *Illustrated Catalogue*, Various contributors, published Novello, London, 1909. (This and the R.M.E. are probably the most important of all English catalogues.)

The Horniman Museum. *The Adam Carse Collection of Musical Wind Instruments.* A list published by the London County Council, 1947. As above a *Catalogue*, illustrated. Published by the L.C.C. 1951.

The Galpin Society. British Musical Instruments, an Exhibition by arrangement with the Arts Council of Great Britain, *Catalogue* 1951.

Boosey and Hawkes Collection. *Catalogue* 1939. (Typescript, privately circulated.)

LUTON. Luton Museum. Exhibition 1947. " Growth of Music." *Catalogue*, 1947 (*stencil*).

MICHIGAN. University of Ann Arbor. The Frederick Stearns Collection. *Catalogue.* A. A. STANLEY, 1921.

MILAN. Museo del Conservatorio. *Gli strumenti musicali nel Museo.* EUGENOI DE GUARINONI, 1908.

*Esposizione musicale, sotto il partocinio di S.M. la Regina. Atti del congresso dei Musicisti italiani, riunito in Milano dal* 16 *al* 22 *Guigon,* 1881.

MUNICH. Baiersches Nationalmuseum. *Catalogue.* K. A. BIERDIMPFL, 1883.

NEW YORK. Crosby Brown Collection. The Metropolitan Museum of Art. *Catalogue* 1902.

PARIS. Musée du Conservatoire National. *Catalogue raisonné.* G. CHOUQUET, 1884. Supplements 1894, 1899, 1903.

Conservatoire des Arts et Métiers. *General Catalogue* in course of reprinting in 1948.

*Catalogue du Musée instrumental de M. Adolphe Sax,* 1877.

L'Industrie. *Exposition de* 1834. STEPHEN FLACHAT.

*Histoire illustrée de l'Exposition Universelle, par catégories d'industries, avec notices sur les exposants.* 1855. (Vol. I refers to the musical section.) CHARLES ROBIN.

*La Musique à l' Exposition Universelle de* 1867. MARQUIS DE PONTÉCOULANT. Published 1868.

*La Musique, les Musiciens, et les Instruments de Musique . . . Archive complètes . . . l'Expositiona Internationale de* 1867. OSCAR COMETTANT. Published 1869.

*Exposition Universelle de Paris, en* 1855. *Fabrication des Instruments de Musique, rapport.* F. J. FÉTIS. Published 1856.

*La facture instrumentale à l' Exposition Universelle de* 1889 *. . . etc.* CONSTANT PIERRE. Published 1890.

Exposition universelle internationale de 1878 à Paris. *Les instruments de musique etc.* G. CHOUQUET. Published 1880.

Exposition universelle internationale de 1900 à Paris. *Instruments de musique. Rapport.* E. BRIQUEVILLE.

PRAGUE. National Museum. An exhibition of musical instruments. *Catalogue.* ALEXANDER BUCHNER, 1952.

SALZBURG. Museum Carolino Augusteum. *Catalogue.* C. GEIRINGER (Leipzig), 1931.

STOCKHOLM. Musikhistoriska Museet. *Catalogue.* J. SVANBERG, 1902.

VERONA. *Catalogo de Instrumentos do municipio de Verona.*

VIENNA. Die Sammlung alter Musikinstrumente. *Beschreibendes Verzeichnis.* J. SCHLOSSER, 1920. (A most important work with many magnificent illustrations.)

Sammlung der K. K. Gesellschaft der Musikfreunde in Wien. *Catalogue.* E. MANDYCZEWSKI, 1912.

*Rapport sur les Instruments de Musique à l'Exposition de Vienne en 1837.* LISSAJOUS. Published 1895.

YORK. The Castle Museum. Musical section. *Catalogue.*

# Condensed Subject Index

# Index of Names

(Excluding those found in the Introduction and Appendices)

*Proper names in the following table are arranged alphabetic-*
*ally. International celebrities are indicated by surname only.*
*In other cases where pre-names are known, these are either*
*printed at length or represented by initials according to which is*
*the commoner usage in conversational reference to the person*
*concerned. Biographical entries are indicated by bold figures.*

# Index of Instruments

THIS BOOK IS SET
IN ELEVEN POINT IMPRINT TYPE
AND PRINTED IN GREAT BRITAIN BY
RICHARD CLAY & COMPANY LIMITED
AT THE CHAUCER PRESS
BUNGAY · SUFFOLK